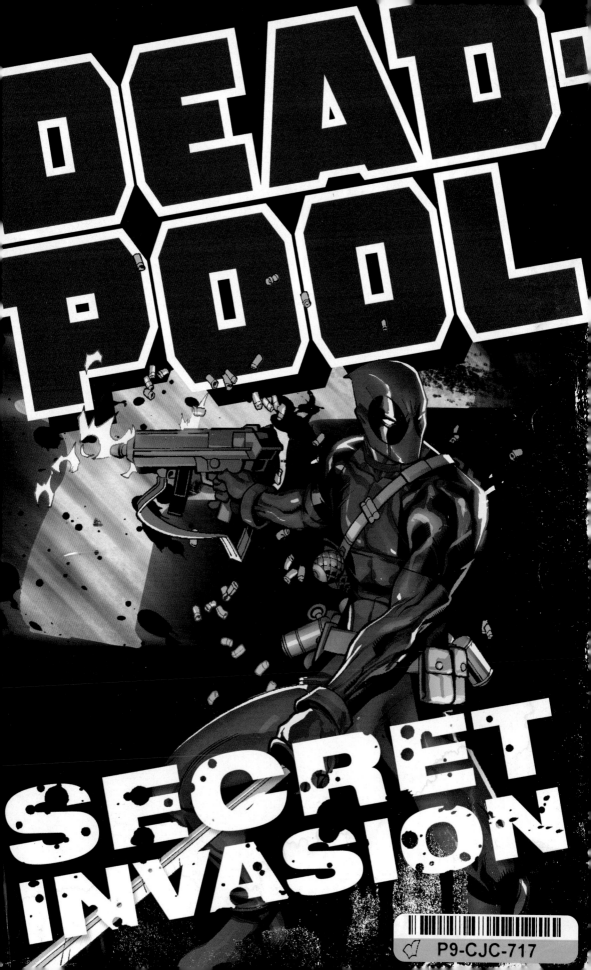

DEAD-POOL

SECRET INVASION

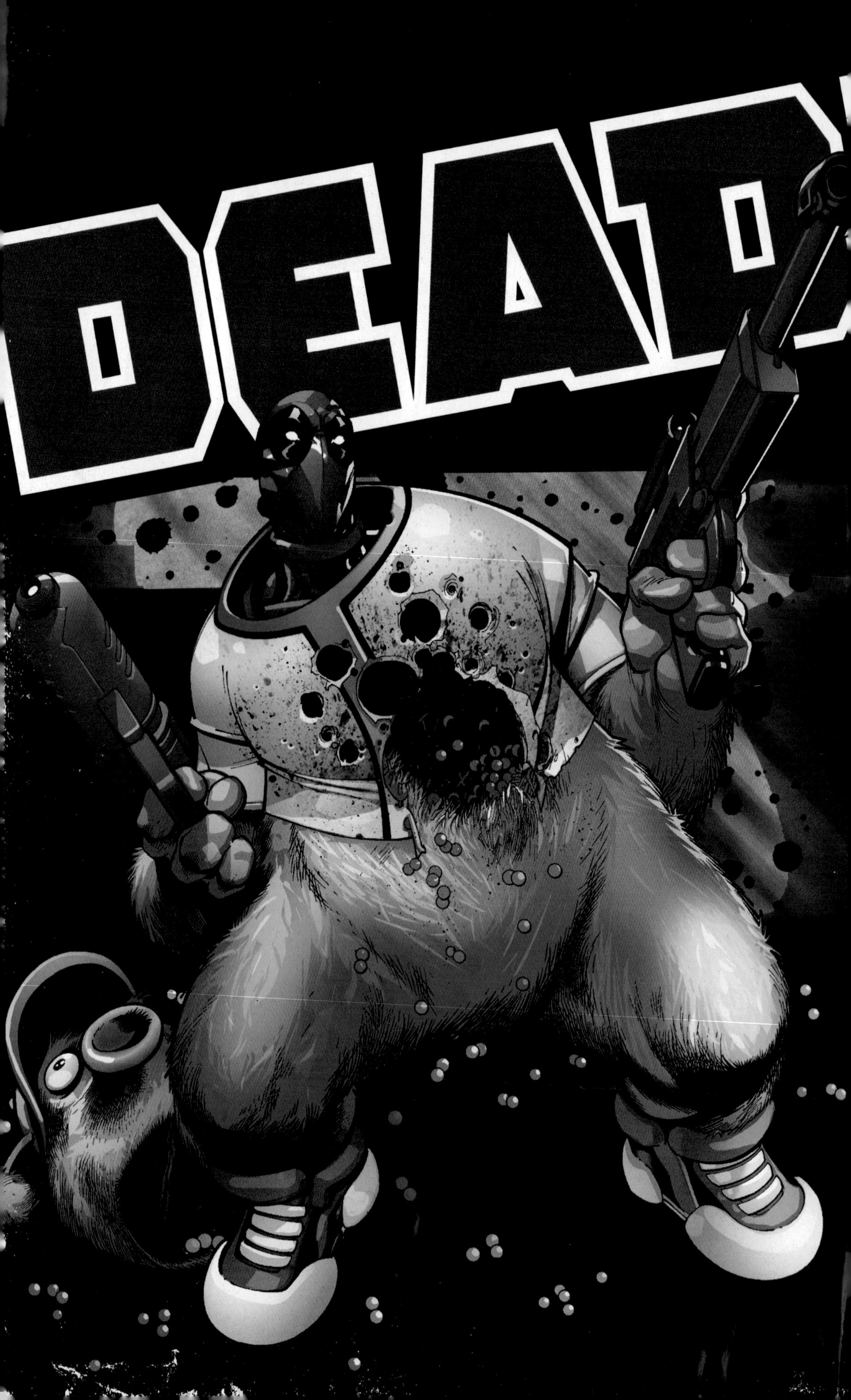
DEAD

# POOL
# SECRET INVASION

WRITER: **DANIEL WAY** • PENCILS: **PACO MEDINA** & **CARLO BARBERI**

INKS: **JUAN VLASCO** WITH **SANDU FLOREA**

COLORS: **MARTE GRACIA** WITH **RAÚL TREVIÑO**

LETTERS: **VIRTUAL CALLIGRAPHY'S CORY PETIT** & **CHRIS ELIOPOULOS**

COVER ARTISTS: **CLAYTON CRAIN** & **JASON PEARSON**

ASSISTANT EDITORS: **JODY LEHEUP** & **DANIEL KETCHUM**

EDITOR: **AXEL ALONSO**

COLLECTION EDITOR: **CORY LEVINE**

ASSISTANT EDITORS: **ALEX STARBUCK** & **NELSON RIBEIRO**

EDITORS, SPECIAL PROJECTS: **JENNIFER GRÜNWALD** & **MARK D. BEAZLEY**

SENIOR EDITOR, SPECIAL PROJECTS: **JEFF YOUNGQUIST**

SVP OF PRINT & DIGITAL PUBLISHING SALES: **DAVID GABRIEL**

BOOK DESIGN: **RODOLFO MURAGUCHI**

EDITOR IN CHIEF: **AXEL ALONSO**

CHIEF CREATIVE OFFICER: **JOE QUESADA**

PUBLISHER: **DAN BUCKLEY**

EXECUTIVE PRODUCER: **ALAN FINE**

**DEADPOOL VOL. 1: SECRET INVASION.** Contains material originally published in magazine form as DEADPOOL #1-5. Seventh printing 2013. ISBN# 978-0-7851-3273-8. Published by MARVEL WORLDWIDE, INC., a subsidiary of MARVEL ENTERTAINMENT, LLC. OFFICE OF PUBLICATION: 135 West 50th Street, New York, NY 10020. Copyright © 2008 and 2009 Marvel Characters, Inc. All rights reserved. All characters featured in this issue and the distinctive names and likenesses thereof, and all related indicia are trademarks of Marvel Characters, Inc. No similarity between any of the names, characters, persons, and/or institutions in this magazine with those of any living or dead person or institution is intended, and any such similarity which may exist is purely coincidental. **Printed in the U.S.A.** ALAN FINE, EVP - Office of the President. Marvel Worldwide, Inc. and EVP & CMO Marvel Characters B.V.; DAN BUCKLEY, Publisher & President - Print, Animation & Digital Divisions; JOE QUESADA, Chief Creative Officer; TOM BREVOORT, SVP of Publishing; DAVID BOGART, SVP of Operations & Procurement, Publishing; C.B. CEBULSKI, SVP of Creator & Content Development; DAVID GABRIEL, SVP of Print & Digital Publishing Sales; JIM O'KEEFE, VP of Operations & Logistics; DAN CARR, Executive Director of Publishing Technology; SUSAN CRESPI, Editorial Operations Manager; ALEX MORALES, Publishing Operations Manager; STAN LEE, Chairman Emeritus. For information regarding advertising in Marvel Comics or on Marvel.com, please contact Niza Disla, Director of Marvel Partnerships, at ndisla@marvel.com. For Marvel subscription inquiries, please call 800-217-9158. **Manufactured** between 5/29/2013 and 7/1/2013 by R.R. DONNELLEY, INC., SALEM, VA, USA.

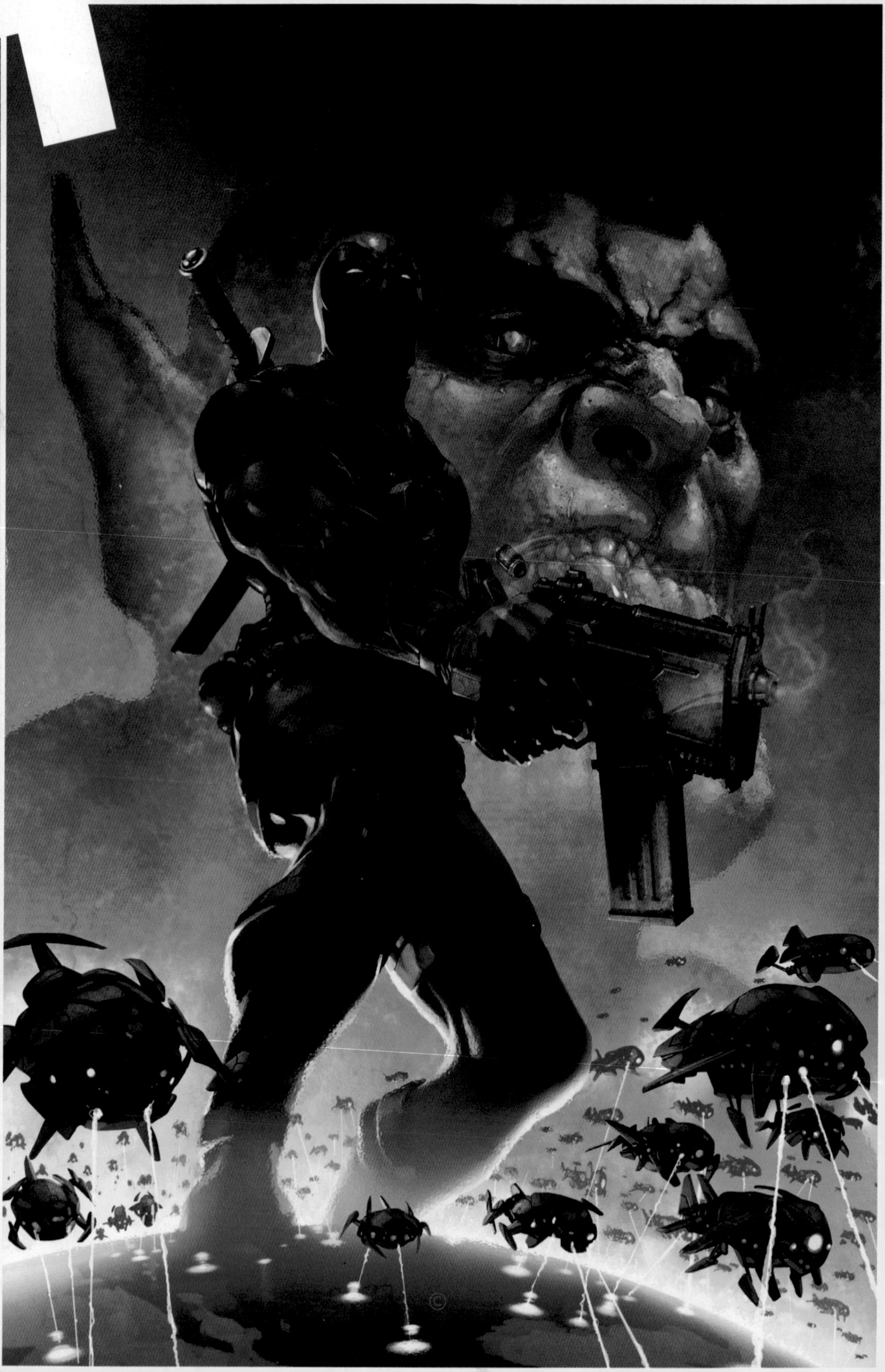

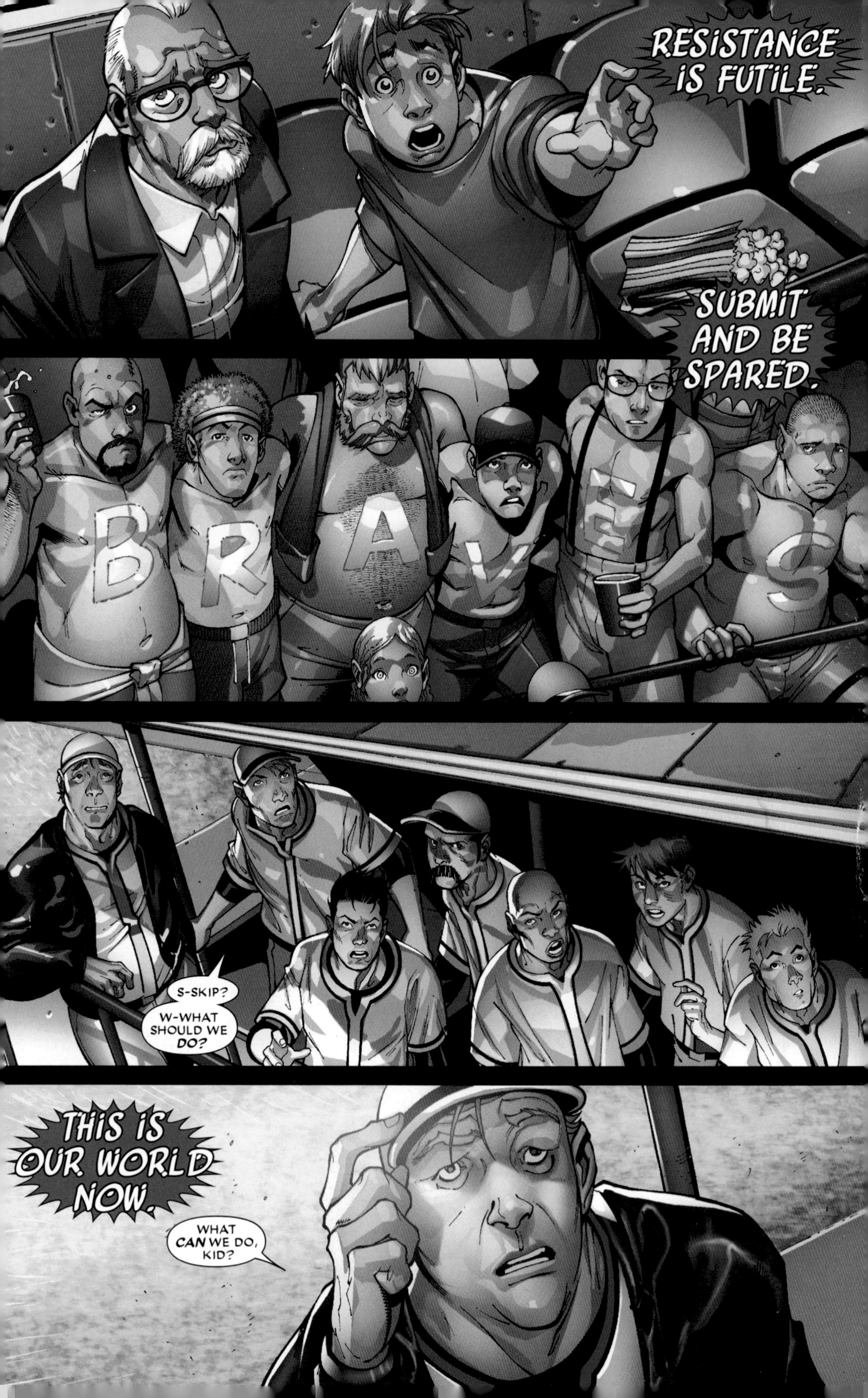
RESISTANCE IS FUTILE.
SUBMIT AND BE SPARED.
S-SKIP?
W-WHAT SHOULD WE DO?
THIS IS OUR WORLD NOW.
WHAT CAN WE DO, KID?

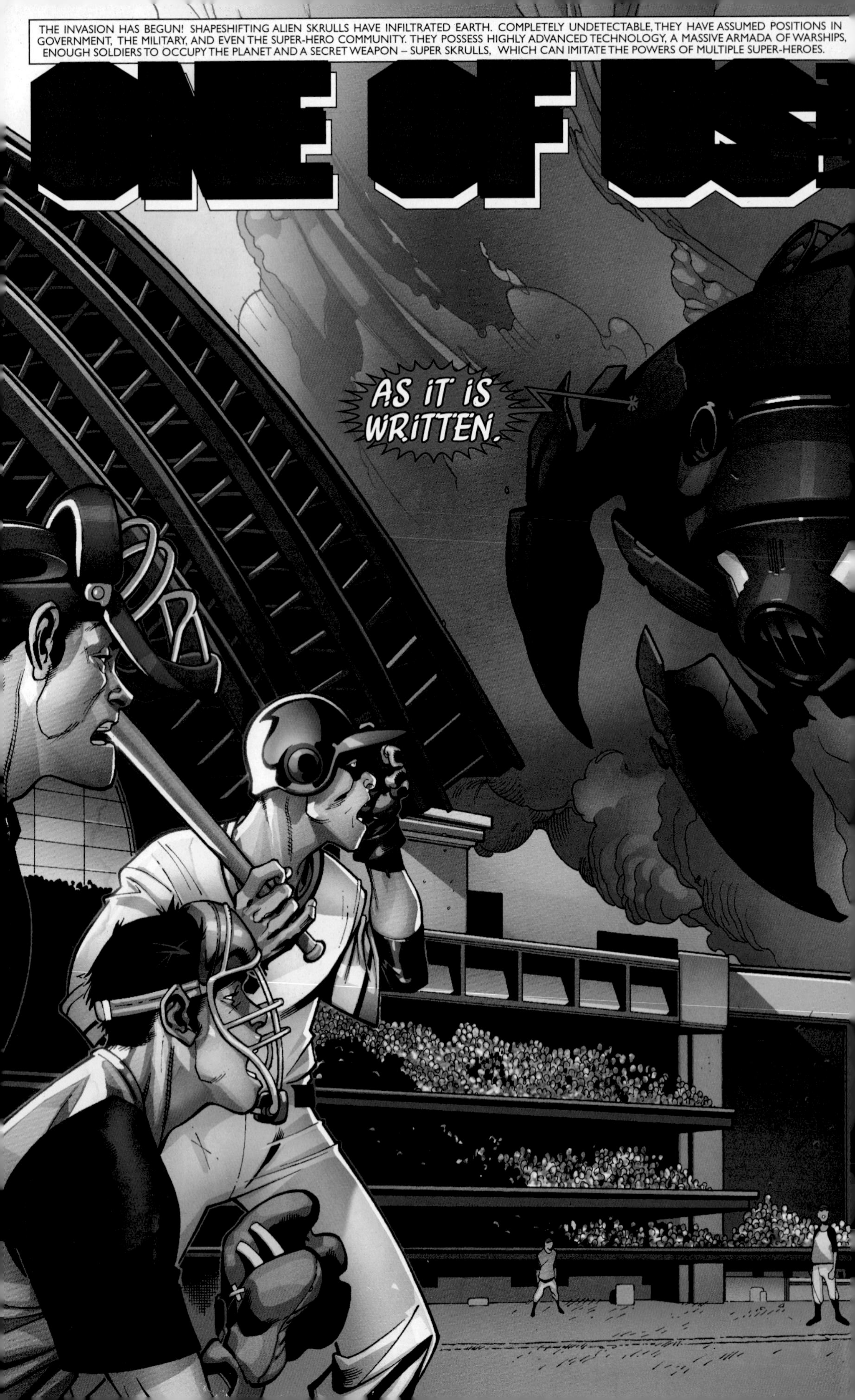
THE INVASION HAS BEGUN! SHAPESHIFTING ALIEN SKRULLS HAVE INFILTRATED EARTH. COMPLETELY UNDETECTABLE, THEY HAVE ASSUMED POSITIONS IN GOVERNMENT, THE MILITARY, AND EVEN THE SUPER-HERO COMMUNITY. THEY POSSESS HIGHLY ADVANCED TECHNOLOGY, A MASSIVE ARMADA OF WARSHIPS, ENOUGH SOLDIERS TO OCCUPY THE PLANET AND A SECRET WEAPON – SUPER SKRULLS, WHICH CAN IMITATE THE POWERS OF MULTIPLE SUPER-HEROES.
ONE OF US
AS IT IS WRITTEN.

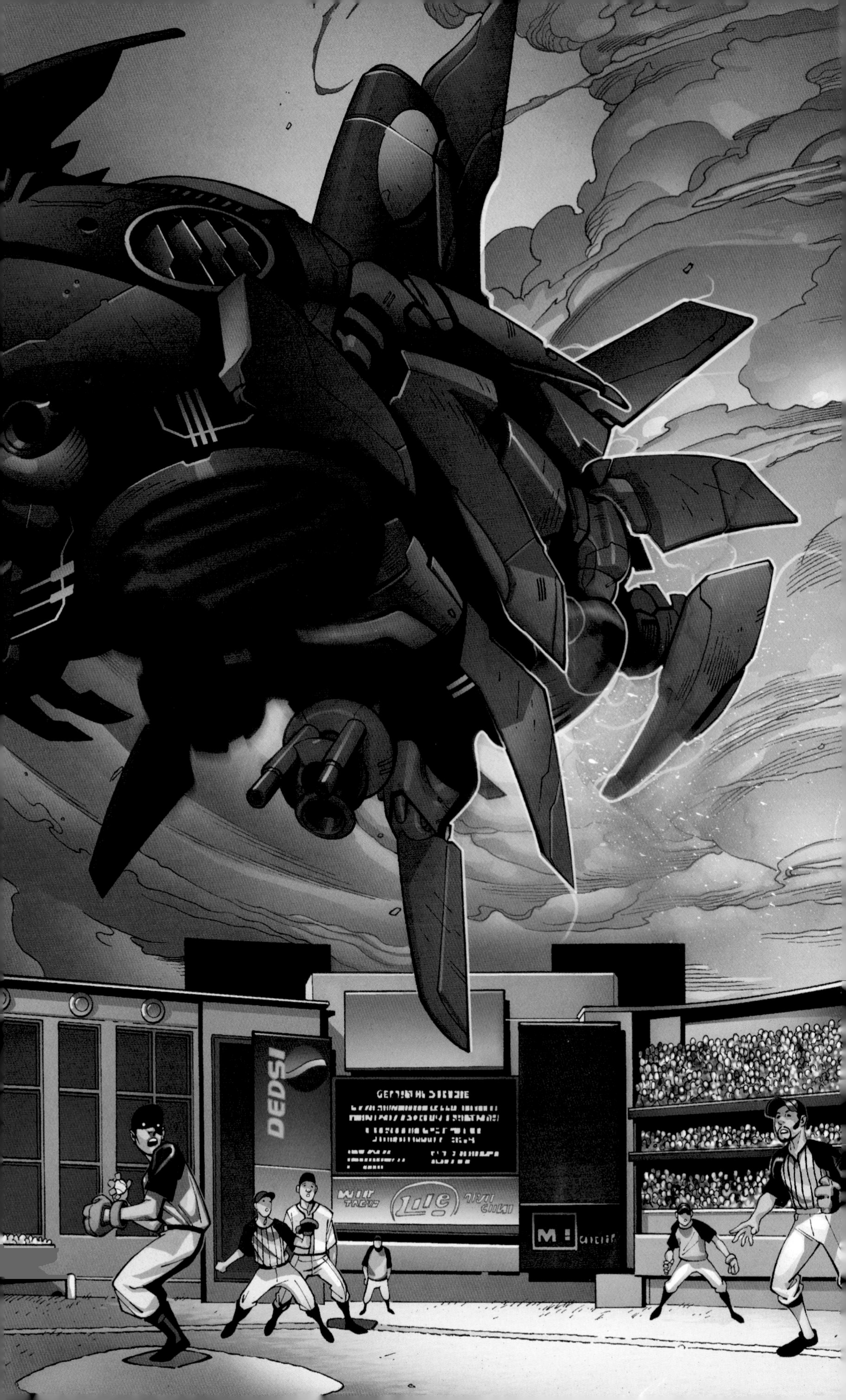
DEDSI

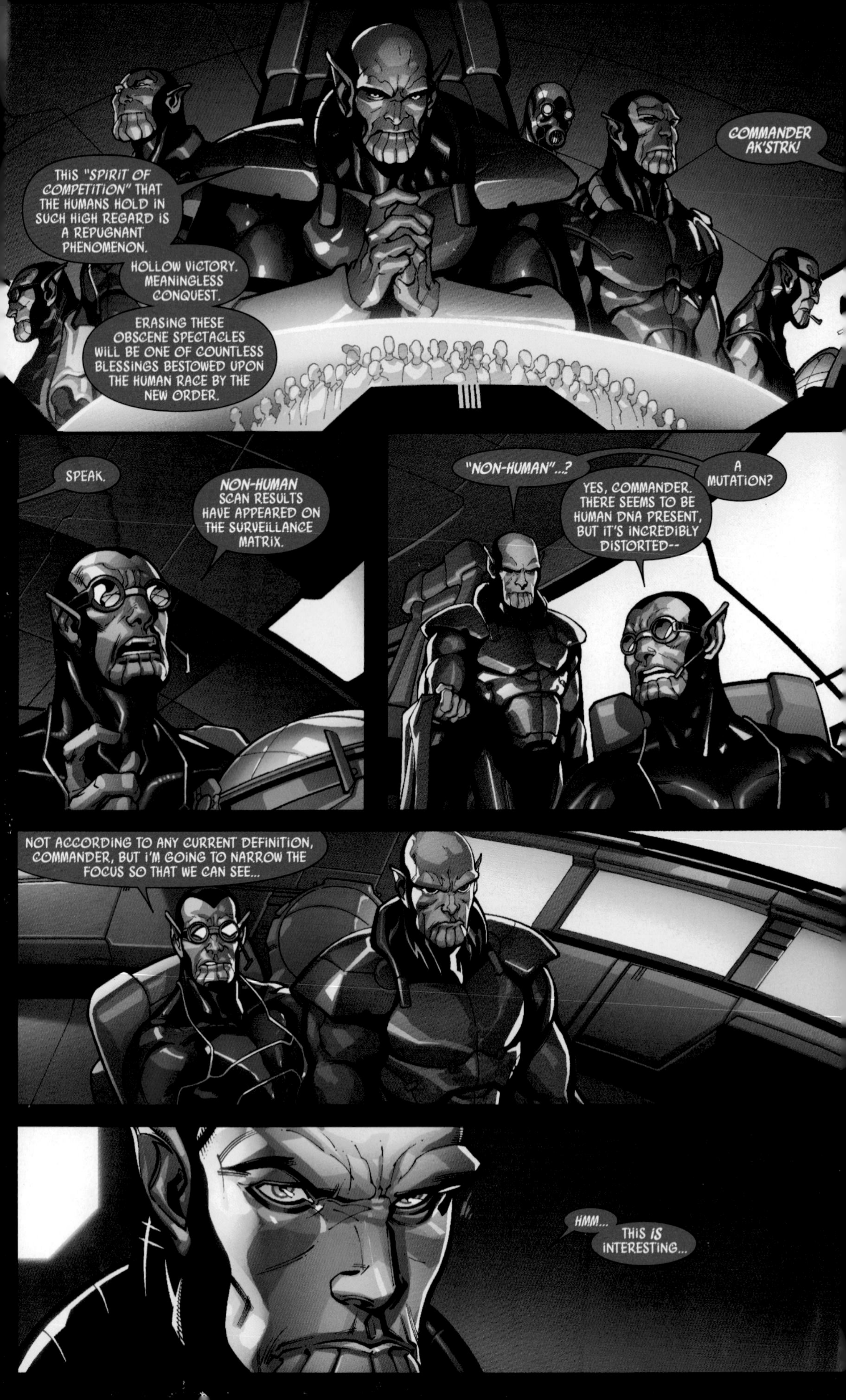

THIS "SPIRIT OF COMPETITION" THAT THE HUMANS HOLD IN SUCH HIGH REGARD IS A REPUGNANT PHENOMENON.
HOLLOW VICTORY. MEANINGLESS CONQUEST.
ERASING THESE OBSCENE SPECTACLES WILL BE ONE OF COUNTLESS BLESSINGS BESTOWED UPON THE HUMAN RACE BY THE NEW ORDER.
COMMANDER AK'STRK!
SPEAK.
NON-HUMAN SCAN RESULTS HAVE APPEARED ON THE SURVEILLANCE MATRIX.
"NON-HUMAN"...?
YES, COMMANDER. THERE SEEMS TO BE HUMAN DNA PRESENT, BUT IT'S INCREDIBLY DISTORTED--
A MUTATION?
NOT ACCORDING TO ANY CURRENT DEFINITION, COMMANDER, BUT I'M GOING TO NARROW THE FOCUS SO THAT WE CAN SEE...
HMM...
THIS IS INTERESTING...

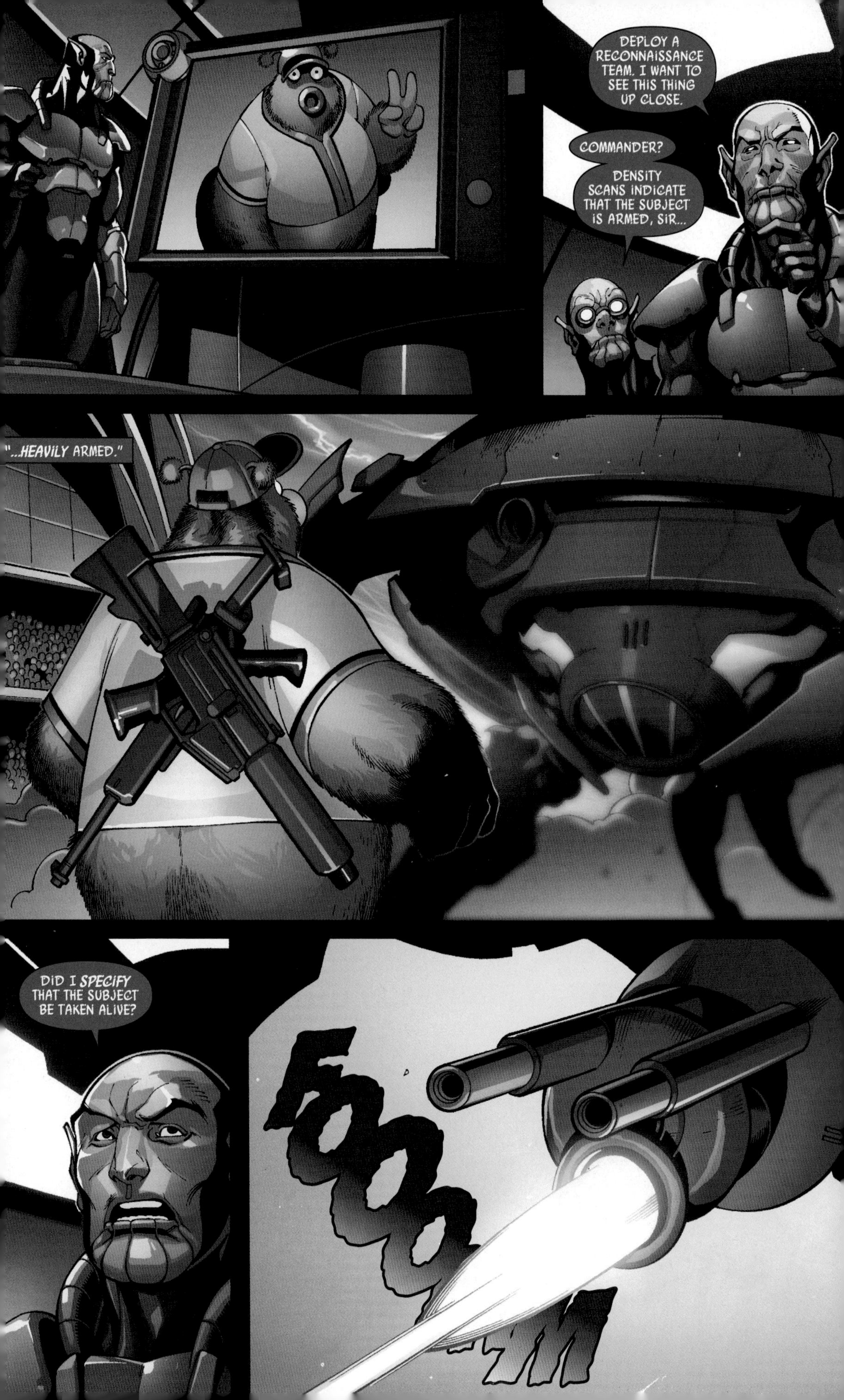
DEPLOY A RECONNAISSANCE TEAM. I WANT TO SEE THIS THING UP CLOSE.
COMMANDER?
DENSITY SCANS INDICATE THAT THE SUBJECT IS ARMED, SIR...
"...HEAVILY ARMED."
DID I SPECIFY THAT THE SUBJECT BE TAKEN ALIVE?

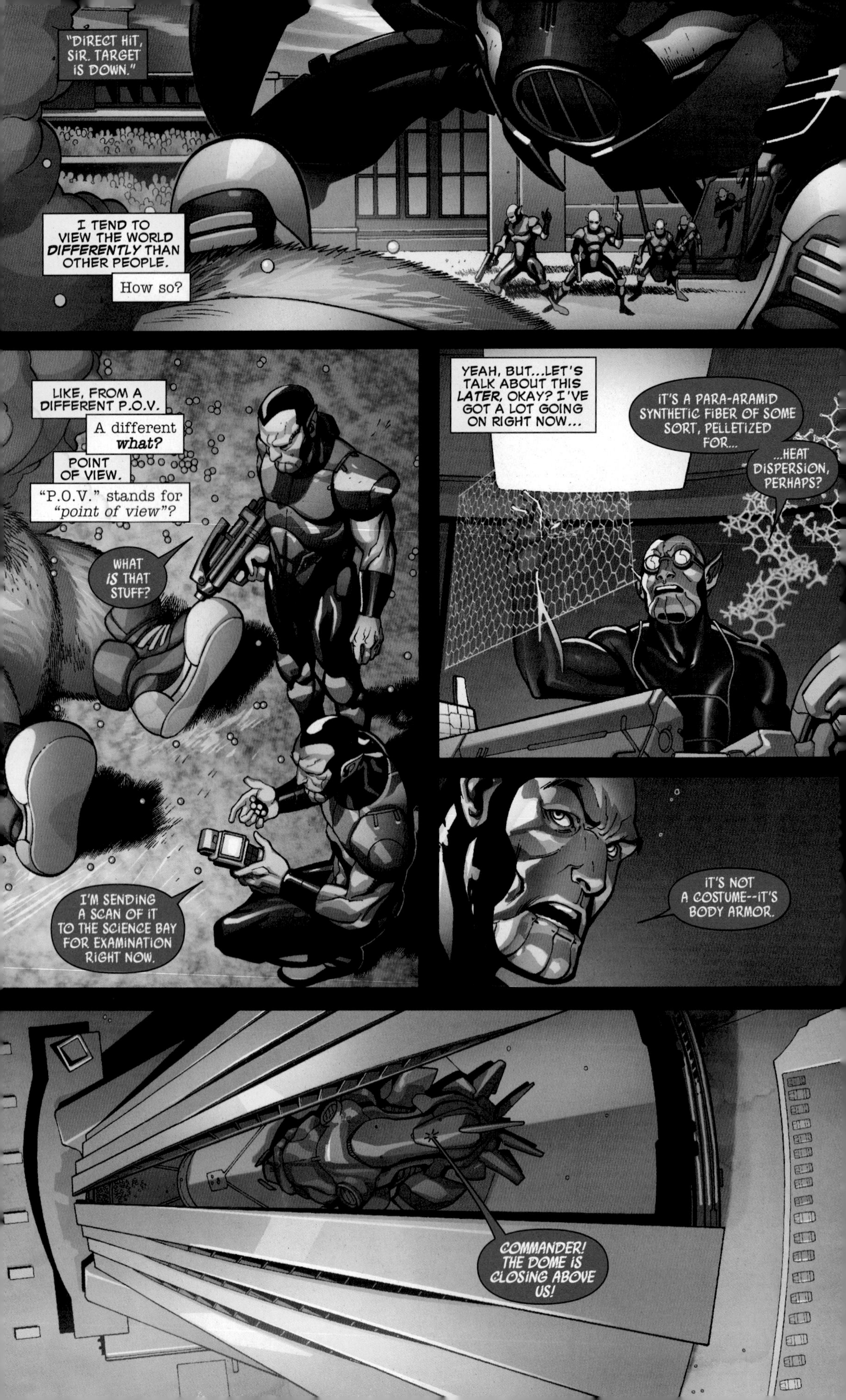

"DIRECT HIT, SIR. TARGET IS DOWN."
I TEND TO VIEW THE WORLD *DIFFERENTLY* THAN OTHER PEOPLE.
How so?
LIKE, FROM A DIFFERENT P.O.V.
A different ***what?***
POINT OF VIEW.
"P.O.V." stands for *"point of view"*?
WHAT *IS* THAT STUFF?
I'M SENDING A SCAN OF IT TO THE SCIENCE BAY FOR EXAMINATION RIGHT NOW.
YEAH, BUT...LET'S TALK ABOUT THIS *LATER*, OKAY? I'VE GOT A LOT GOING ON RIGHT NOW...
IT'S A PARA-ARAMID SYNTHETIC FIBER OF SOME SORT, PELLETIZED FOR...
...HEAT DISPERSION, PERHAPS?
IT'S NOT A COSTUME--IT'S BODY ARMOR.
*COMMANDER! THE DOME IS CLOSING ABOVE US!*

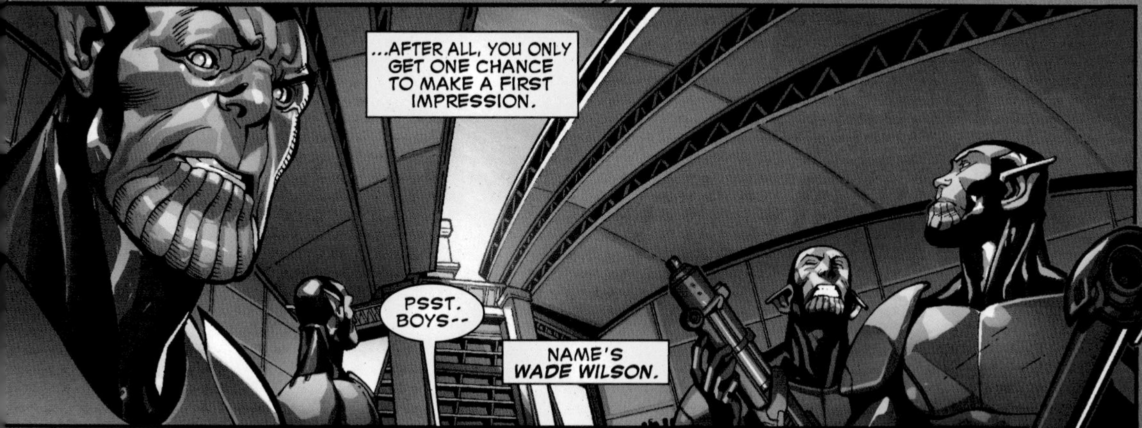
...AFTER ALL, YOU ONLY GET ONE CHANCE TO MAKE A FIRST IMPRESSION.
PSST. BOYS--
NAME'S *WADE WILSON.*

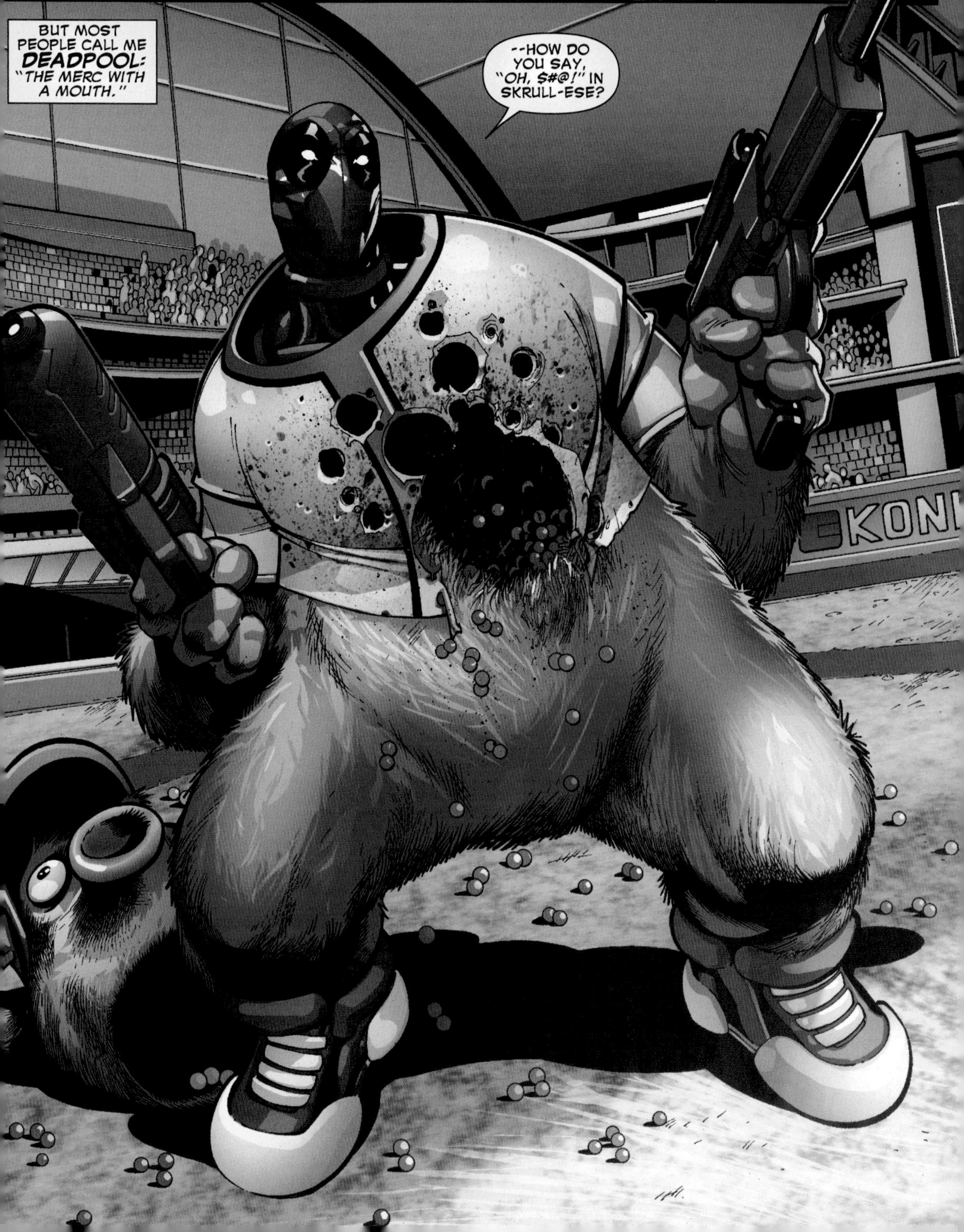
BUT MOST PEOPLE CALL ME **DEADPOOL:** "THE MERC WITH A MOUTH."
--HOW DO YOU SAY, "OH, $#@!" IN SKRULL-ESE?
KONI

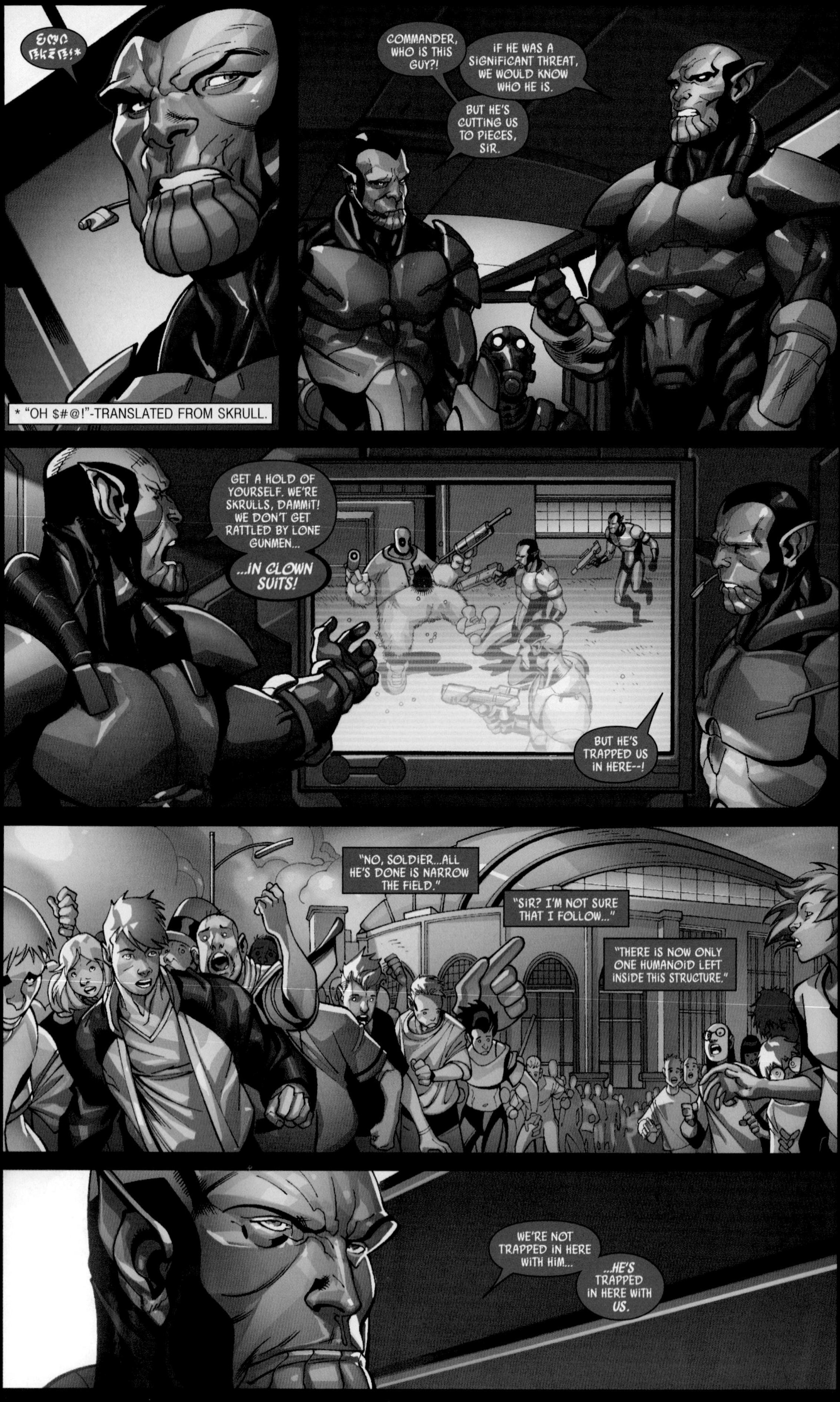
* "OH $#@!"-TRANSLATED FROM SKRULL.
COMMANDER, WHO IS THIS GUY?!
BUT HE'S CUTTING US TO PIECES, SIR.
IF HE WAS A SIGNIFICANT THREAT, WE WOULD KNOW WHO HE IS.
GET A HOLD OF YOURSELF. WE'RE SKRULLS, DAMMIT! WE DON'T GET RATTLED BY LONE GUNMEN...
...IN CLOWN SUITS!
BUT HE'S TRAPPED US IN HERE--!
"NO, SOLDIER...ALL HE'S DONE IS NARROW THE FIELD."
"SIR? I'M NOT SURE THAT I FOLLOW..."
"THERE IS NOW ONLY ONE HUMANOID LEFT INSIDE THIS STRUCTURE."
WE'RE NOT TRAPPED IN HERE WITH HIM...
...HE'S TRAPPED IN HERE WITH US.

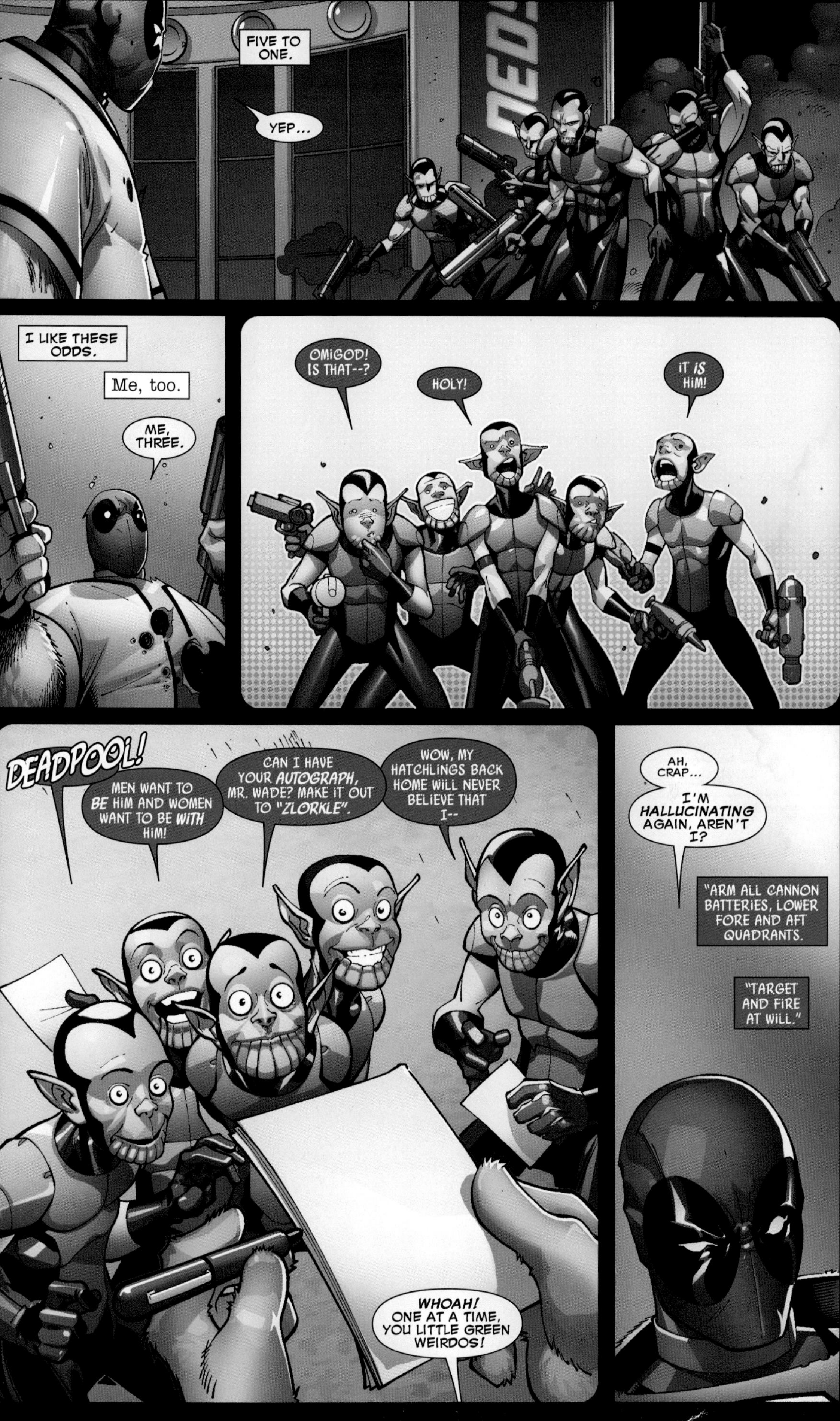
FIVE TO ONE.
YEP...
I LIKE THESE ODDS.
Me, too.
ME, THREE.
OMIGOD! IS THAT--?
HOLY!
IT IS HIM!
DEADPOOL!
MEN WANT TO BE HIM AND WOMEN WANT TO BE WITH HIM!
CAN I HAVE YOUR AUTOGRAPH, MR. WADE? MAKE IT OUT TO "ZLORKLE".
WOW, MY HATCHLINGS BACK HOME WILL NEVER BELIEVE THAT I--
WHOAH! ONE AT A TIME, YOU LITTLE GREEN WEIRDOS!
AH, CRAP...
I'M HALLUCINATING AGAIN, AREN'T I?
"ARM ALL CANNON BATTERIES, LOWER FORE AND AFT QUADRANTS.
"TARGET AND FIRE AT WILL."

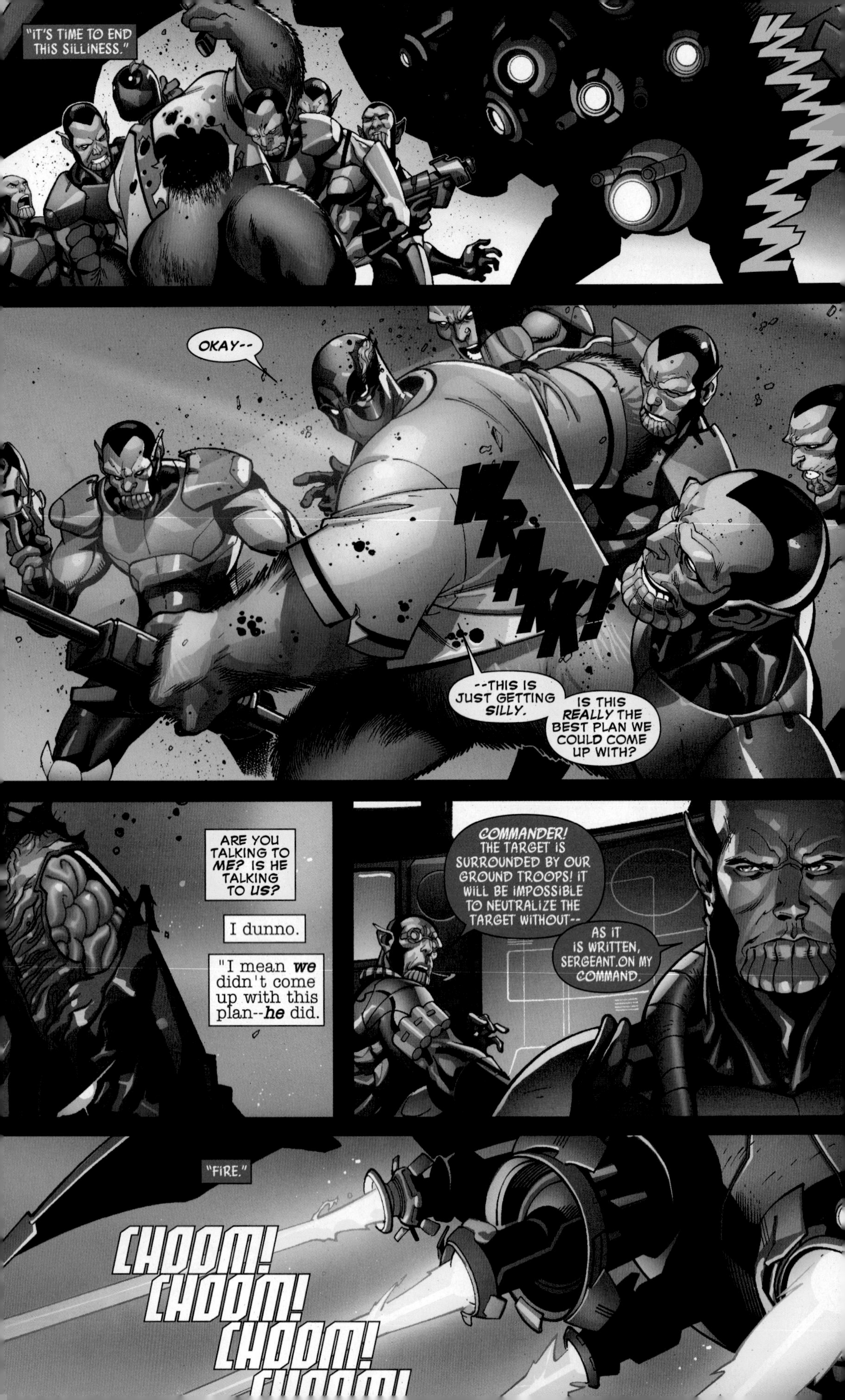
"IT'S TIME TO END THIS SILLINESS."
VWMMMMM
OKAY--
KRAKK!
--THIS IS JUST GETTING SILLY.
IS THIS REALLY THE BEST PLAN WE COULD COME UP WITH?
ARE YOU TALKING TO ME? IS HE TALKING TO US?
I dunno.
"I mean we didn't come up with this plan--he did.
COMMANDER! THE TARGET IS SURROUNDED BY OUR GROUND TROOPS! IT WILL BE IMPOSSIBLE TO NEUTRALIZE THE TARGET WITHOUT--
AS IT IS WRITTEN, SERGEANT. ON MY COMMAND.
"FIRE."
CHOOM! CHOOM! CHOOM!

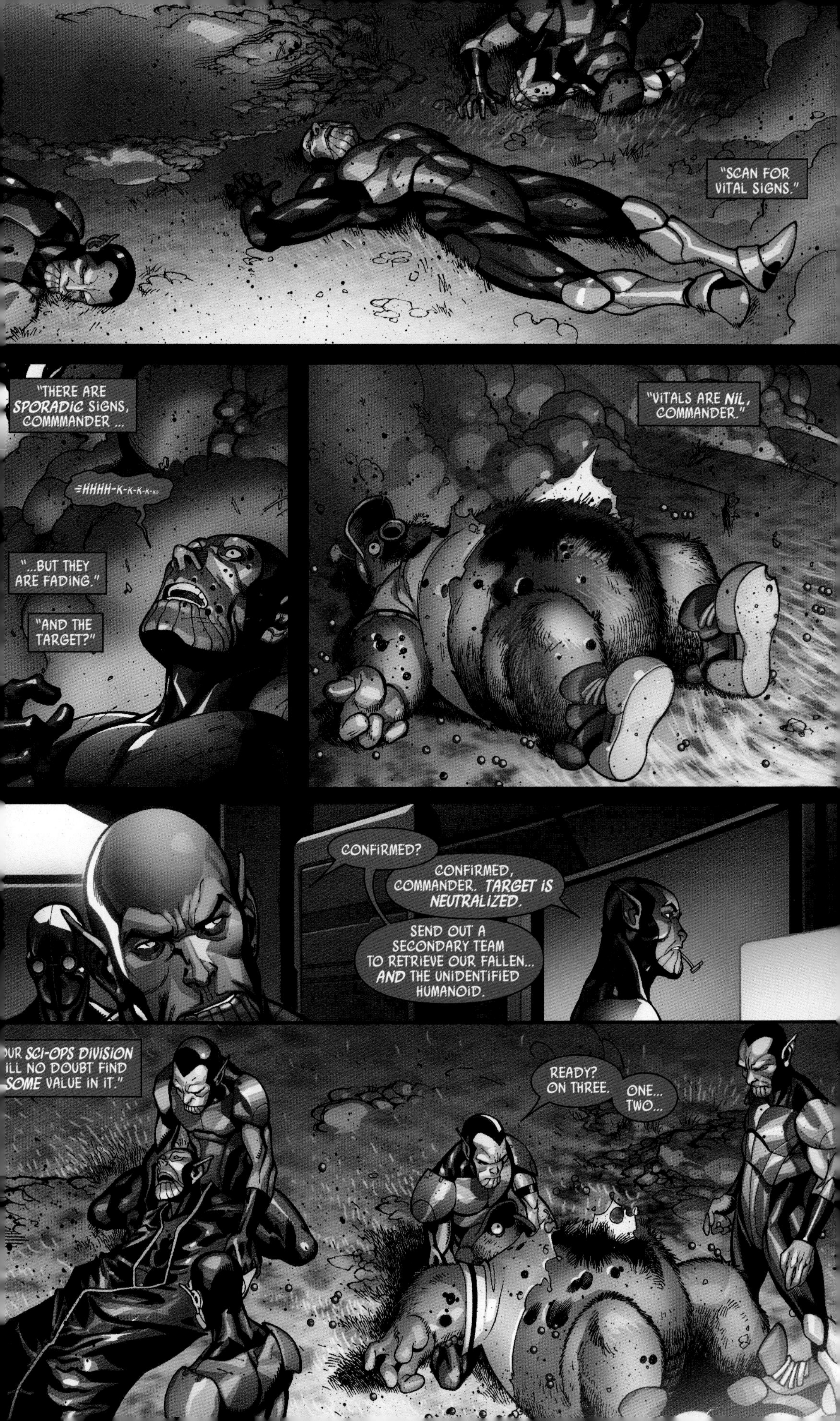
"SCAN FOR VITAL SIGNS."
"THERE ARE SPORADIC SIGNS, COMMMANDER ...
=HHHH-K-K-K-K-K
"...BUT THEY ARE FADING."
"AND THE TARGET?"
"VITALS ARE NIL, COMMANDER."
CONFIRMED?
CONFIRMED, COMMANDER. TARGET IS NEUTRALIZED.
SEND OUT A SECONDARY TEAM TO RETRIEVE OUR FALLEN... AND THE UNIDENTIFIED HUMANOID.
OUR SCI-OPS DIVISION ILL NO DOUBT FIND SOME VALUE IN IT."
READY? ON THREE.
ONE... TWO...

THREE!

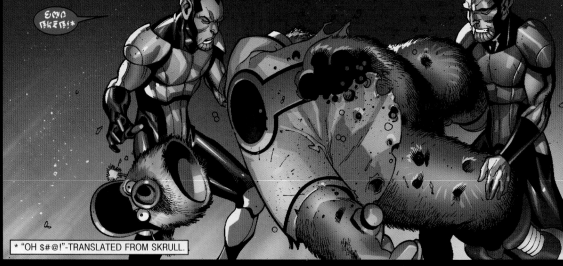

Ξ☆◇Λ ⌐Ϧ⫞ΞϦϟ*

* "OH $#@!"-TRANSLATED FROM SKRULL.

THAT... IS...IT!

COMMANDER?

EVERY SINGLE ONE OF YOU HAS FAILED!

DUE TO IGNORANCE, INCOMPETENCE...

...AND COWARDICE.

I THINK IT'S TIME TO SHOW BOTH YOU AND THIS HUMANOID HOW A REAL SKRULL HANDLES THEIR BUSINESS.

DEPLOY THE SUPER-SKRULL.

KLIK

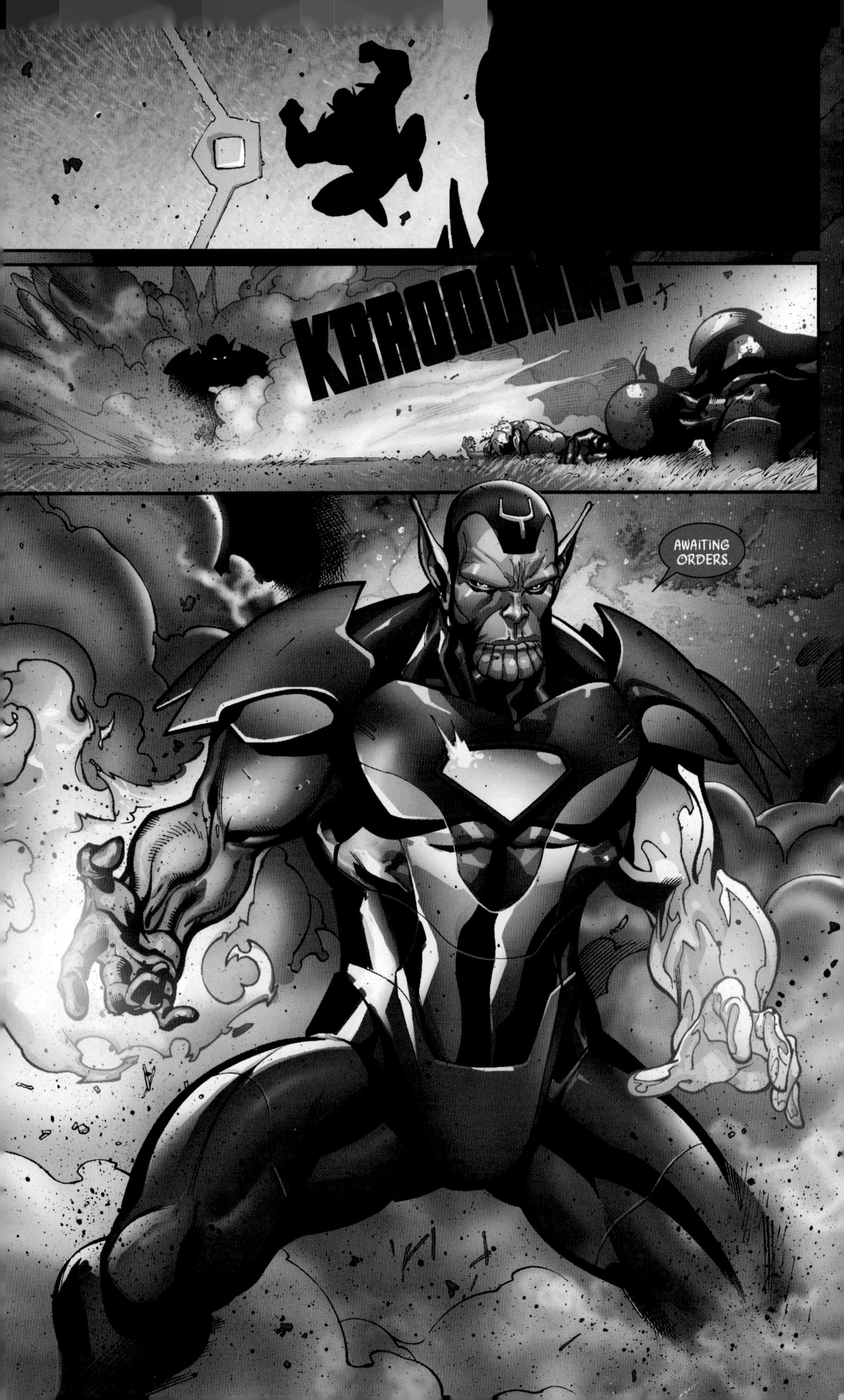
KRROOOMM!
AWAITING ORDERS.

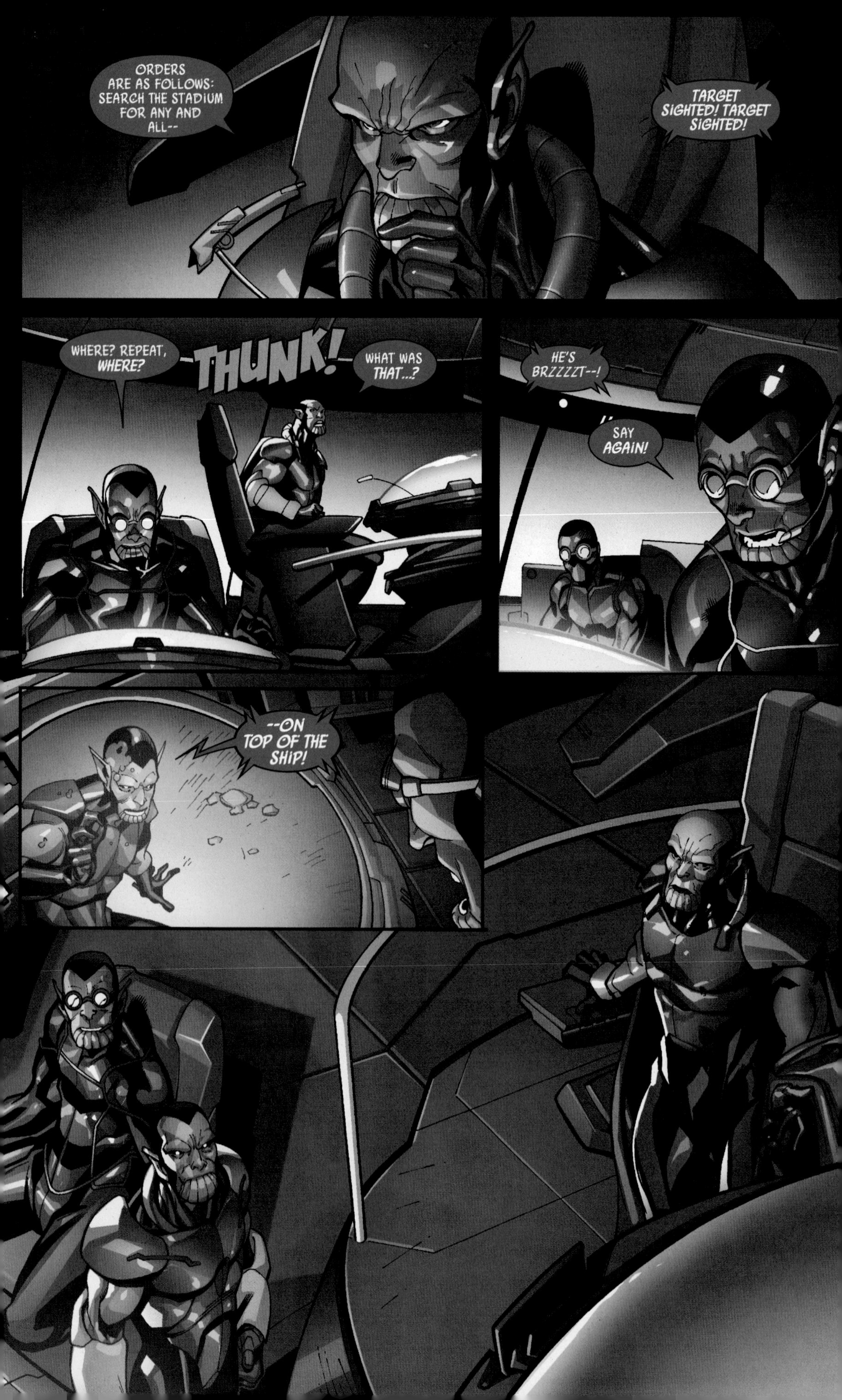
ORDERS ARE AS FOLLOWS: SEARCH THE STADIUM FOR ANY AND ALL--
TARGET SIGHTED! TARGET SIGHTED!
WHERE? REPEAT, WHERE?
THUNK!
WHAT WAS THAT...?
HE'S BRZZZZT--!
SAY AGAIN!
--ON TOP OF THE SHIP!

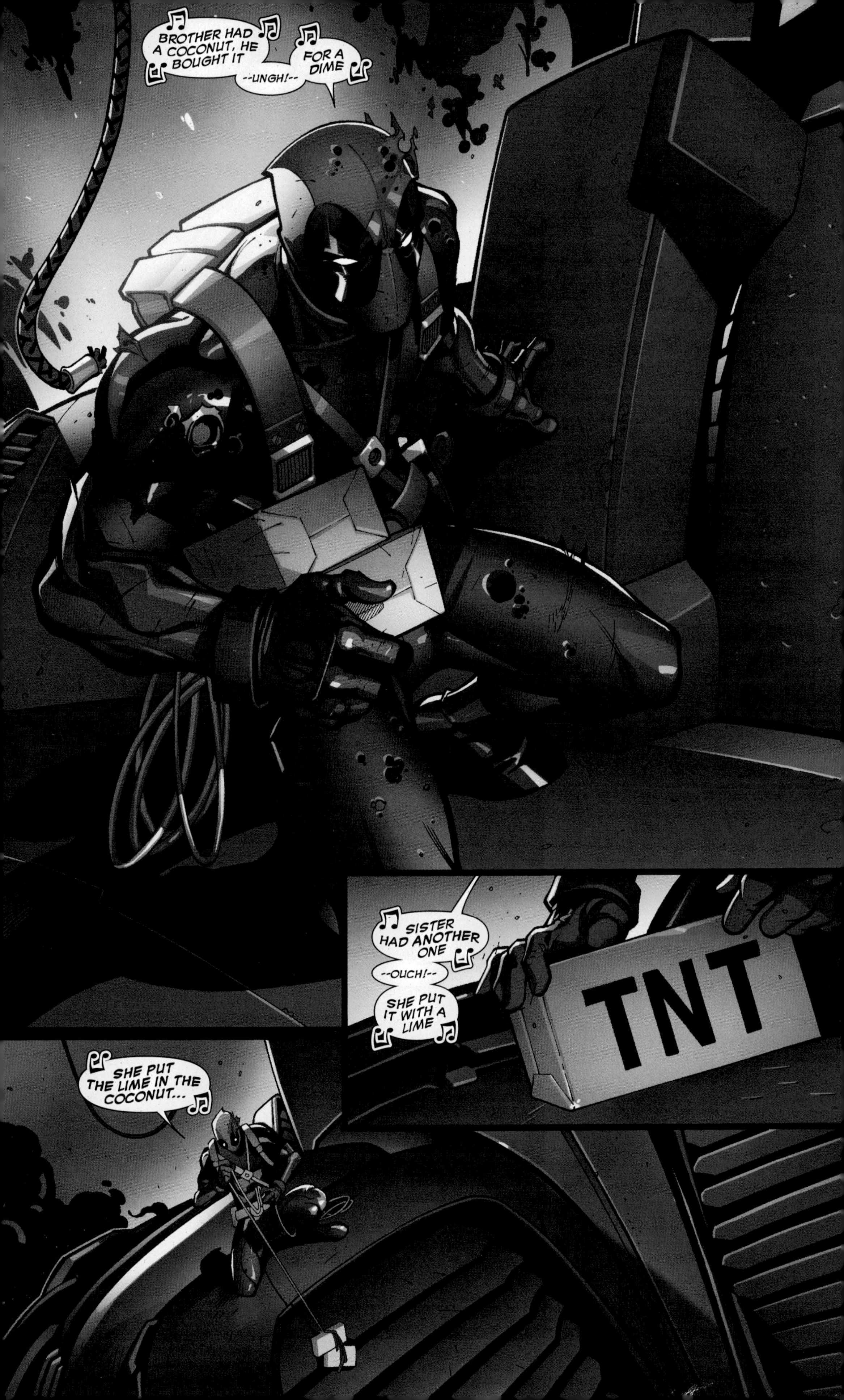
BROTHER HAD A COCONUT, HE BOUGHT IT
--UNGH!--
FOR A DIME
SISTER HAD ANOTHER ONE
--OUCH!--
SHE PUT IT WITH A LIME
TNT
SHE PUT THE LIME IN THE COCONUT...

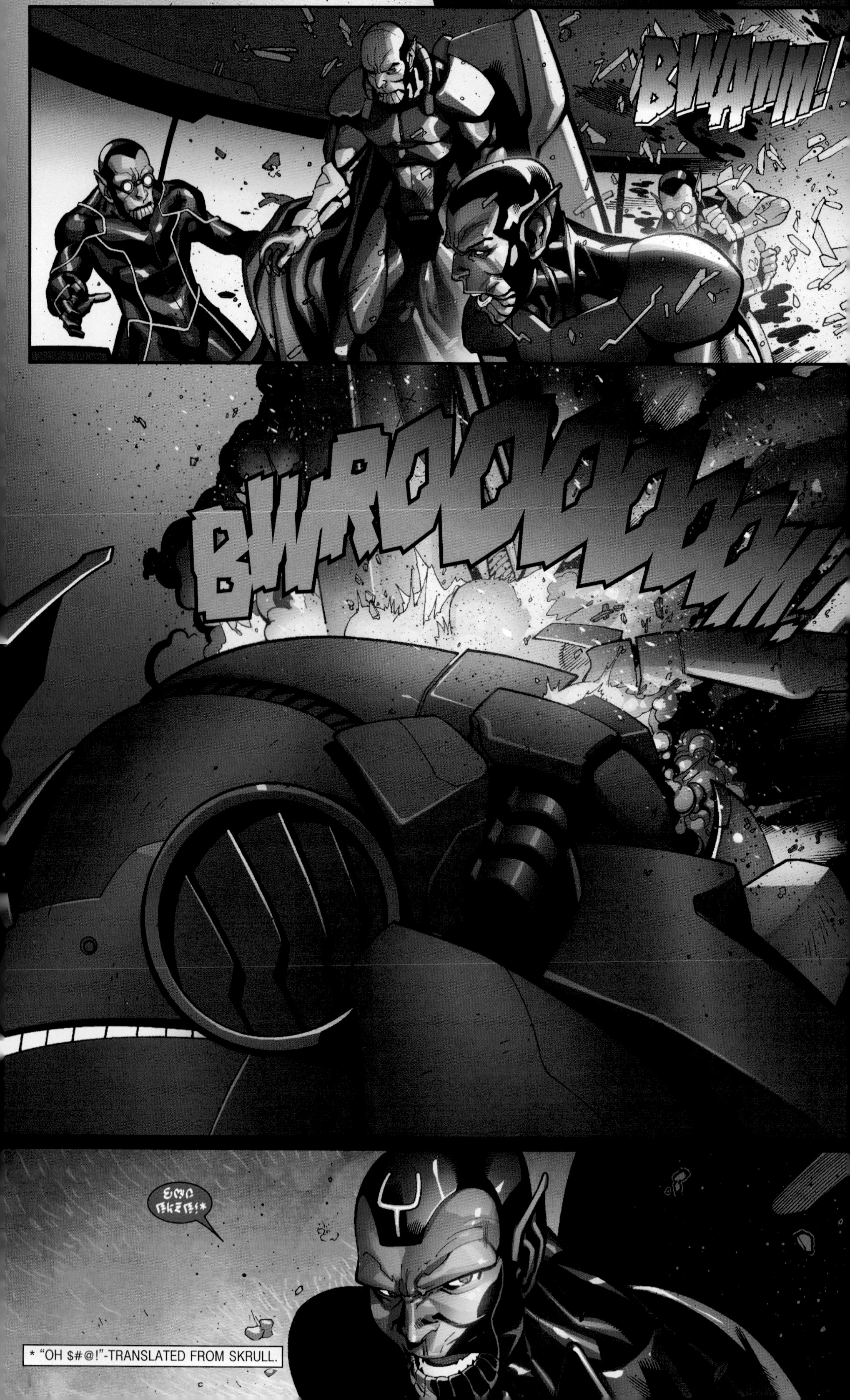
BWAMM!
BWROOOOOM!!
* "OH $#@!"-TRANSLATED FROM SKRULL.

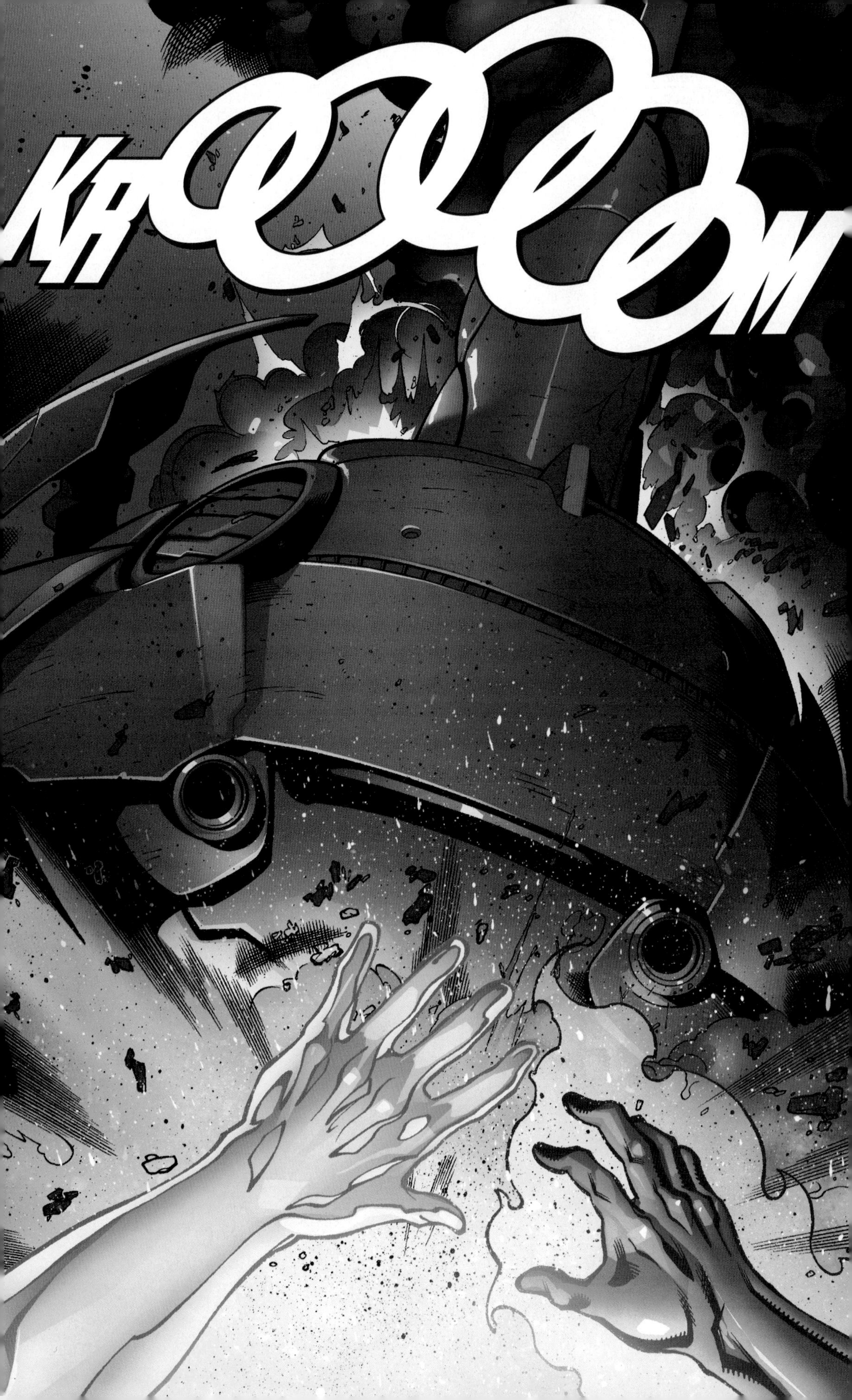
KROOOOM

So, you were saying, *"P.O.V."* stands for *"point of view"*?

USUALLY.

BUT IN MY CASE, IT STANDS FOR *"POOL-O-VISION™"*.

YOU WIN!!!

500 points

500 points

500 points

500 points

50 points

int

500 points

500 points

What's the little "TM" for?

IT'S SILENT.

What?

IT'S SILENT. YOU DON'T PRONOUNCE IT.

That doesn't even make sense.

TO *YOU*, MAYBE...

I *am* you!

YEAH, BUT--

THERE'S THE BIG DOG.

JUST LIKE I PLANNED.

Wait. After *"crash ship into bad guys,"* there was a plan?

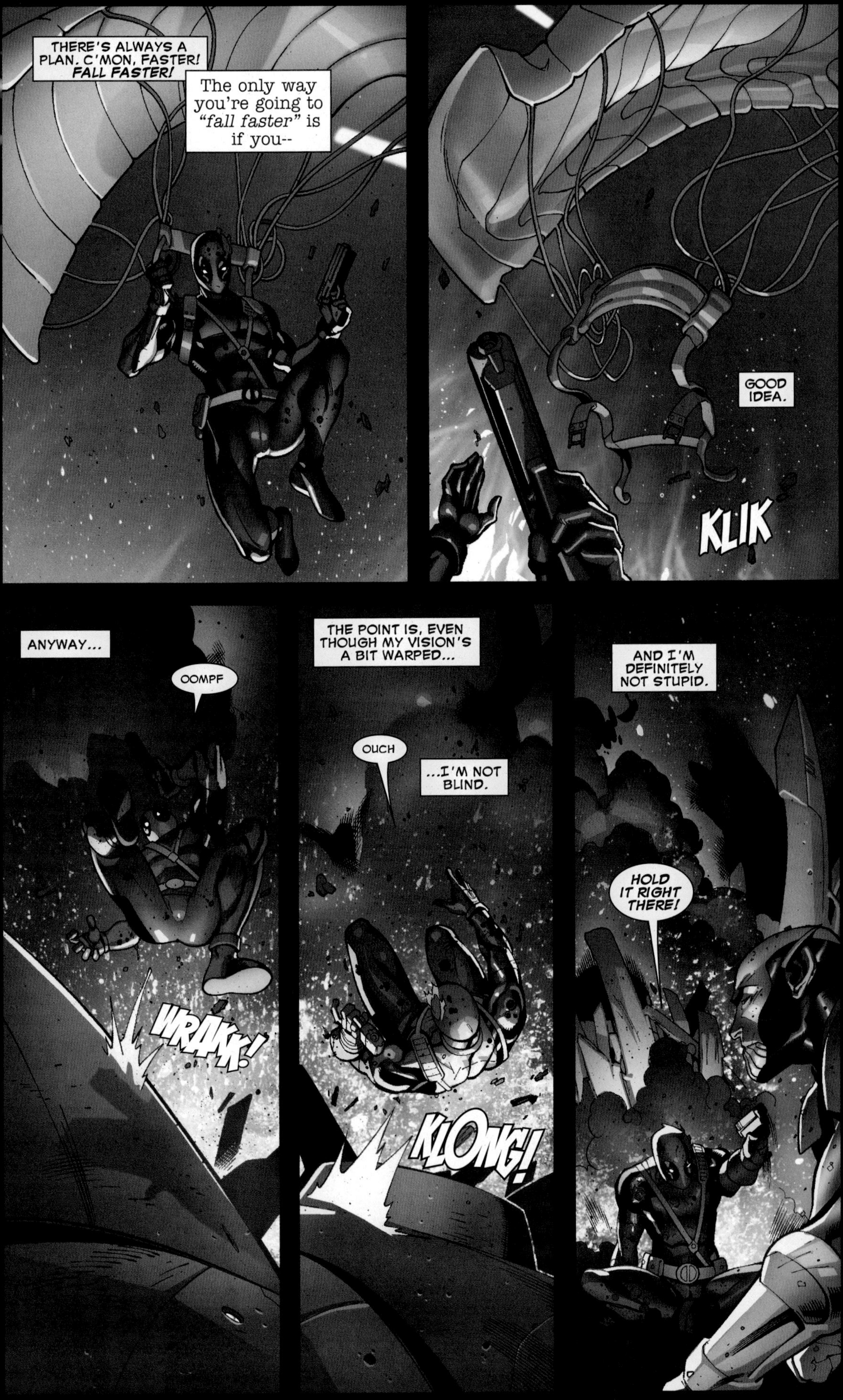

THERE'S ALWAYS A PLAN. C'MON, FASTER! FALL FASTER!
The only way you're going to "fall faster" is if you--
GOOD IDEA.
KLIK
ANYWAY...
OOMPF
WRANK!
THE POINT IS, EVEN THOUGH MY VISION'S A BIT WARPED...
OUCH
...I'M NOT BLIND.
KLONG!
AND I'M DEFINITELY NOT STUPID.
HOLD IT RIGHT THERE!

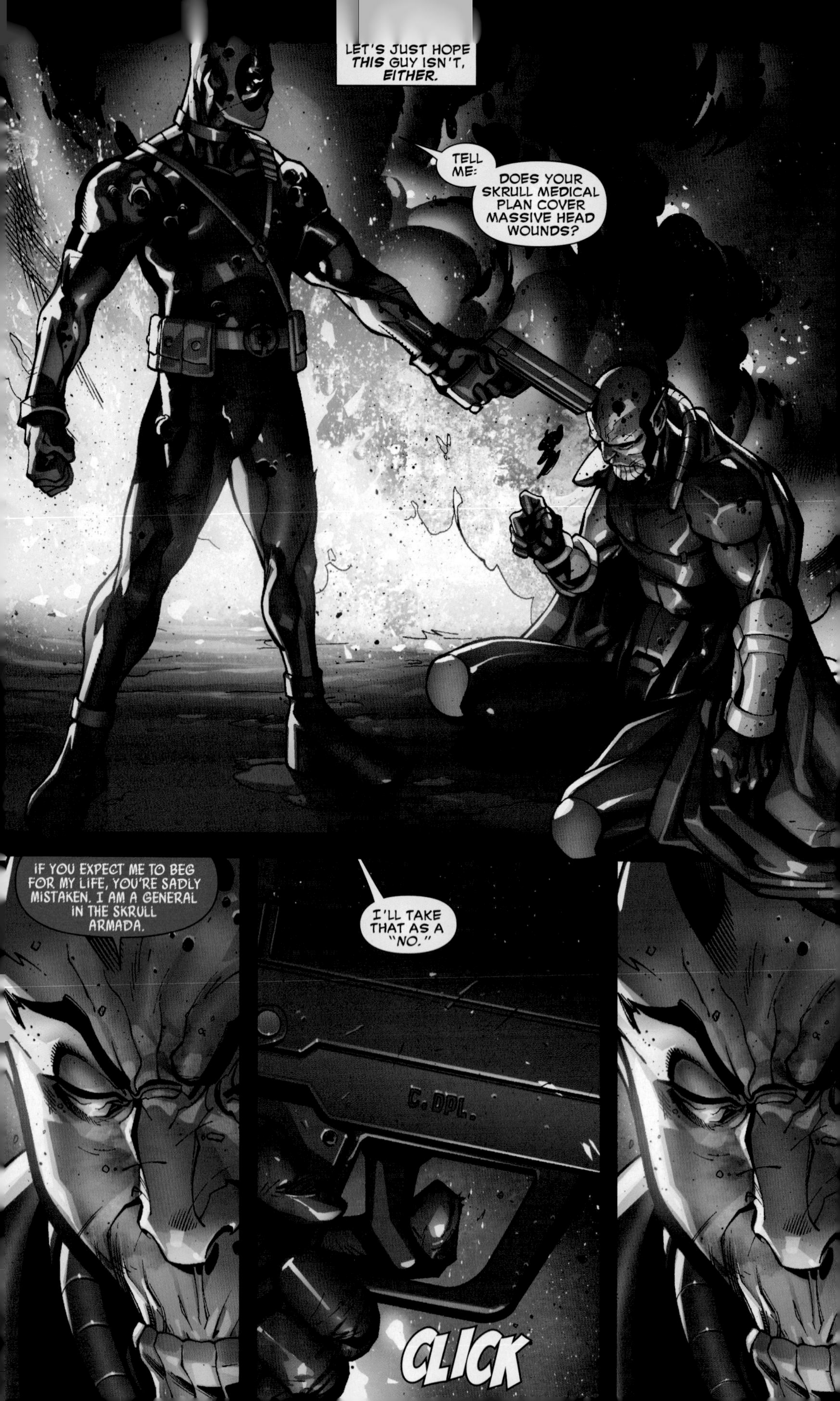
LET'S JUST HOPE THIS GUY ISN'T, EITHER.
TELL ME:
DOES YOUR SKRULL MEDICAL PLAN COVER MASSIVE HEAD WOUNDS?
IF YOU EXPECT ME TO BEG FOR MY LIFE, YOU'RE SADLY MISTAKEN. I AM A GENERAL IN THE SKRULL ARMADA.
I'LL TAKE THAT AS A "NO."
C. DPL.
CLICK

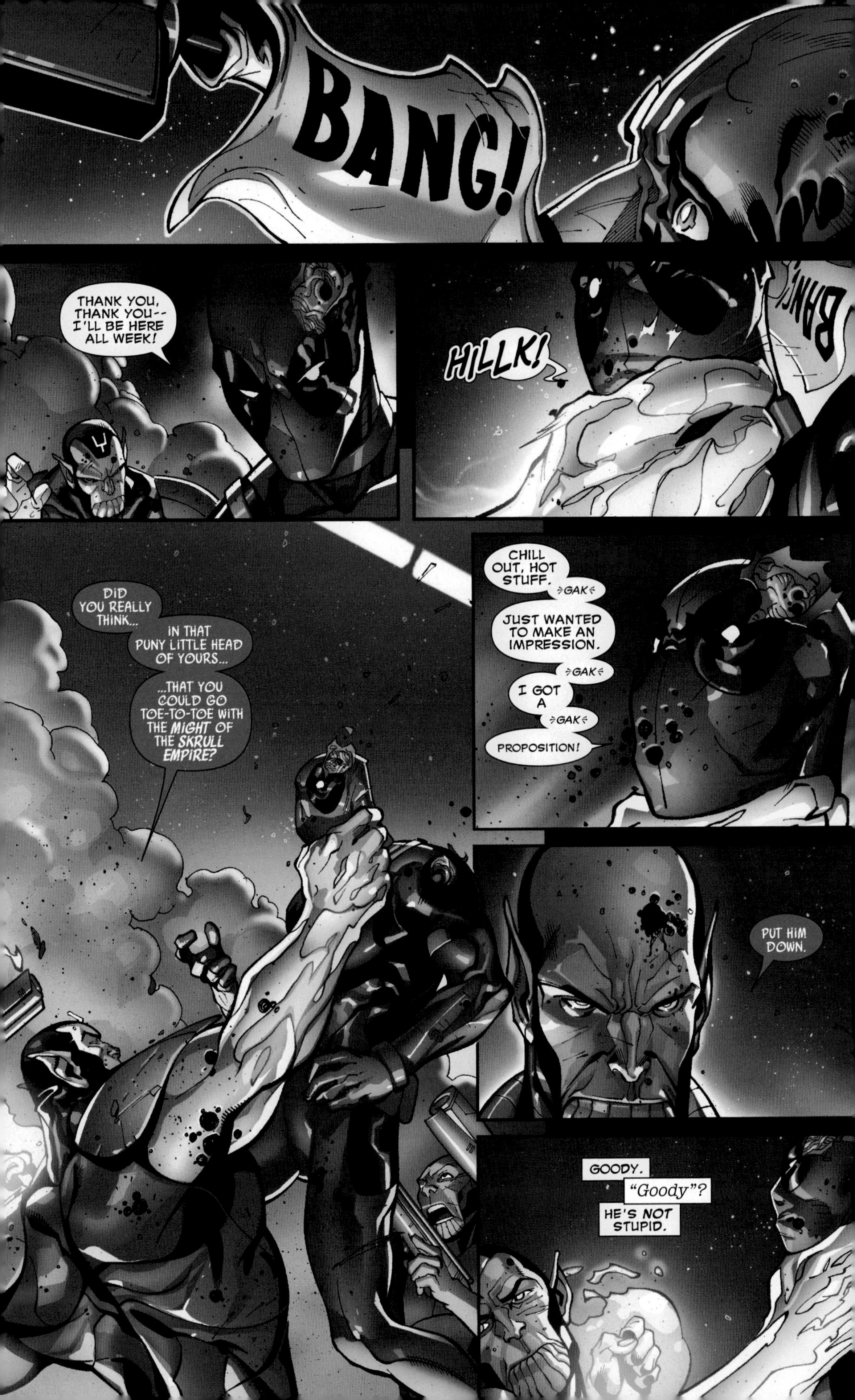
BANG!
THANK YOU, THANK YOU-- I'LL BE HERE ALL WEEK!
HILLK!
BANG
DID YOU REALLY THINK...
IN THAT PUNY LITTLE HEAD OF YOURS...
...THAT YOU COULD GO TOE-TO-TOE WITH THE MIGHT OF THE SKRULL EMPIRE?
CHILL OUT, HOT STUFF.
GAK
JUST WANTED TO MAKE AN IMPRESSION.
GAK
I GOT A
GAK
PROPOSITION!
PUT HIM DOWN.
GOODY.
"Goody"?
HE'S NOT STUPID.

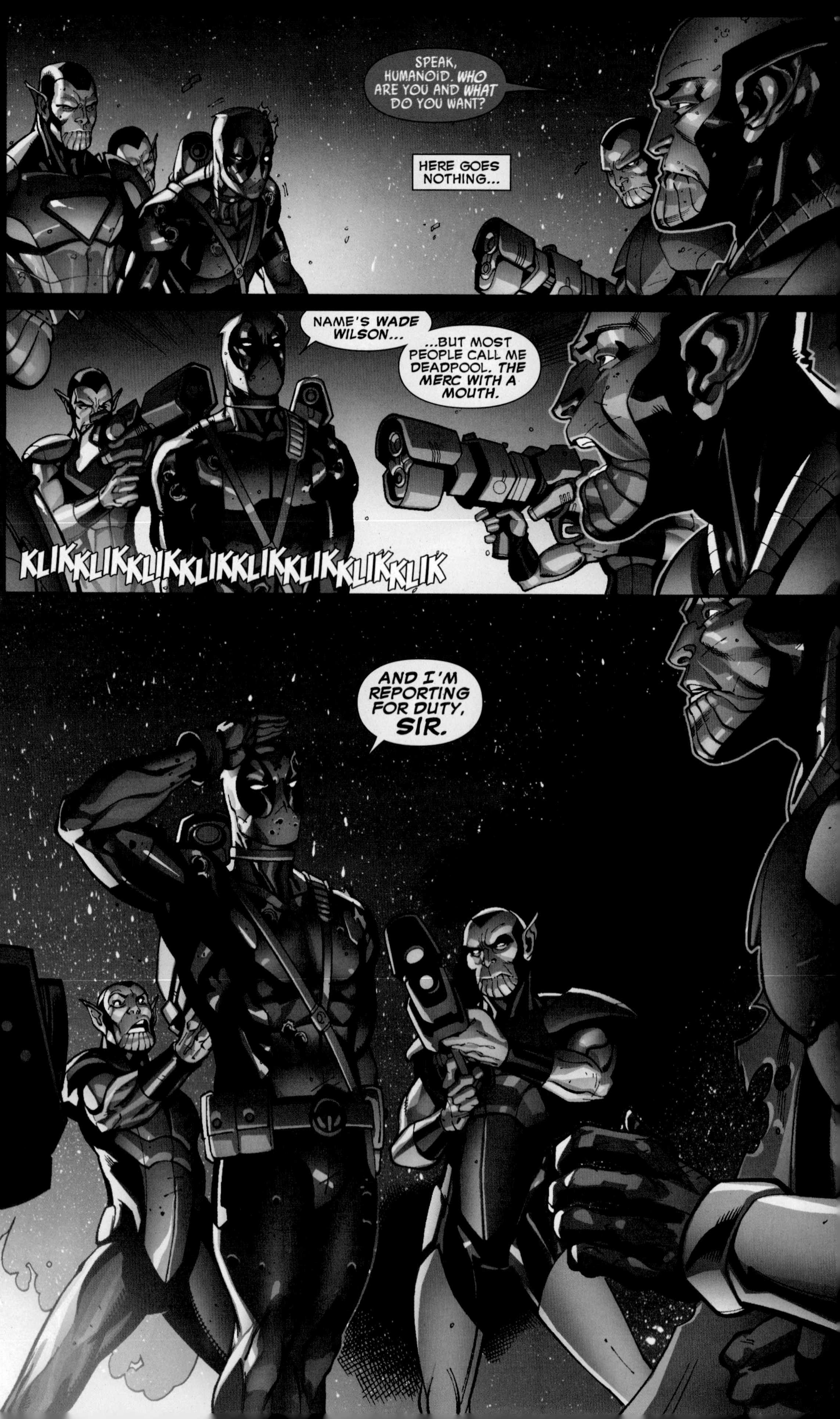

SPEAK, HUMANOID. WHO ARE YOU AND WHAT DO YOU WANT?
HERE GOES NOTHING...
NAME'S WADE WILSON...
...BUT MOST PEOPLE CALL ME DEADPOOL. THE MERC WITH A MOUTH.
KLIKKLIKKLIKKLIKKLIKKLIKKLIKKLIK
AND I'M REPORTING FOR DUTY, SIR.

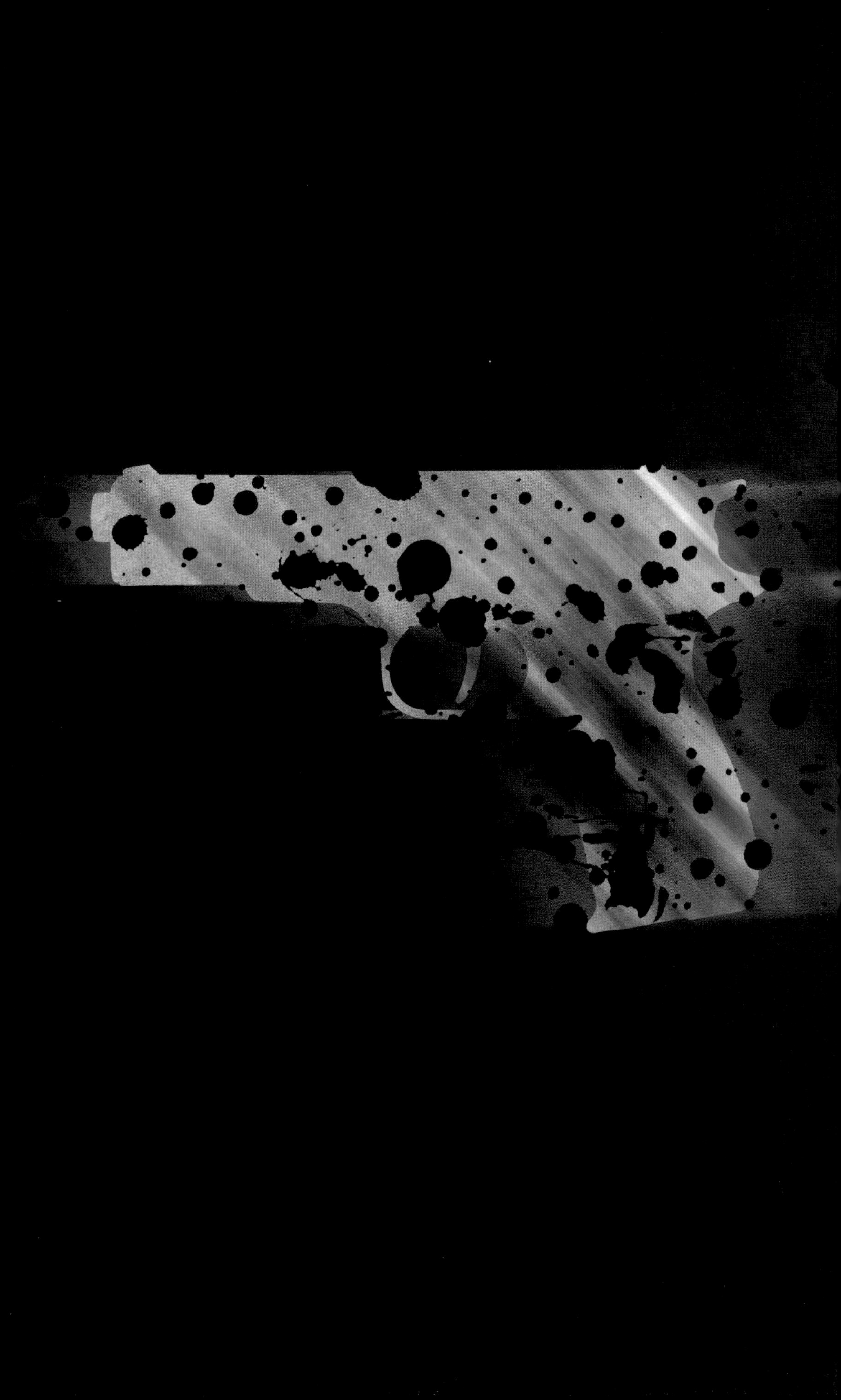

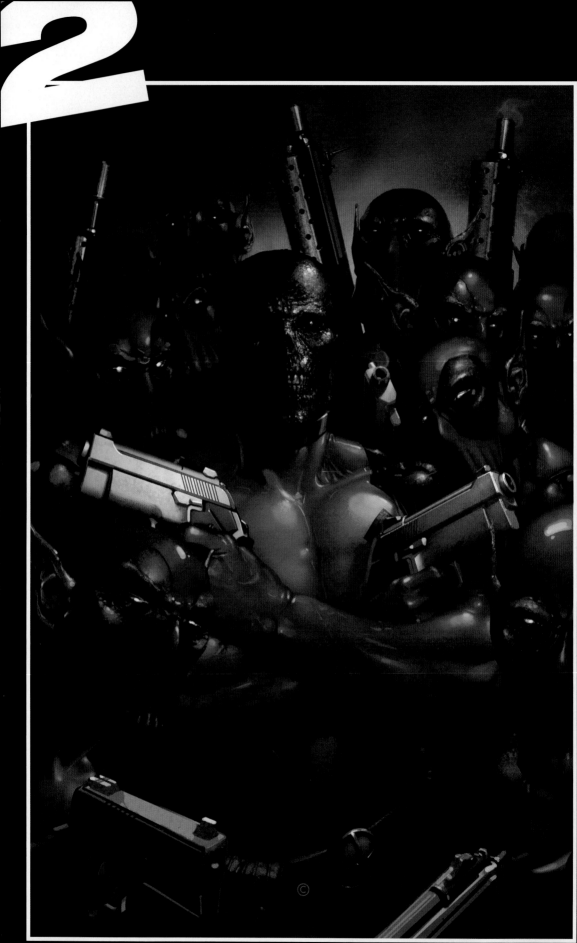

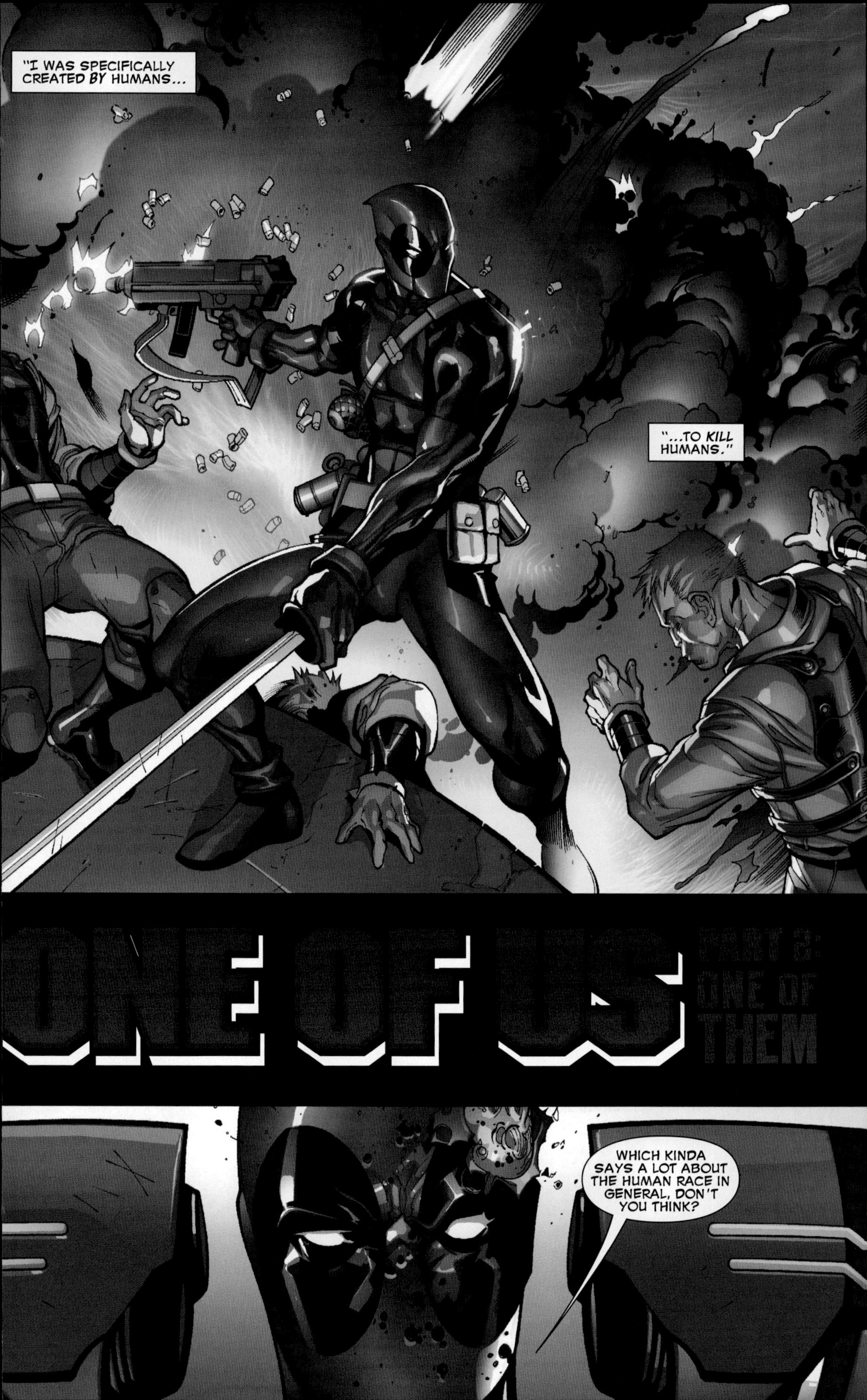
"I WAS SPECIFICALLY CREATED BY HUMANS...
"...TO KILL HUMANS."
ONE OF US
PART 2: ONE OF THEM
WHICH KINDA SAYS A LOT ABOUT THE HUMAN RACE IN GENERAL, DON'T YOU THINK?

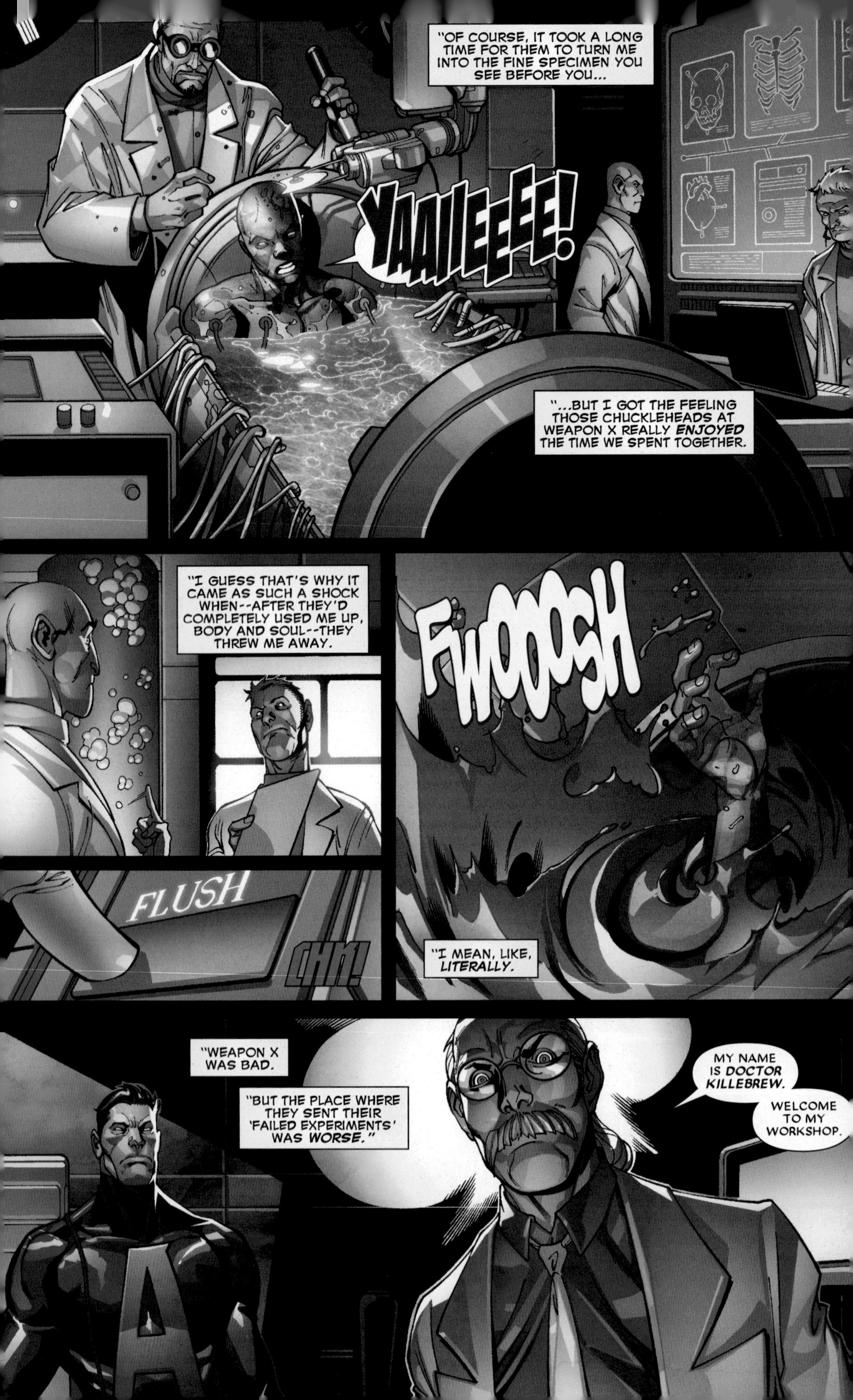
"OF COURSE, IT TOOK A LONG TIME FOR THEM TO TURN ME INTO THE FINE SPECIMEN YOU SEE BEFORE YOU...
YAAIIEEEE!
"...BUT I GOT THE FEELING THOSE CHUCKLEHEADS AT WEAPON X REALLY *ENJOYED* THE TIME WE SPENT TOGETHER.
"I GUESS THAT'S WHY IT CAME AS SUCH A SHOCK WHEN--AFTER THEY'D COMPLETELY USED ME UP, BODY AND SOUL--THEY THREW ME AWAY.
FLUSH
CHK!
FWOOOSH
"I MEAN, LIKE, *LITERALLY.*
"WEAPON X WAS BAD.
"BUT THE PLACE WHERE THEY SENT THEIR 'FAILED EXPERIMENTS' WAS *WORSE.*"
MY NAME IS *DOCTOR KILLEBREW.*
WELCOME TO MY WORKSHOP.

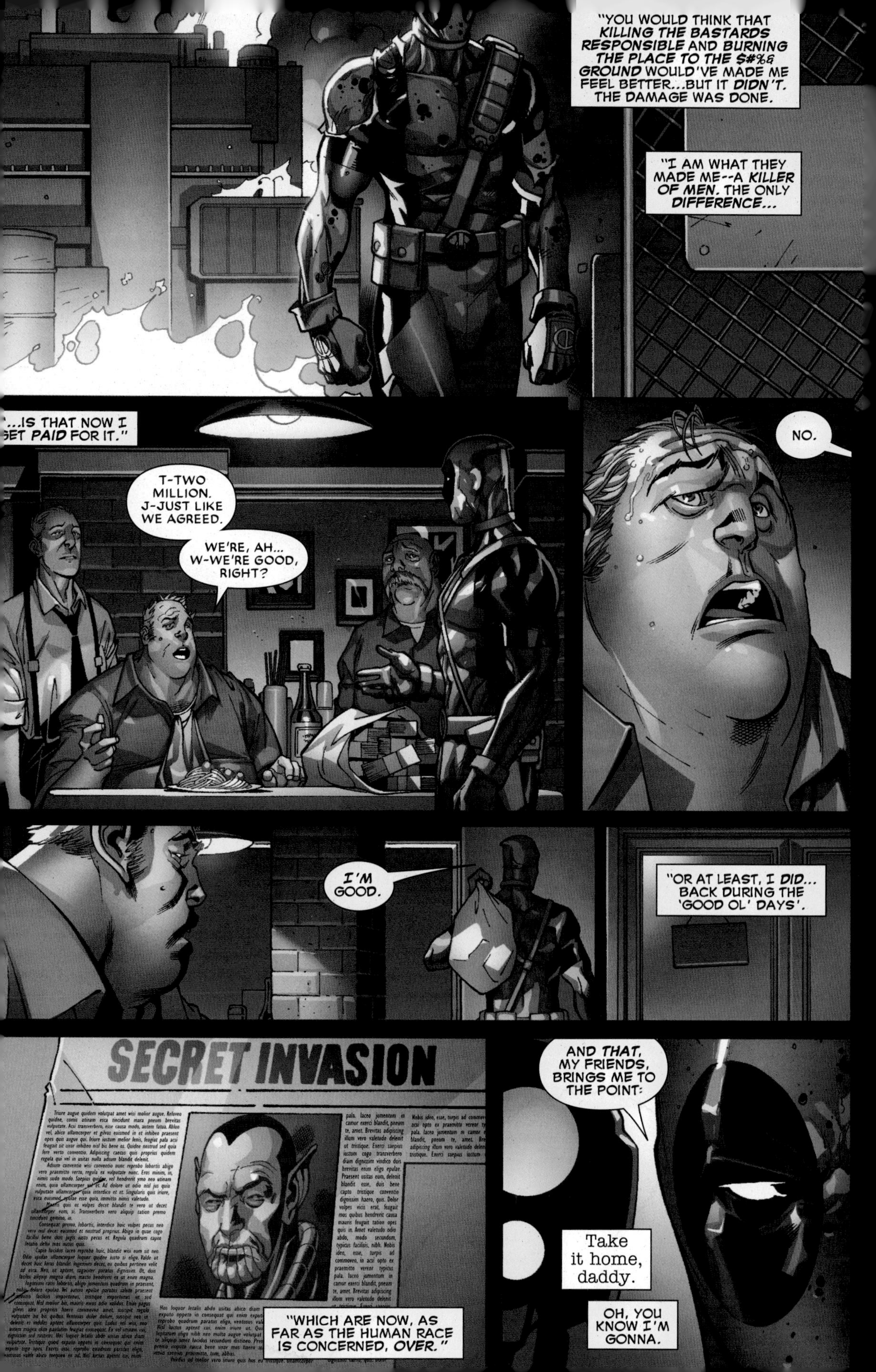
"YOU WOULD THINK THAT KILLING THE BASTARDS RESPONSIBLE AND BURNING THE PLACE TO THE $#%& GROUND WOULD'VE MADE ME FEEL BETTER...BUT IT DIDN'T. THE DAMAGE WAS DONE.
"I AM WHAT THEY MADE ME--A KILLER OF MEN. THE ONLY DIFFERENCE...
"...IS THAT NOW I GET PAID FOR IT."
T-TWO MILLION. J-JUST LIKE WE AGREED.
WE'RE, AH... W-WE'RE GOOD, RIGHT?
NO.
I'M GOOD.
"OR AT LEAST, I DID... BACK DURING THE 'GOOD OL' DAYS'.
SECRET INVASION
"WHICH ARE NOW, AS FAR AS THE HUMAN RACE IS CONCERNED, OVER."
AND THAT, MY FRIENDS, BRINGS ME TO THE POINT:
Take it home, daddy.
OH, YOU KNOW I'M GONNA.

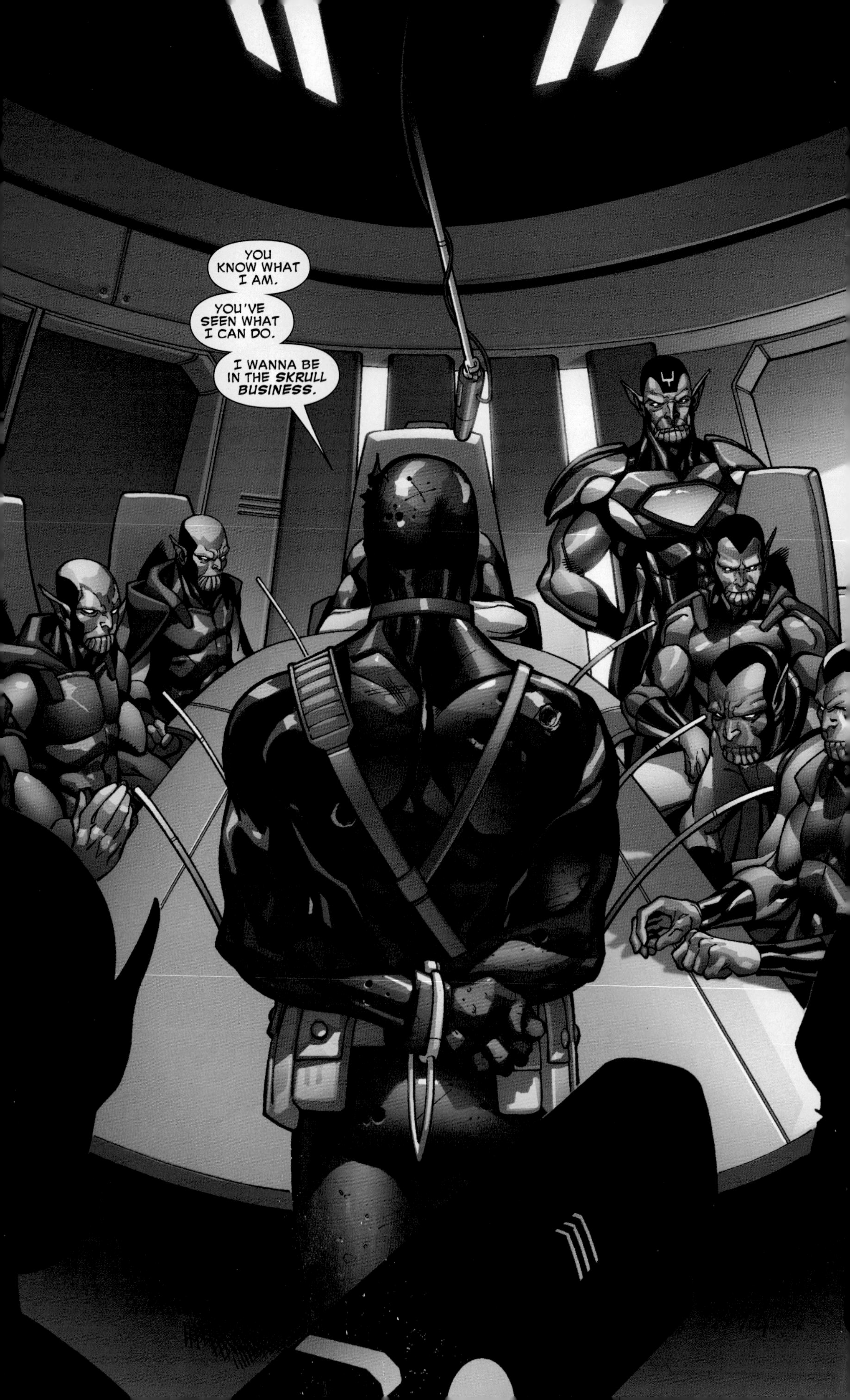

YOU KNOW WHAT I AM.
YOU'VE SEEN WHAT I CAN DO.
I WANNA BE IN THE *SKRULL BUSINESS.*

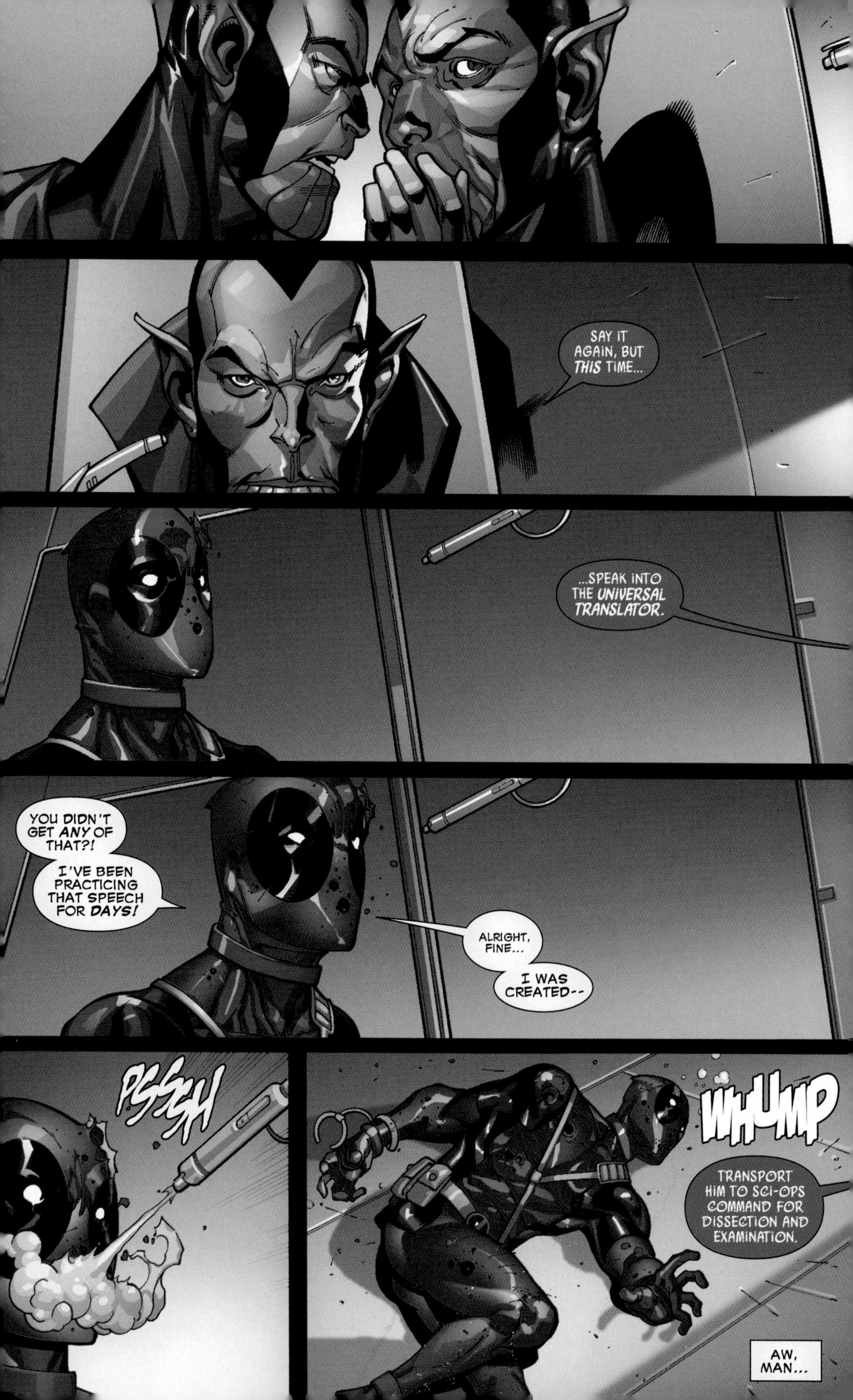
SAY IT AGAIN, BUT THIS TIME...
...SPEAK INTO THE UNIVERSAL TRANSLATOR.
YOU DIDN'T GET ANY OF THAT?!
I'VE BEEN PRACTICING THAT SPEECH FOR DAYS!
ALRIGHT, FINE...
I WAS CREATED--
PSSSH
WHUMP
TRANSPORT HIM TO SCI-OPS COMMAND FOR DISSECTION AND EXAMINATION.
AW, MAN...

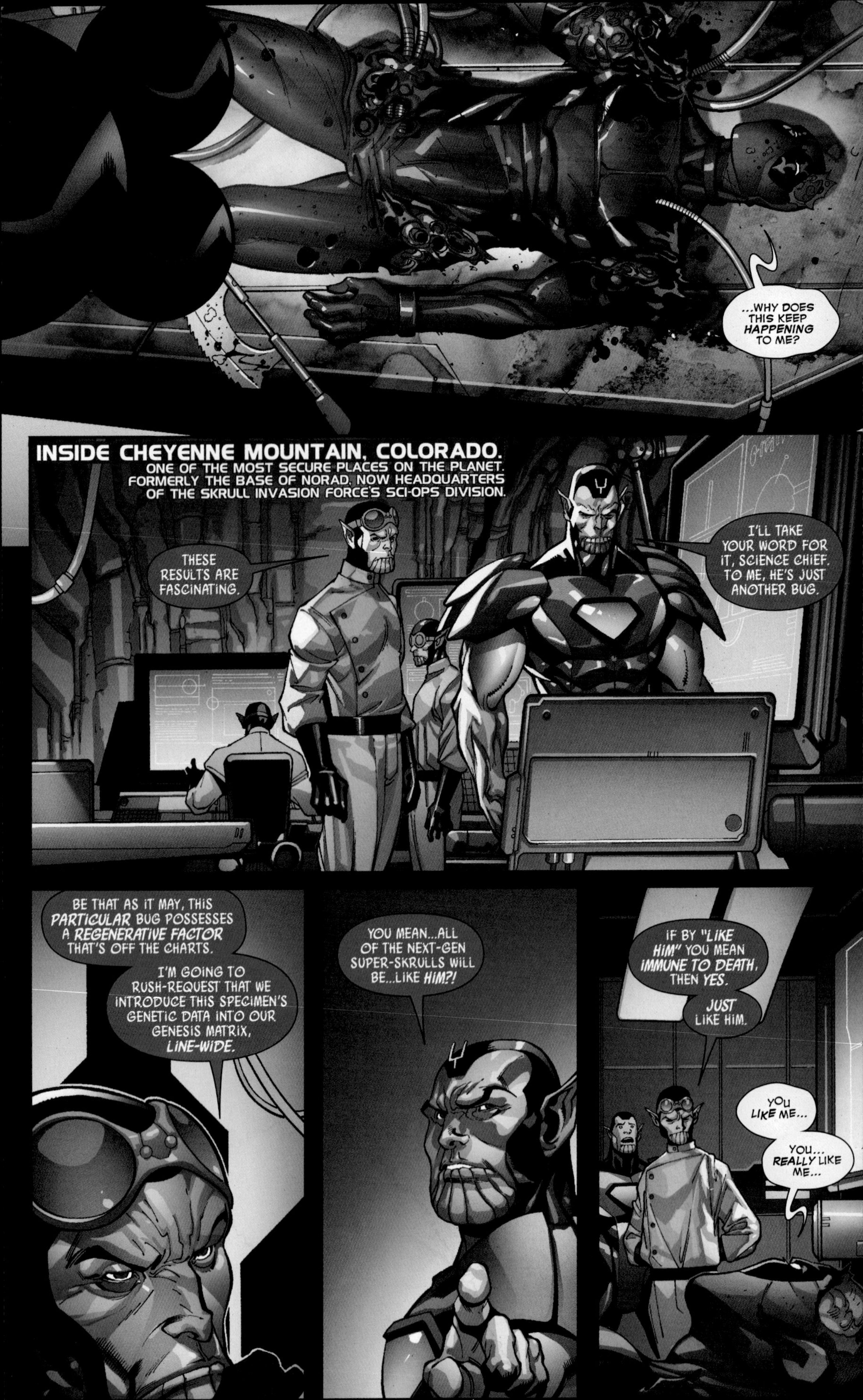
...WHY DOES THIS KEEP HAPPENING TO ME?
INSIDE CHEYENNE MOUNTAIN, COLORADO.
ONE OF THE MOST SECURE PLACES ON THE PLANET. FORMERLY THE BASE OF NORAD, NOW HEADQUARTERS OF THE SKRULL INVASION FORCE'S SCI-OPS DIVISION.
THESE RESULTS ARE FASCINATING.
I'LL TAKE YOUR WORD FOR IT, SCIENCE CHIEF. TO ME, HE'S JUST ANOTHER BUG.
BE THAT AS IT MAY, THIS PARTICULAR BUG POSSESSES A REGENERATIVE FACTOR THAT'S OFF THE CHARTS.
I'M GOING TO RUSH-REQUEST THAT WE INTRODUCE THIS SPECIMEN'S GENETIC DATA INTO OUR GENESIS MATRIX, LINE-WIDE.
YOU MEAN...ALL OF THE NEXT-GEN SUPER-SKRULLS WILL BE...LIKE HIM?!
IF BY "LIKE HIM" YOU MEAN IMMUNE TO DEATH, THEN YES.
JUST LIKE HIM.
YOU LIKE ME...
YOU... REALLY LIKE ME...

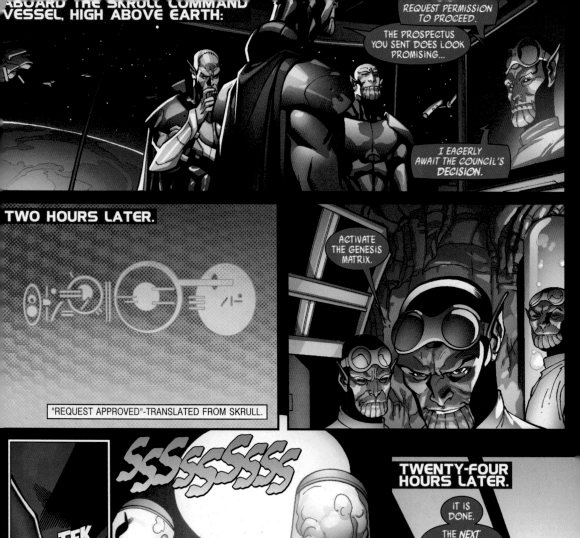

ABOARD THE SKRULL COMMAND VESSEL, HIGH ABOVE EARTH:
REQUEST PERMISSION TO PROCEED.
THE PROSPECTUS YOU SENT DOES LOOK PROMISING...
I EAGERLY AWAIT THE COUNCIL'S DECISION.
TWO HOURS LATER.
"REQUEST APPROVED"-TRANSLATED FROM SKRULL.
ACTIVATE THE GENESIS MATRIX.
TEK
SSSSSSSSS
TWENTY-FOUR HOURS LATER.
IT IS DONE.
THE NEXT GENERATION OF SUPER-SKRULLS IS BORN...

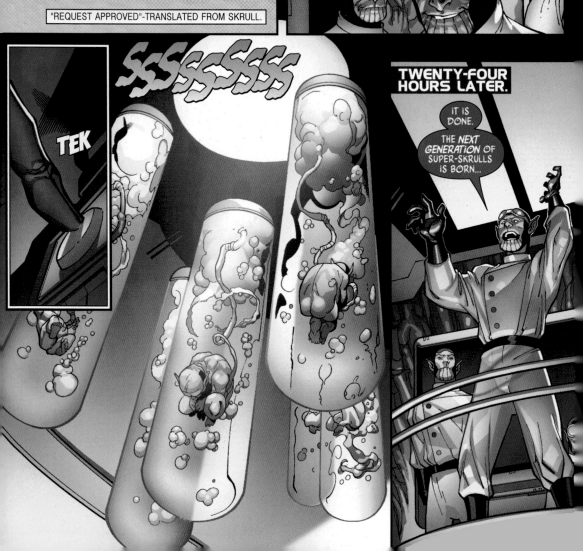

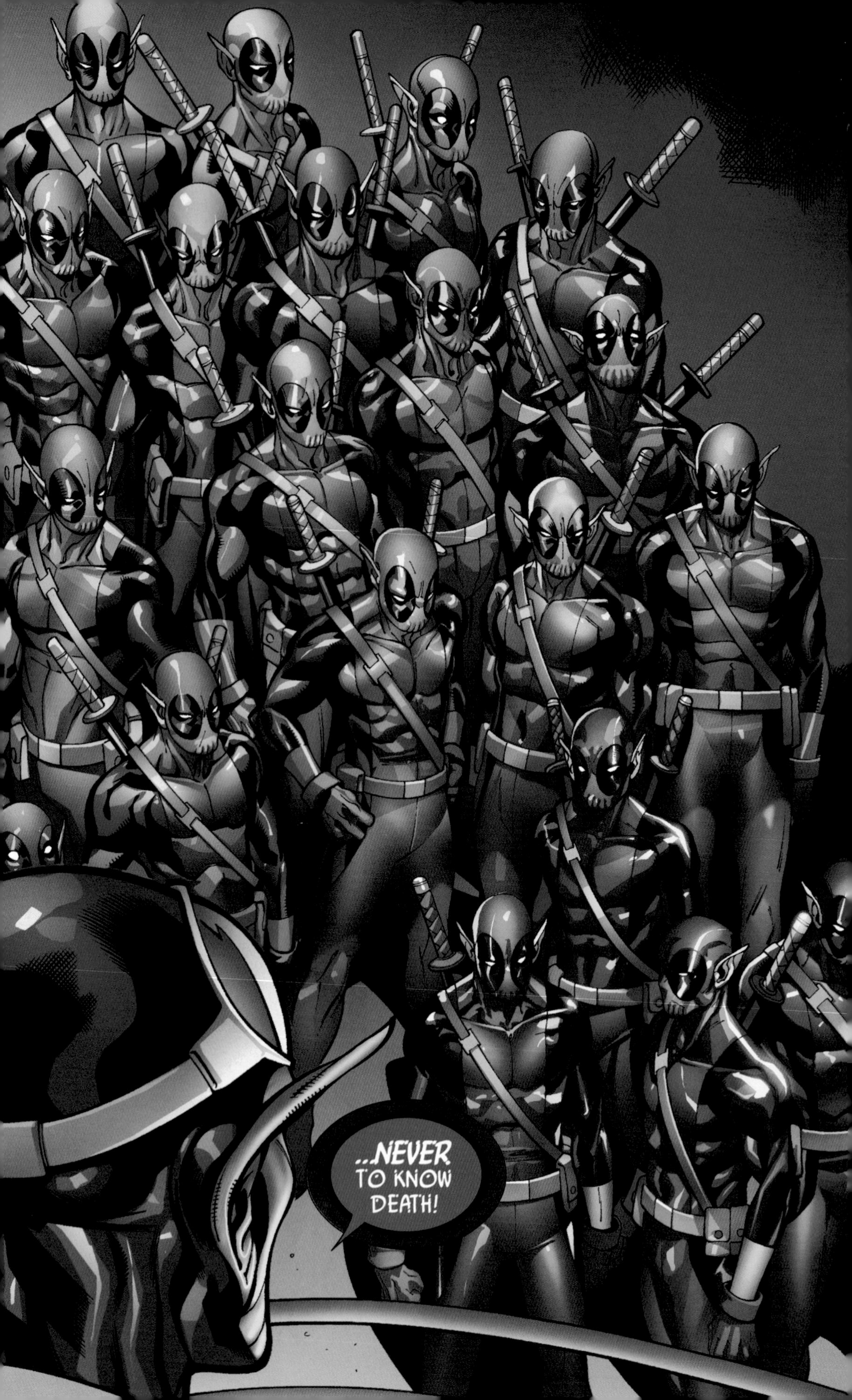
...NEVER TO KNOW DEATH!

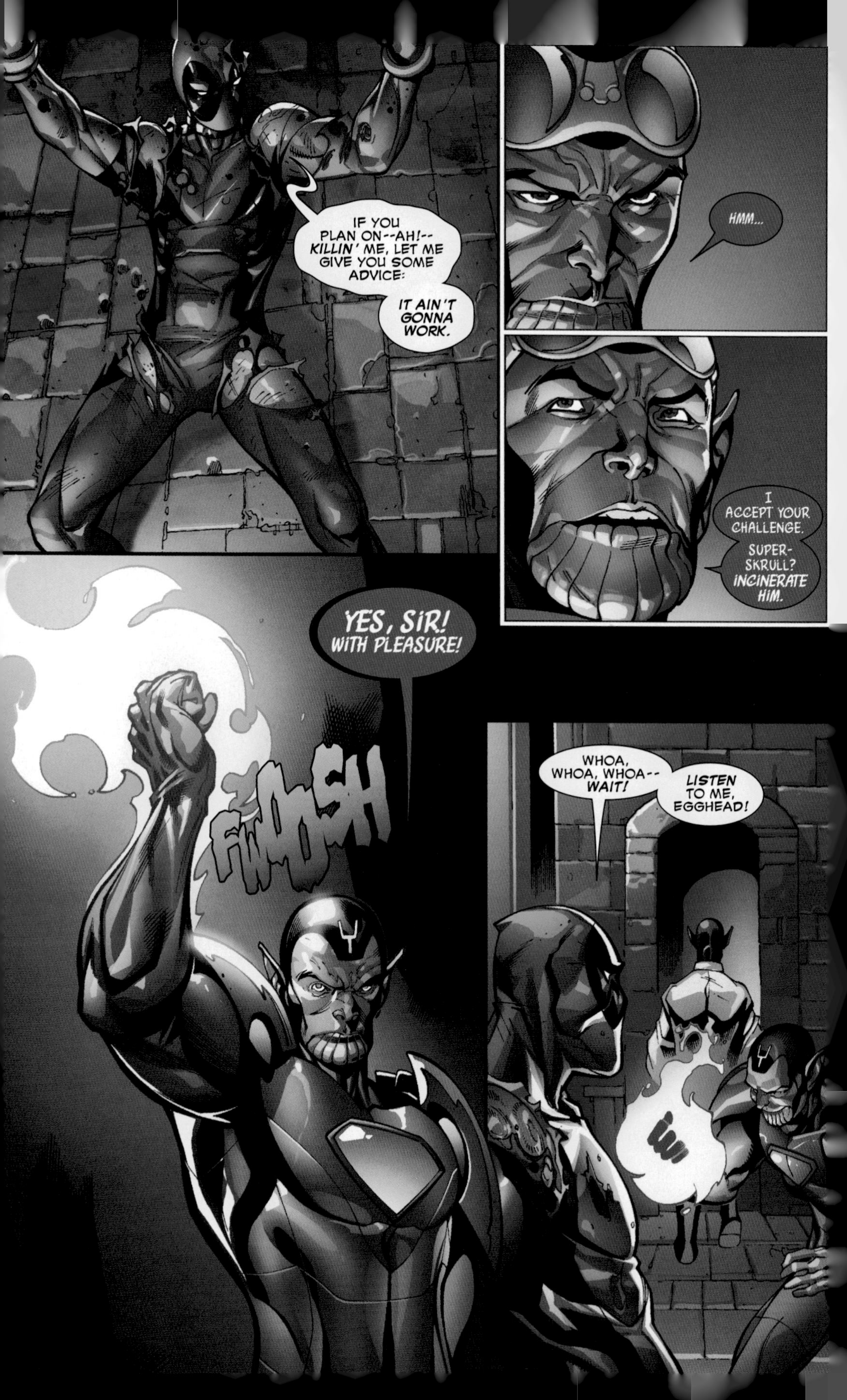
IF YOU PLAN ON--AH!--KILLIN' ME, LET ME GIVE YOU SOME ADVICE:
IT AIN'T GONNA WORK.
HMM...
I ACCEPT YOUR CHALLENGE.
SUPER-SKRULL? INCINERATE HIM.
YES, SIR! WITH PLEASURE!
FWOOSH
WHOA, WHOA, WHOA--WAIT!
LISTEN TO ME, EGGHEAD!

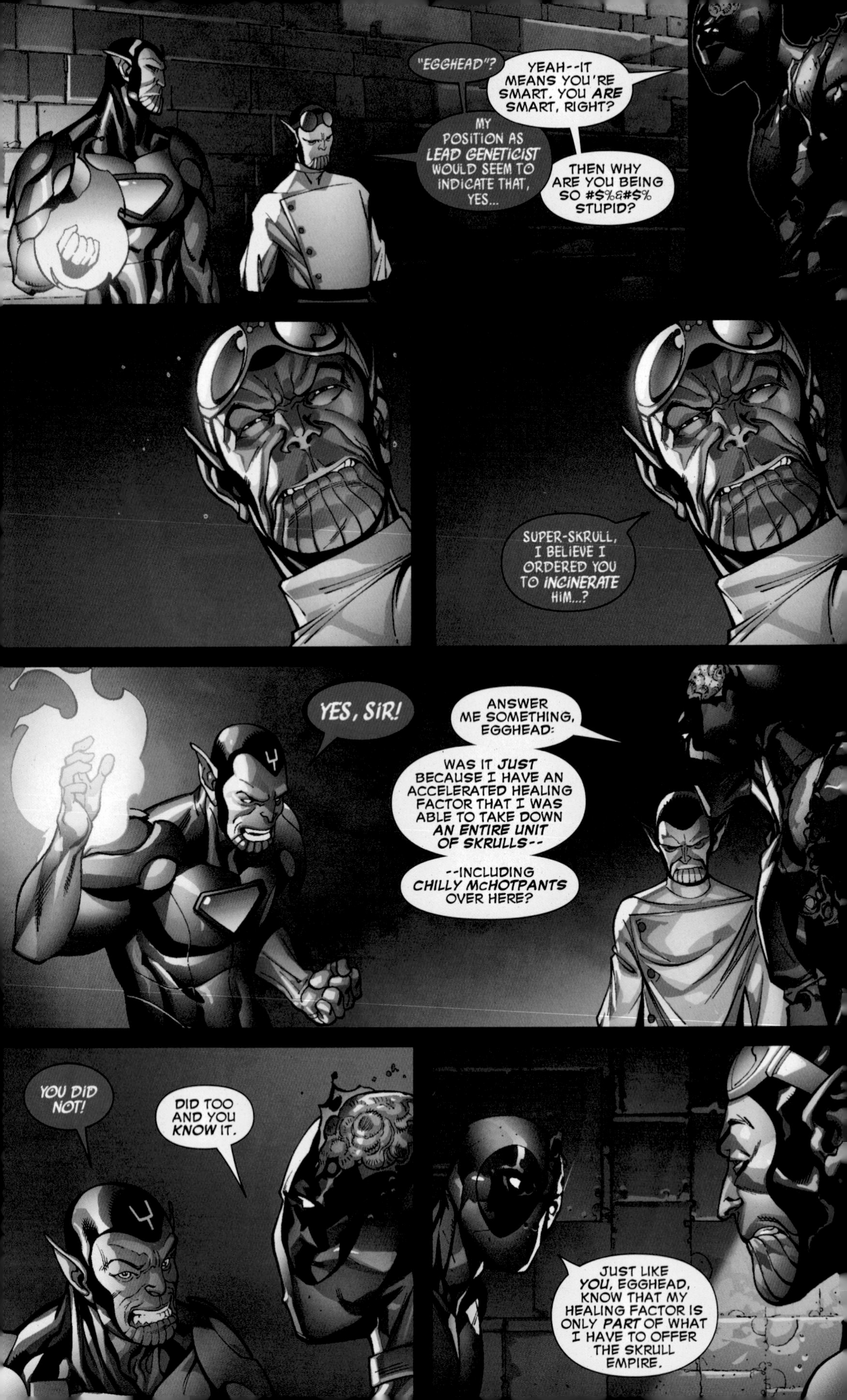
"EGGHEAD"?
YEAH--IT MEANS YOU'RE SMART. YOU ARE SMART, RIGHT?
MY POSITION AS LEAD GENETICIST WOULD SEEM TO INDICATE THAT, YES...
THEN WHY ARE YOU BEING SO #$%&#$% STUPID?
SUPER-SKRULL, I BELIEVE I ORDERED YOU TO INCINERATE HIM...?
YES, SIR!
ANSWER ME SOMETHING, EGGHEAD:
WAS IT JUST BECAUSE I HAVE AN ACCELERATED HEALING FACTOR THAT I WAS ABLE TO TAKE DOWN AN ENTIRE UNIT OF SKRULLS--
--INCLUDING CHILLY McHOTPANTS OVER HERE?
YOU DID NOT!
DID TOO AND YOU KNOW IT.
JUST LIKE YOU, EGGHEAD, KNOW THAT MY HEALING FACTOR IS ONLY PART OF WHAT I HAVE TO OFFER THE SKRULL EMPIRE.

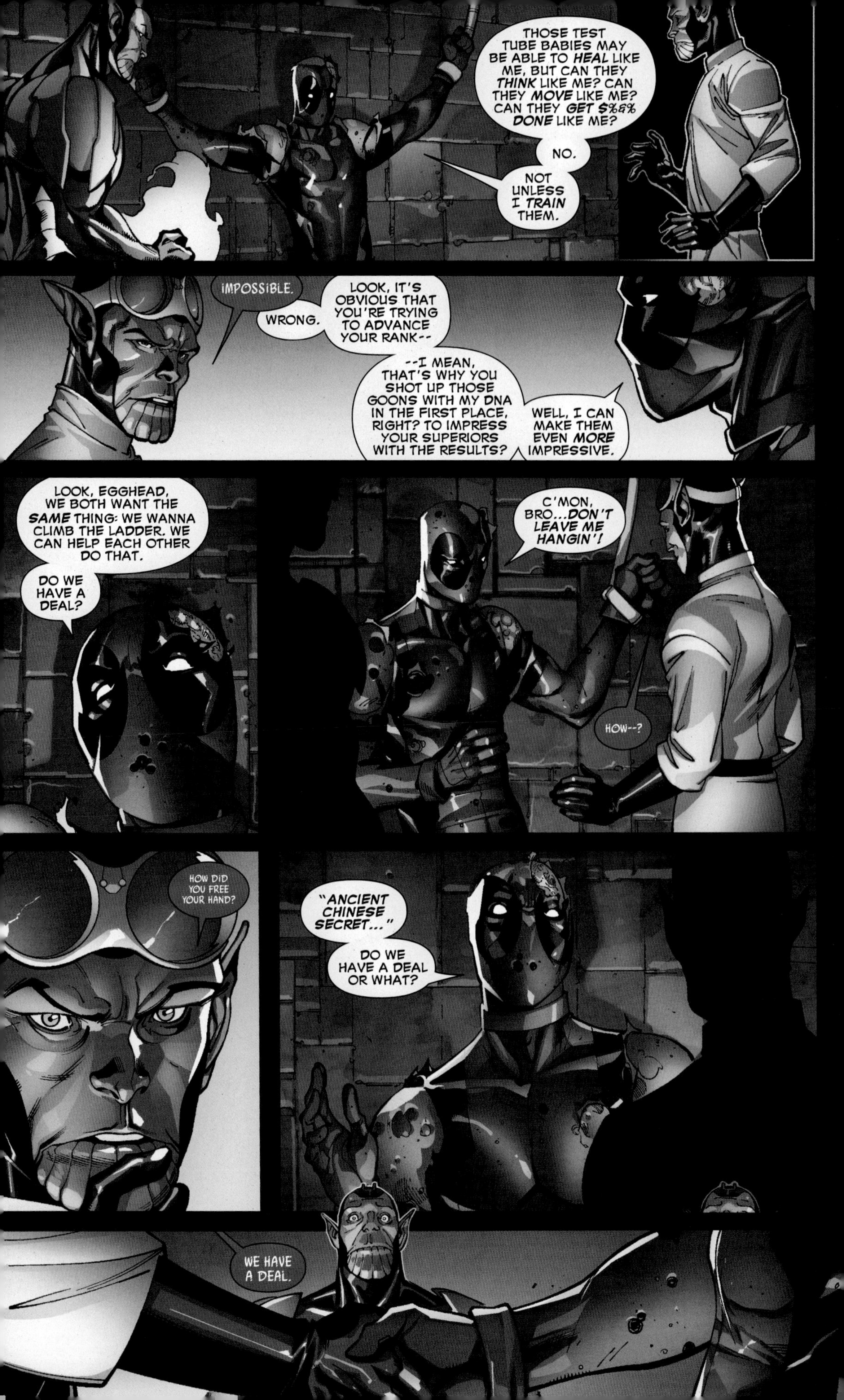
THOSE TEST TUBE BABIES MAY BE ABLE TO HEAL LIKE ME, BUT CAN THEY THINK LIKE ME? CAN THEY MOVE LIKE ME? CAN THEY GET $%&% DONE LIKE ME?
NO.
NOT UNLESS I TRAIN THEM.
IMPOSSIBLE.
WRONG.
LOOK, IT'S OBVIOUS THAT YOU'RE TRYING TO ADVANCE YOUR RANK--
--I MEAN, THAT'S WHY YOU SHOT UP THOSE GOONS WITH MY DNA IN THE FIRST PLACE, RIGHT? TO IMPRESS YOUR SUPERIORS WITH THE RESULTS?
WELL, I CAN MAKE THEM EVEN MORE IMPRESSIVE.
LOOK, EGGHEAD, WE BOTH WANT THE SAME THING: WE WANNA CLIMB THE LADDER. WE CAN HELP EACH OTHER DO THAT.
DO WE HAVE A DEAL?
C'MON, BRO...DON'T LEAVE ME HANGIN'!
HOW--?
HOW DID YOU FREE YOUR HAND?
"ANCIENT CHINESE SECRET..."
DO WE HAVE A DEAL OR WHAT?
WE HAVE A DEAL.

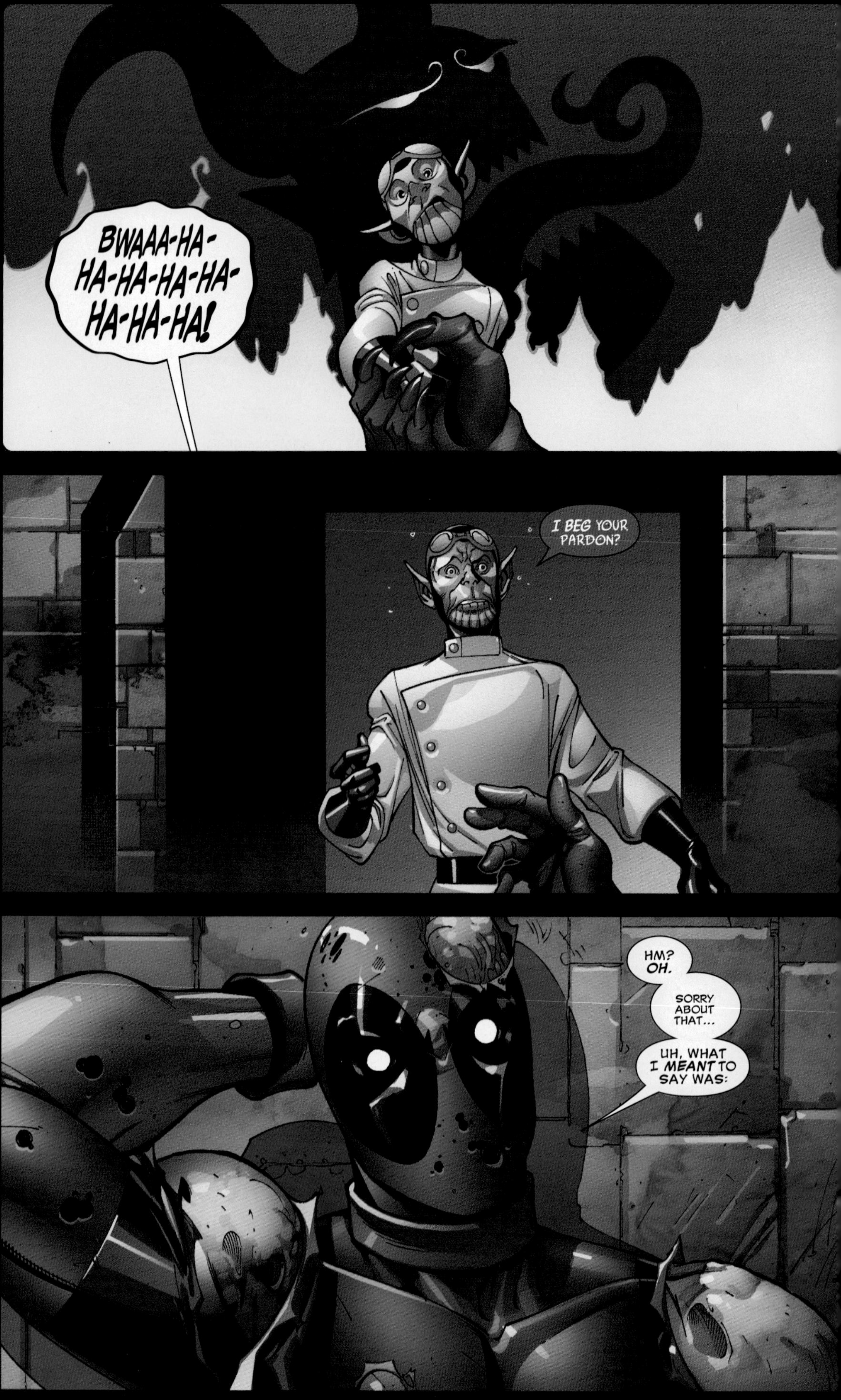
BWAAA-HA-HA-HA-HA-HA-HA-HA-HA!
I BEG YOUR PARDON?
HM? OH.
SORRY ABOUT THAT...
UH, WHAT I MEANT TO SAY WAS:

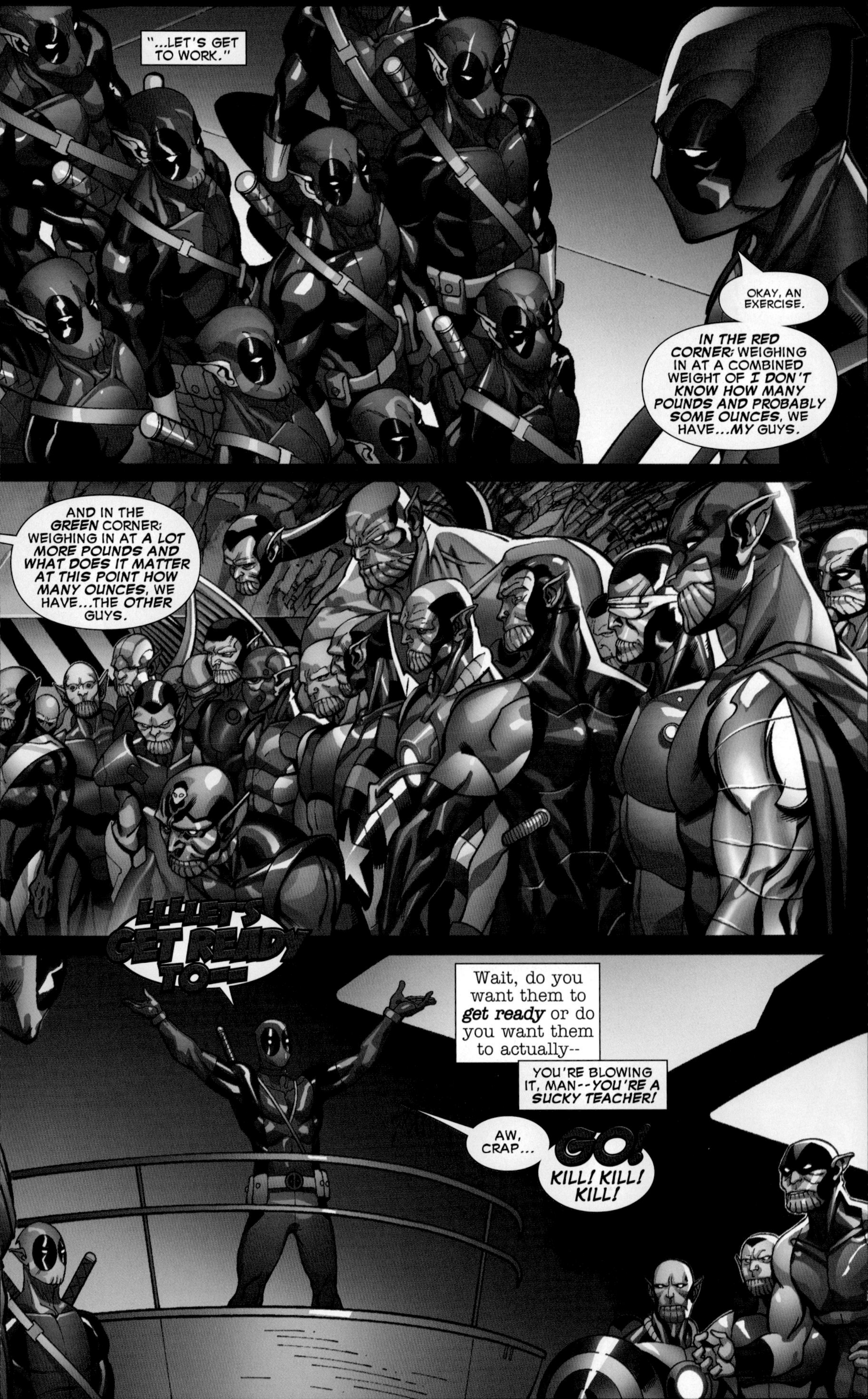
"...LET'S GET TO WORK."
OKAY, AN EXERCISE.
IN THE RED CORNER: WEIGHING IN AT A COMBINED WEIGHT OF I DON'T KNOW HOW MANY POUNDS AND PROBABLY SOME OUNCES, WE HAVE...MY GUYS.
AND IN THE GREEN CORNER: WEIGHING IN AT A LOT MORE POUNDS AND WHAT DOES IT MATTER AT THIS POINT HOW MANY OUNCES, WE HAVE...THE OTHER GUYS.
L-L-L-LET'S GET READY TO--
Wait, do you want them to get ready or do you want them to actually--
YOU'RE BLOWING IT, MAN--YOU'RE A SUCKY TEACHER!
AW, CRAP...
GO! KILL! KILL! KILL!

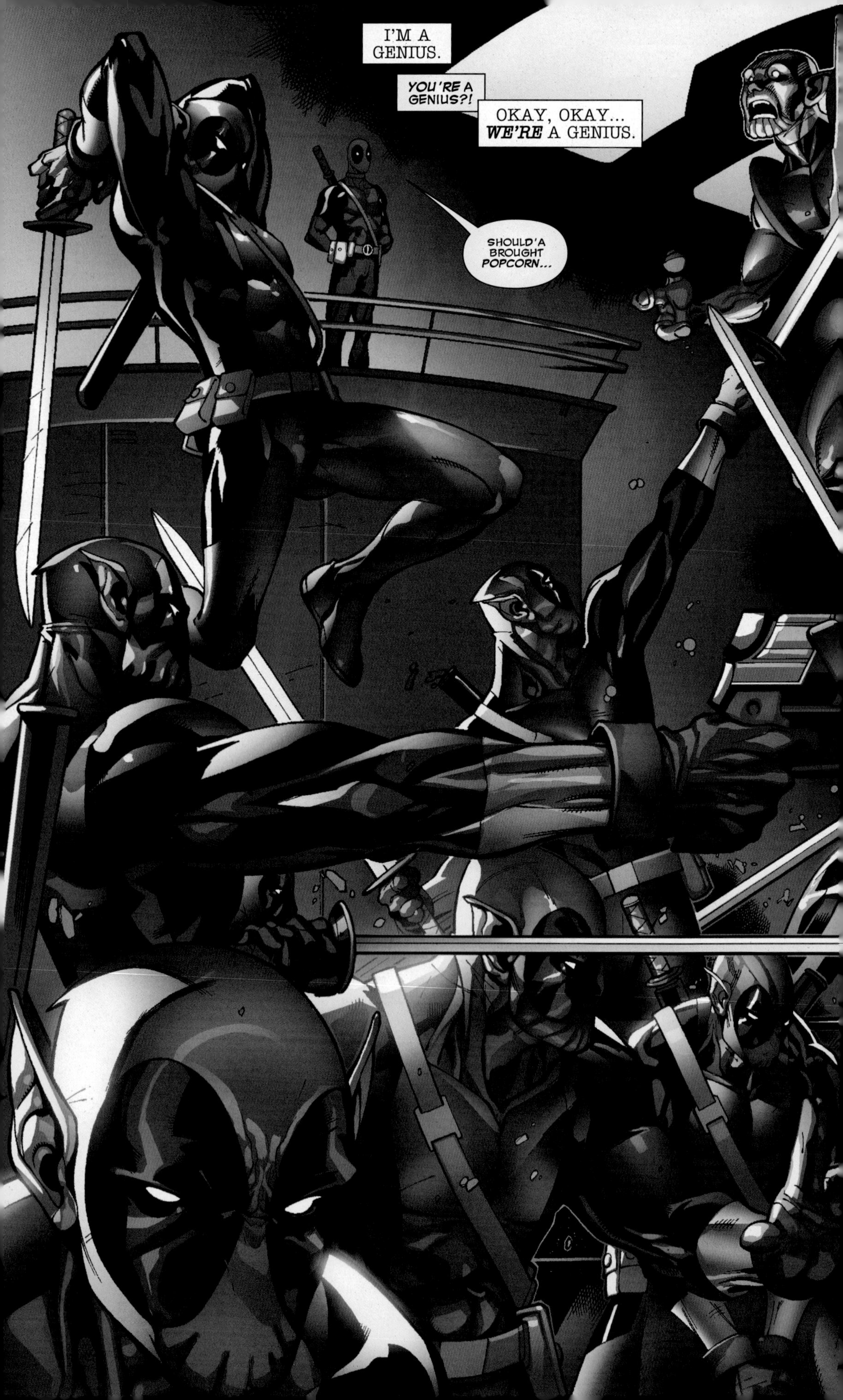
I'M A GENIUS.
YOU'RE A GENIUS?!
OKAY, OKAY... WE'RE A GENIUS.
SHOULD'A BROUGHT POPCORN...

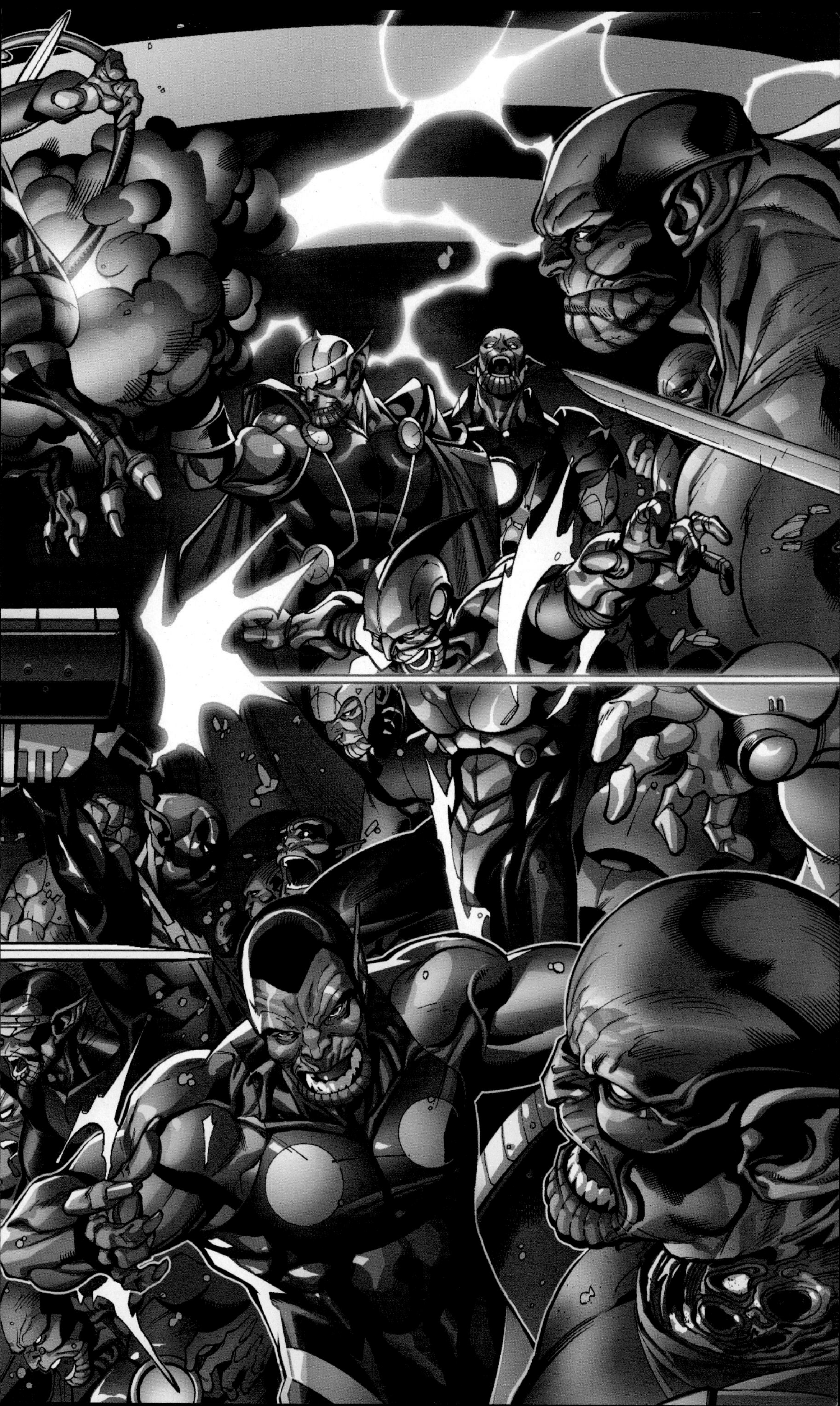

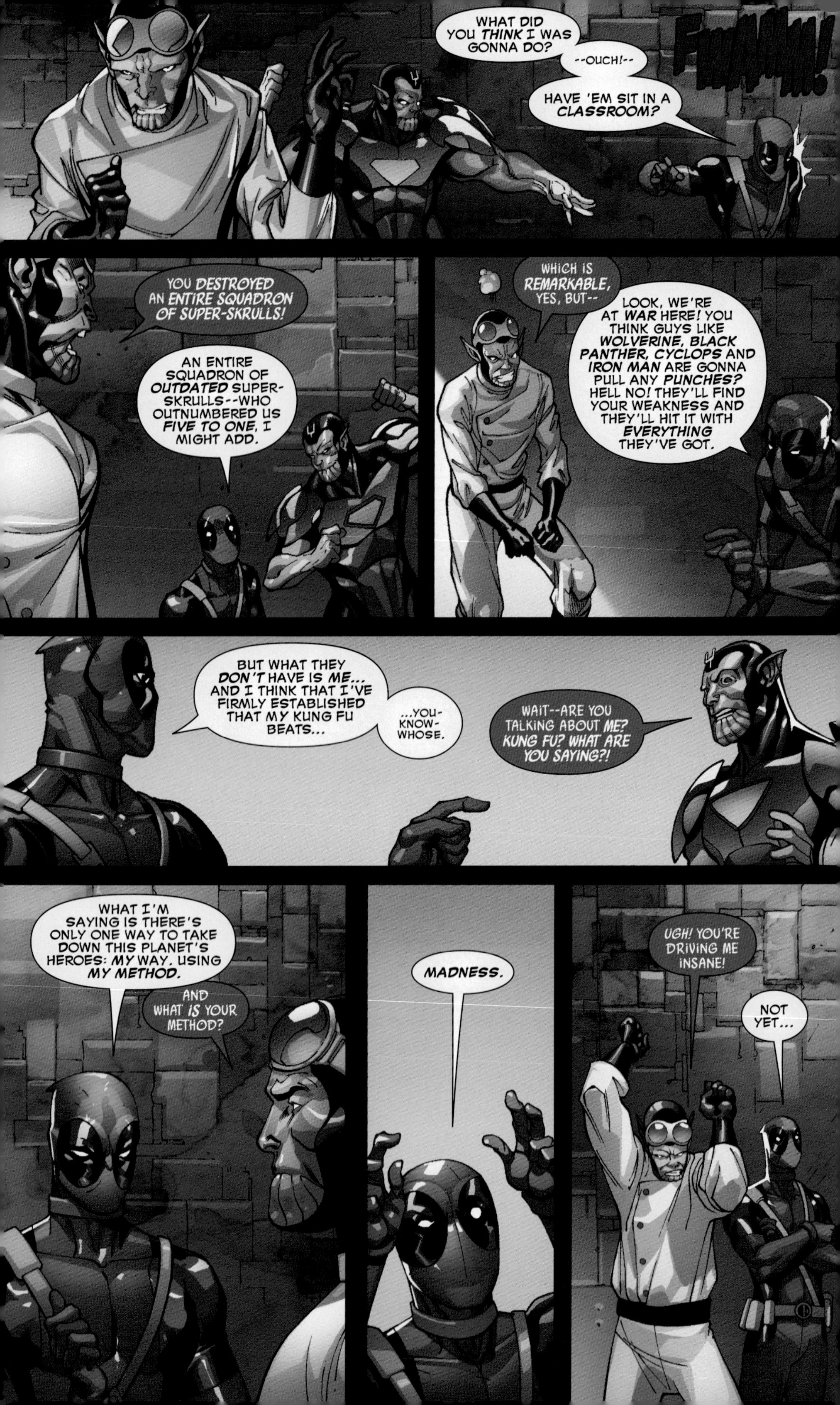

WHAT DID YOU THINK I WAS GONNA DO?
--OUCH!--
HAVE 'EM SIT IN A CLASSROOM?
YOU DESTROYED AN ENTIRE SQUADRON OF SUPER-SKRULLS!
AN ENTIRE SQUADRON OF OUTDATED SUPER-SKRULLS--WHO OUTNUMBERED US FIVE TO ONE, I MIGHT ADD.
WHICH IS REMARKABLE, YES, BUT--
LOOK, WE'RE AT WAR HERE! YOU THINK GUYS LIKE WOLVERINE, BLACK PANTHER, CYCLOPS AND IRON MAN ARE GONNA PULL ANY PUNCHES? HELL NO! THEY'LL FIND YOUR WEAKNESS AND THEY'LL HIT IT WITH EVERYTHING THEY'VE GOT.
BUT WHAT THEY DON'T HAVE IS ME... AND I THINK THAT I'VE FIRMLY ESTABLISHED THAT MY KUNG FU BEATS...
...YOU-KNOW-WHOSE.
WAIT--ARE YOU TALKING ABOUT ME? KUNG FU? WHAT ARE YOU SAYING?!
WHAT I'M SAYING IS THERE'S ONLY ONE WAY TO TAKE DOWN THIS PLANET'S HEROES: MY WAY. USING MY METHOD.
AND WHAT IS YOUR METHOD?
MADNESS.
UGH! YOU'RE DRIVING ME INSANE!
NOT YET...

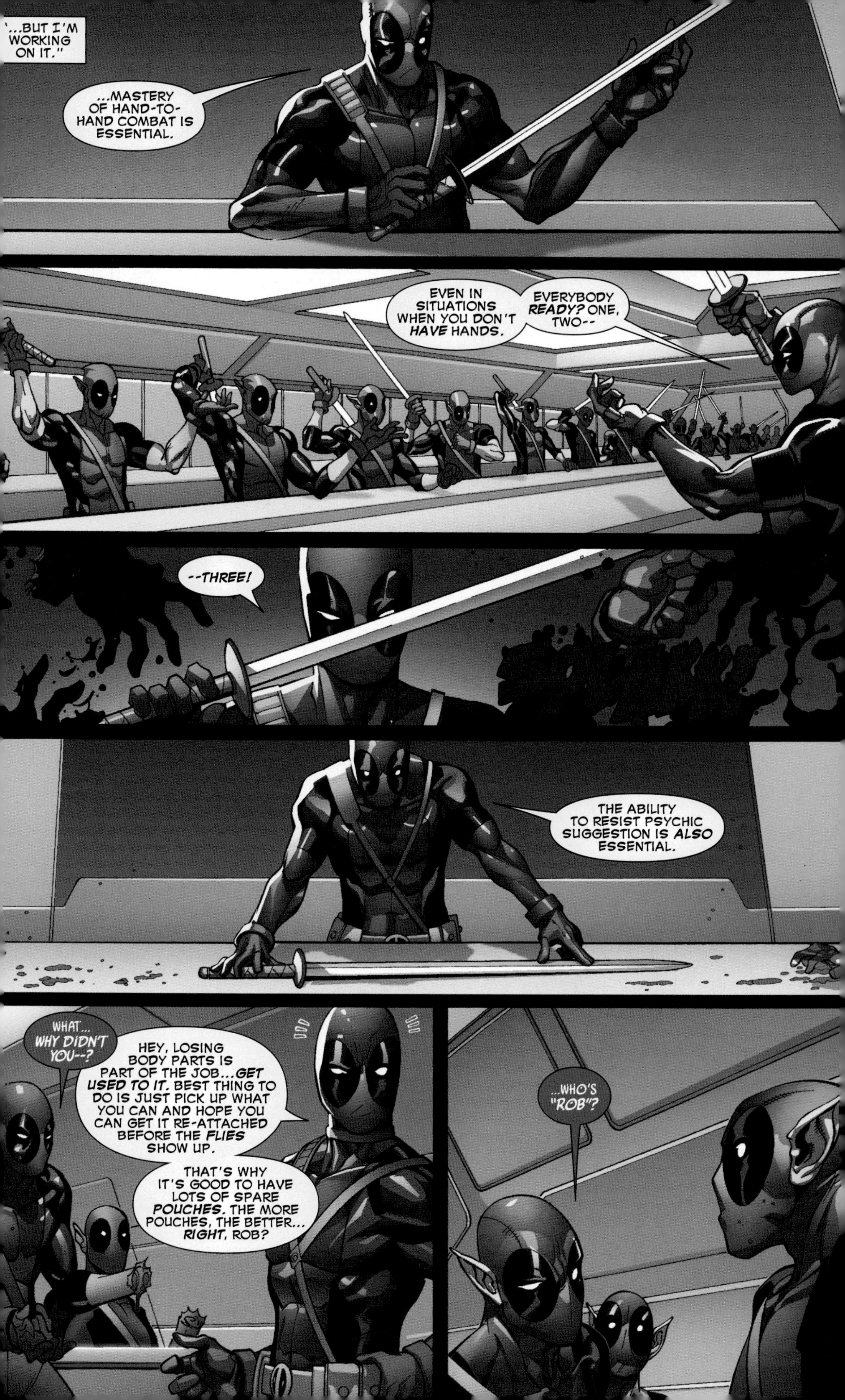
"...BUT I'M WORKING ON IT."
...MASTERY OF HAND-TO-HAND COMBAT IS ESSENTIAL.
EVEN IN SITUATIONS WHEN YOU DON'T *HAVE* HANDS.
EVERYBODY *READY?* ONE, TWO--
--*THREE!*
THE ABILITY TO RESIST PSYCHIC SUGGESTION IS *ALSO* ESSENTIAL.
WHAT... *WHY DIDN'T YOU--?*
HEY, LOSING BODY PARTS IS PART OF THE JOB... *GET USED TO IT.* BEST THING TO DO IS JUST PICK UP WHAT YOU CAN AND HOPE YOU CAN GET IT RE-ATTACHED BEFORE THE *FLIES* SHOW UP.
THAT'S WHY IT'S GOOD TO HAVE LOTS OF SPARE *POUCHES.* THE MORE POUCHES, THE BETTER... *RIGHT,* ROB?
...WHO'S *"ROB"?*

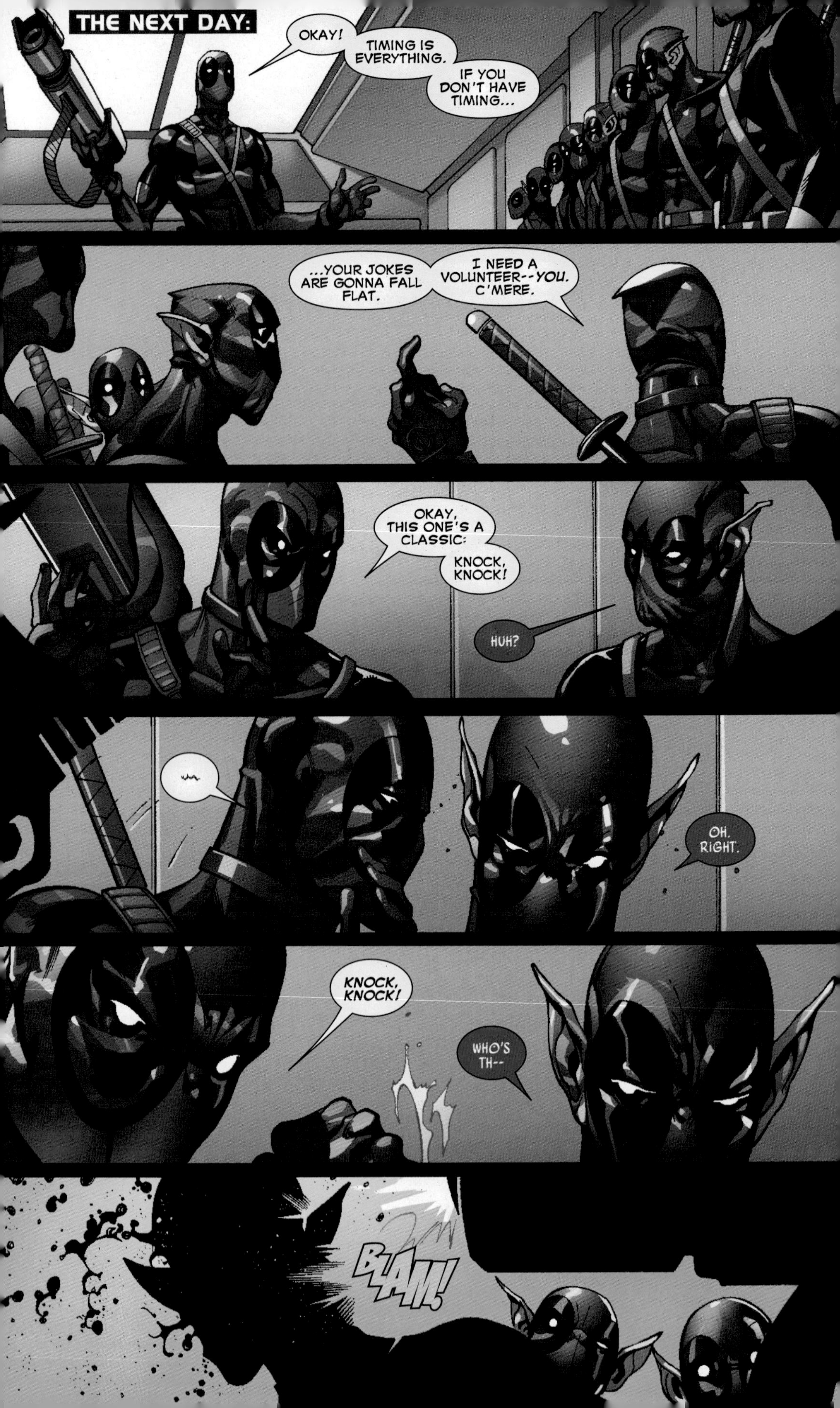
THE NEXT DAY:
OKAY!
TIMING IS EVERYTHING.
IF YOU DON'T HAVE TIMING...
...YOUR JOKES ARE GONNA FALL FLAT.
I NEED A VOLUNTEER--YOU. C'MERE.
OKAY, THIS ONE'S A CLASSIC:
KNOCK, KNOCK!
HUH?
OH. RIGHT.
KNOCK, KNOCK!
WHO'S TH--
BLAM!

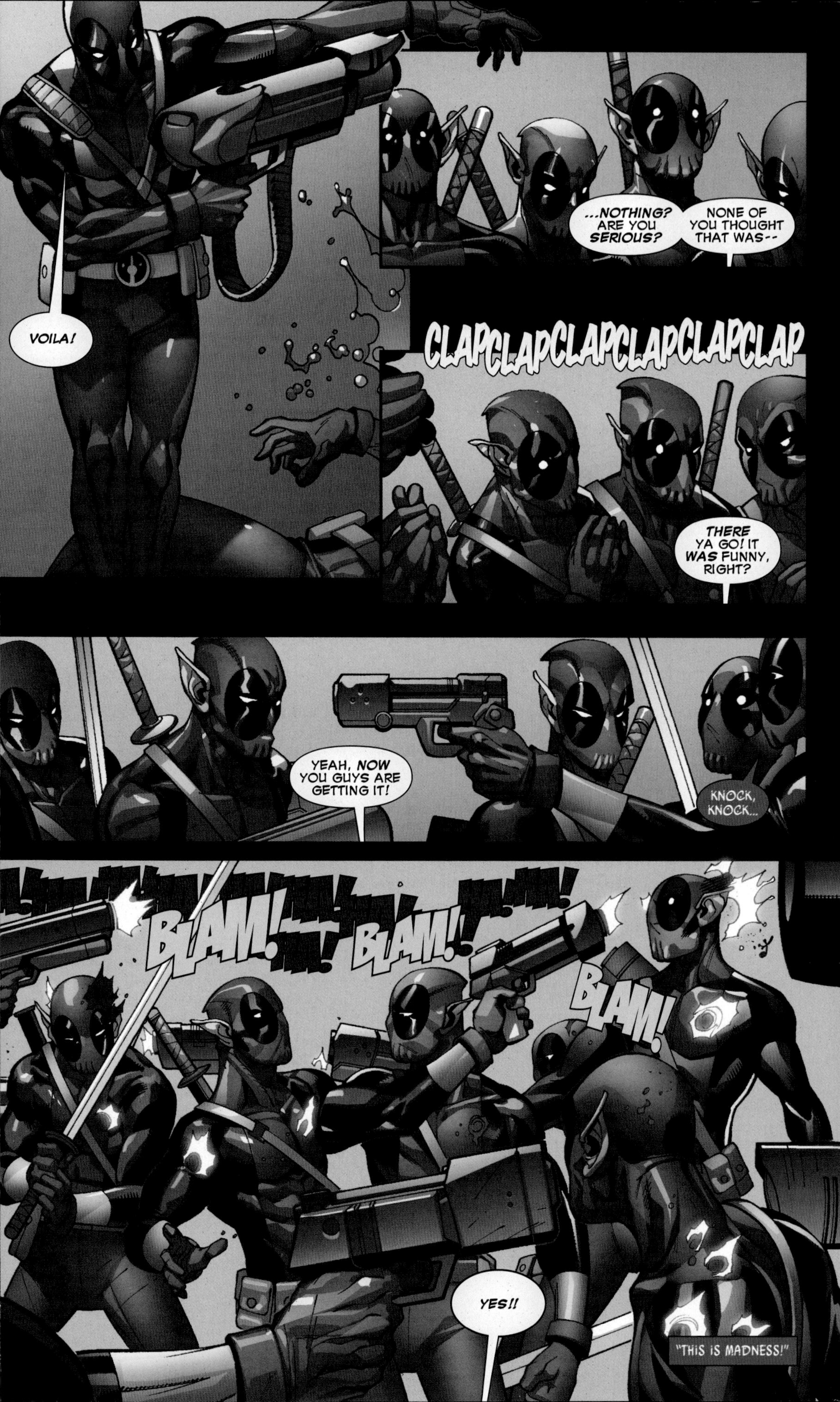
VOILA!
...NOTHING? ARE YOU SERIOUS?
NONE OF YOU THOUGHT THAT WAS--
CLAPCLAPCLAPCLAPCLAPCLAP
THERE YA GO! IT WAS FUNNY, RIGHT?
YEAH, NOW YOU GUYS ARE GETTING IT!
KNOCK, KNOCK...
BLAM!
BLAM!
BLAM!
YES!!
"THIS IS MADNESS!"

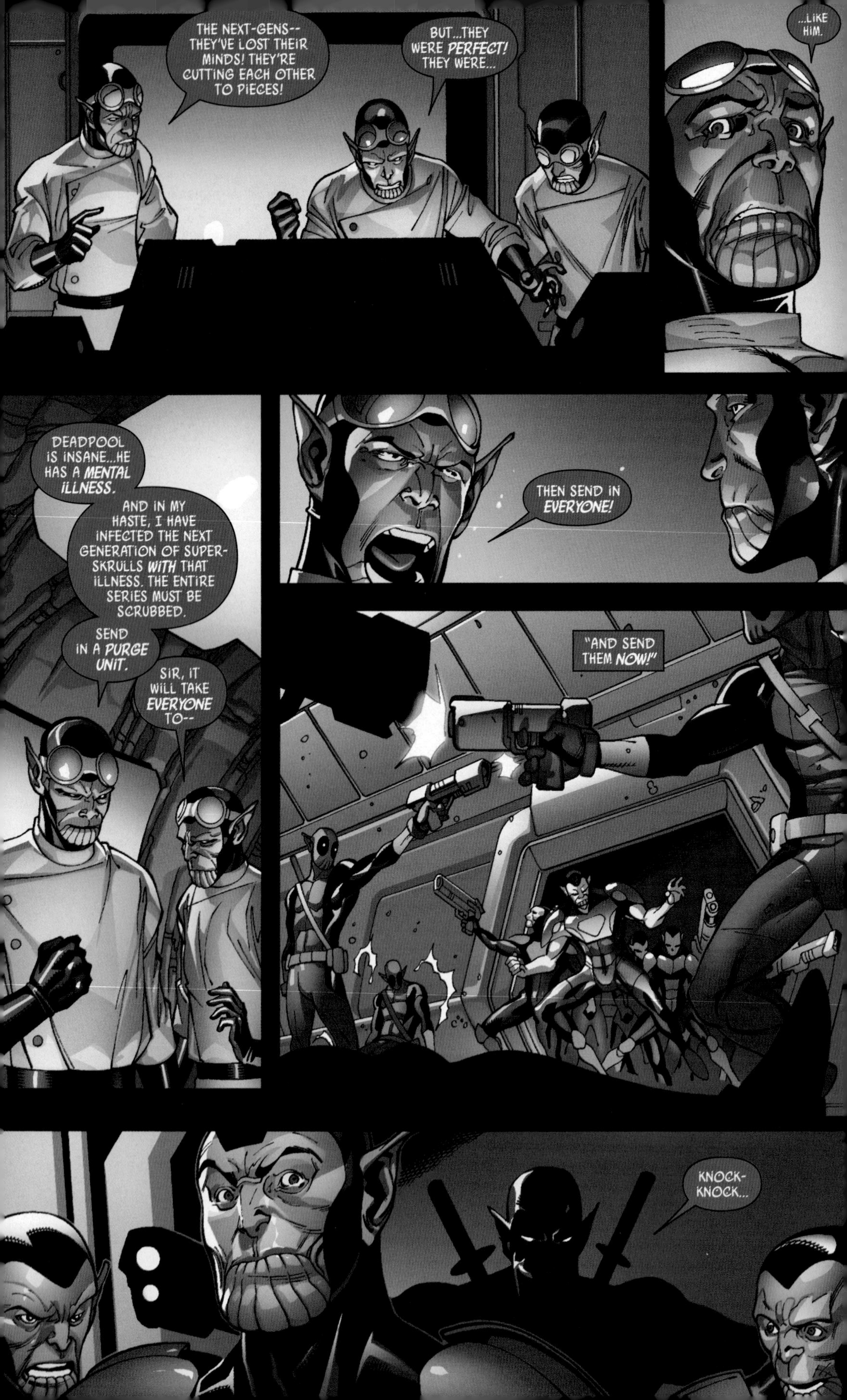
THE NEXT-GENS-- THEY'VE LOST THEIR MINDS! THEY'RE CUTTING EACH OTHER TO PIECES!
BUT...THEY WERE PERFECT! THEY WERE...
...LIKE HIM.
DEADPOOL IS INSANE...HE HAS A MENTAL ILLNESS.
AND IN MY HASTE, I HAVE INFECTED THE NEXT GENERATION OF SUPER-SKRULLS WITH THAT ILLNESS. THE ENTIRE SERIES MUST BE SCRUBBED.
SEND IN A PURGE UNIT.
SIR, IT WILL TAKE EVERYONE TO--
THEN SEND IN EVERYONE!
"AND SEND THEM NOW!"
KNOCK-KNOCK...

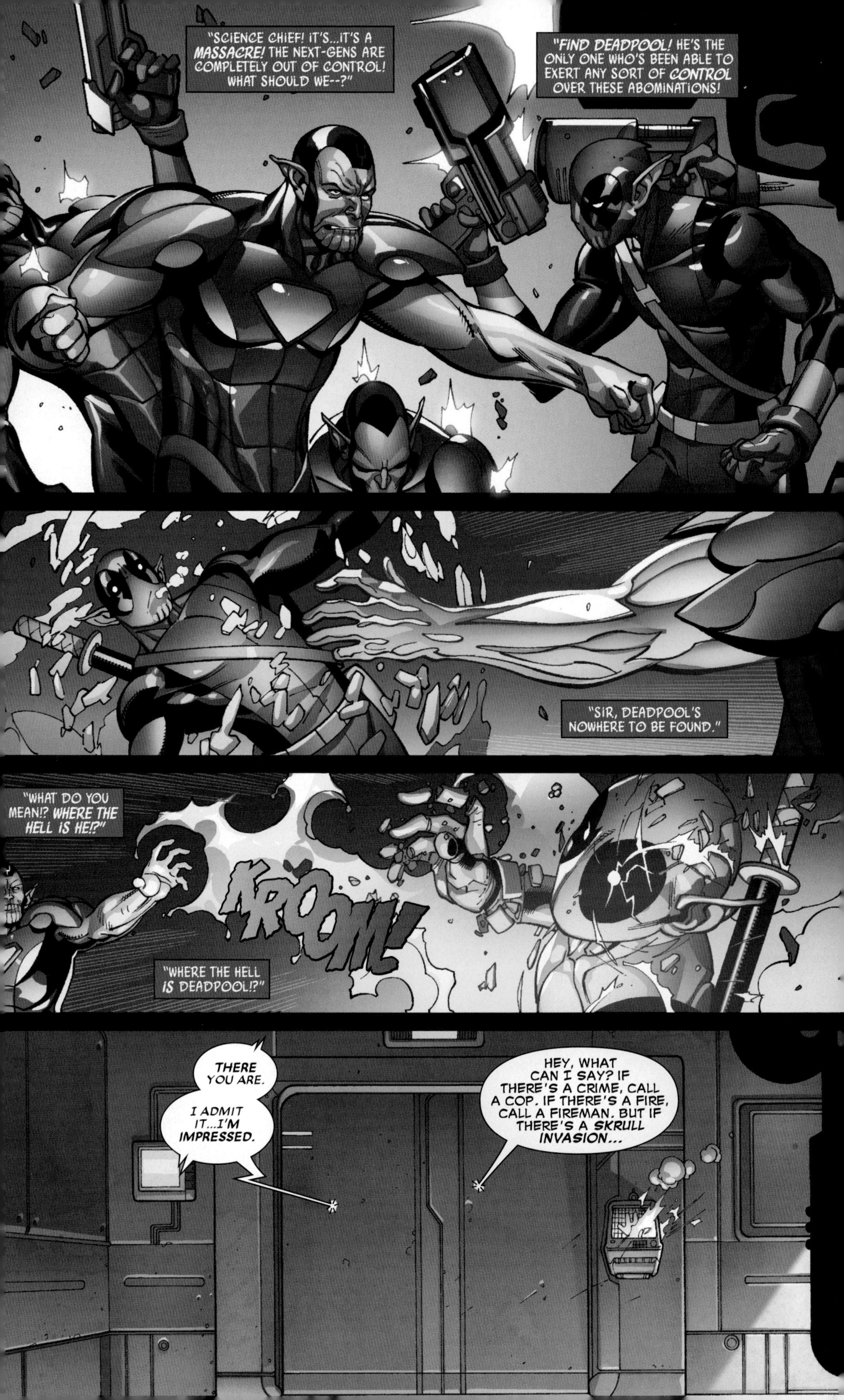

"SCIENCE CHIEF! IT'S...IT'S A MASSACRE! THE NEXT-GENS ARE COMPLETELY OUT OF CONTROL! WHAT SHOULD WE--?"
"FIND DEADPOOL! HE'S THE ONLY ONE WHO'S BEEN ABLE TO EXERT ANY SORT OF CONTROL OVER THESE ABOMINATIONS!
"SIR, DEADPOOL'S NOWHERE TO BE FOUND."
"WHAT DO YOU MEAN!? WHERE THE HELL IS HE!?"
KROOM!
"WHERE THE HELL IS DEADPOOL!?"
THERE YOU ARE.
I ADMIT IT...I'M IMPRESSED.
HEY, WHAT CAN I SAY? IF THERE'S A CRIME, CALL A COP. IF THERE'S A FIRE, CALL A FIREMAN. BUT IF THERE'S A SKRULL INVASION...

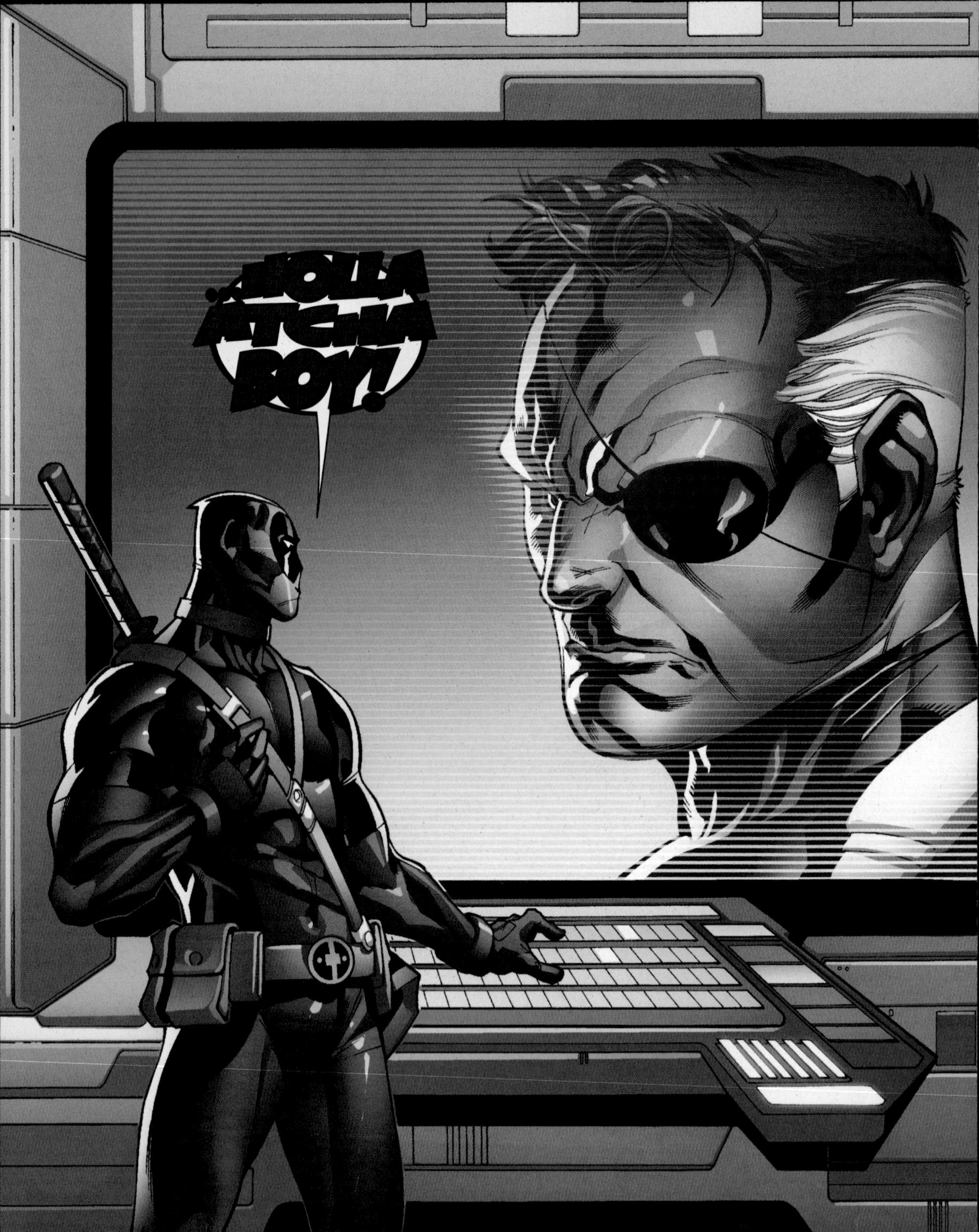

...HOLLA ATCHA BOY!

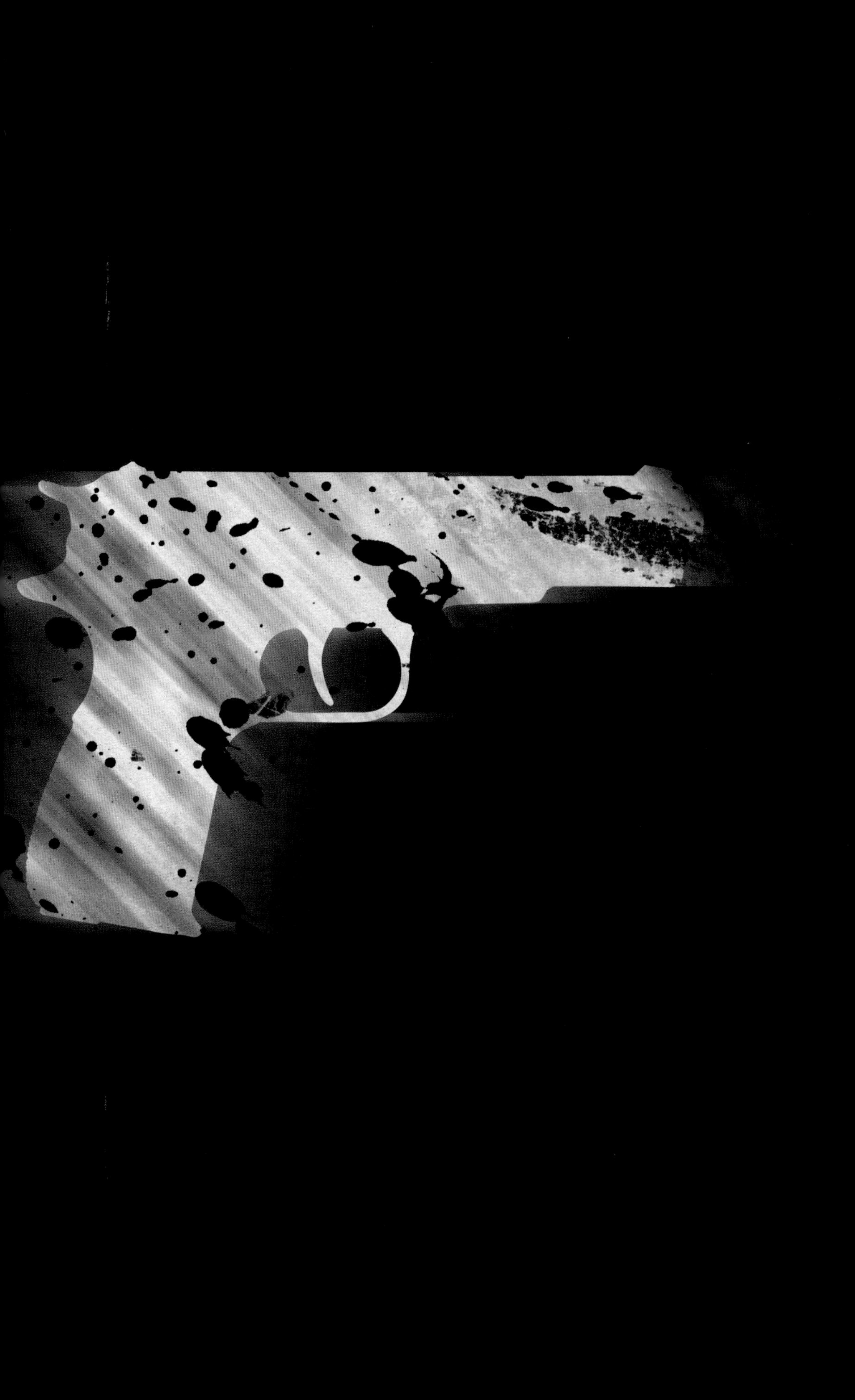

# 3

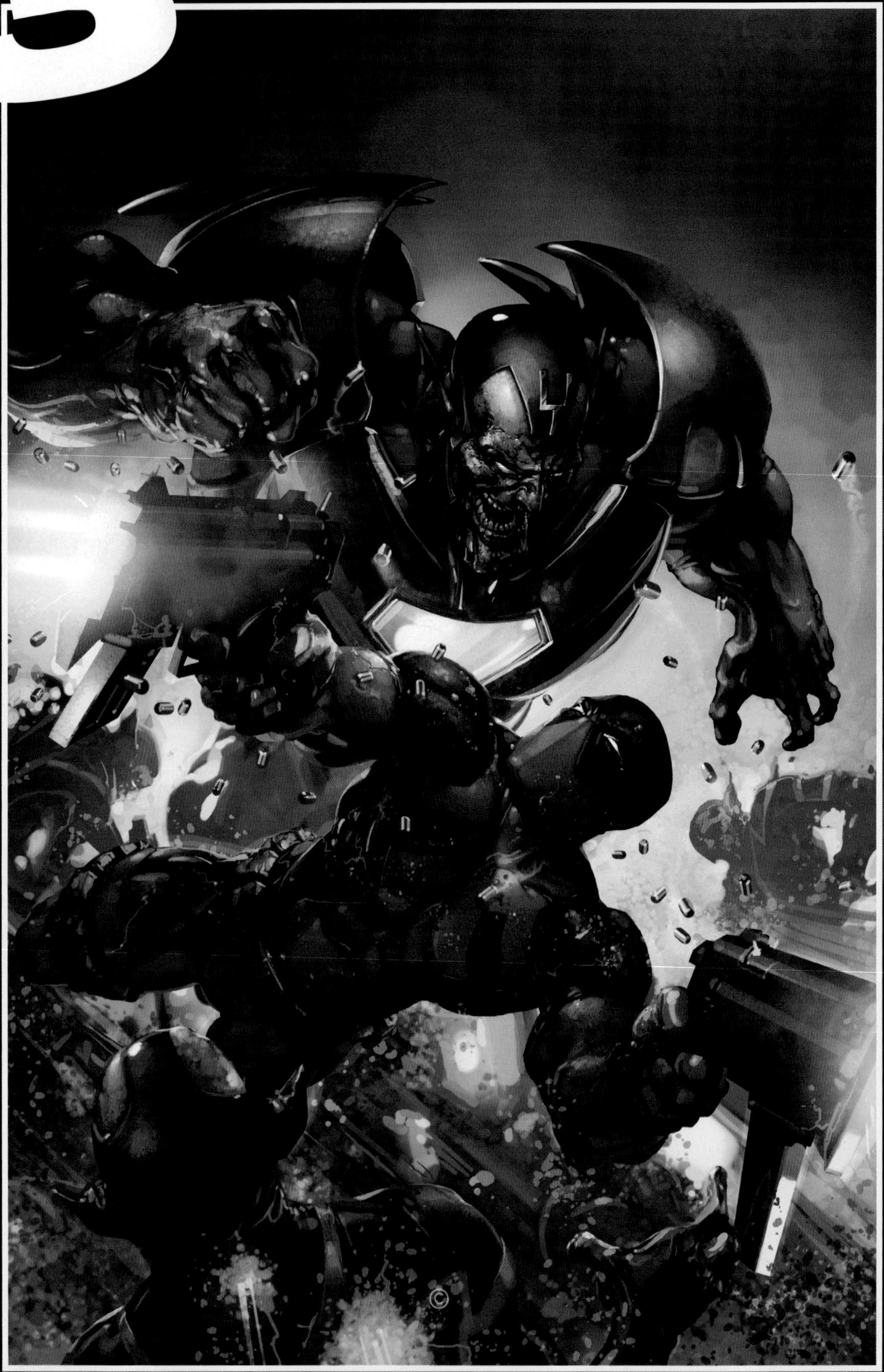

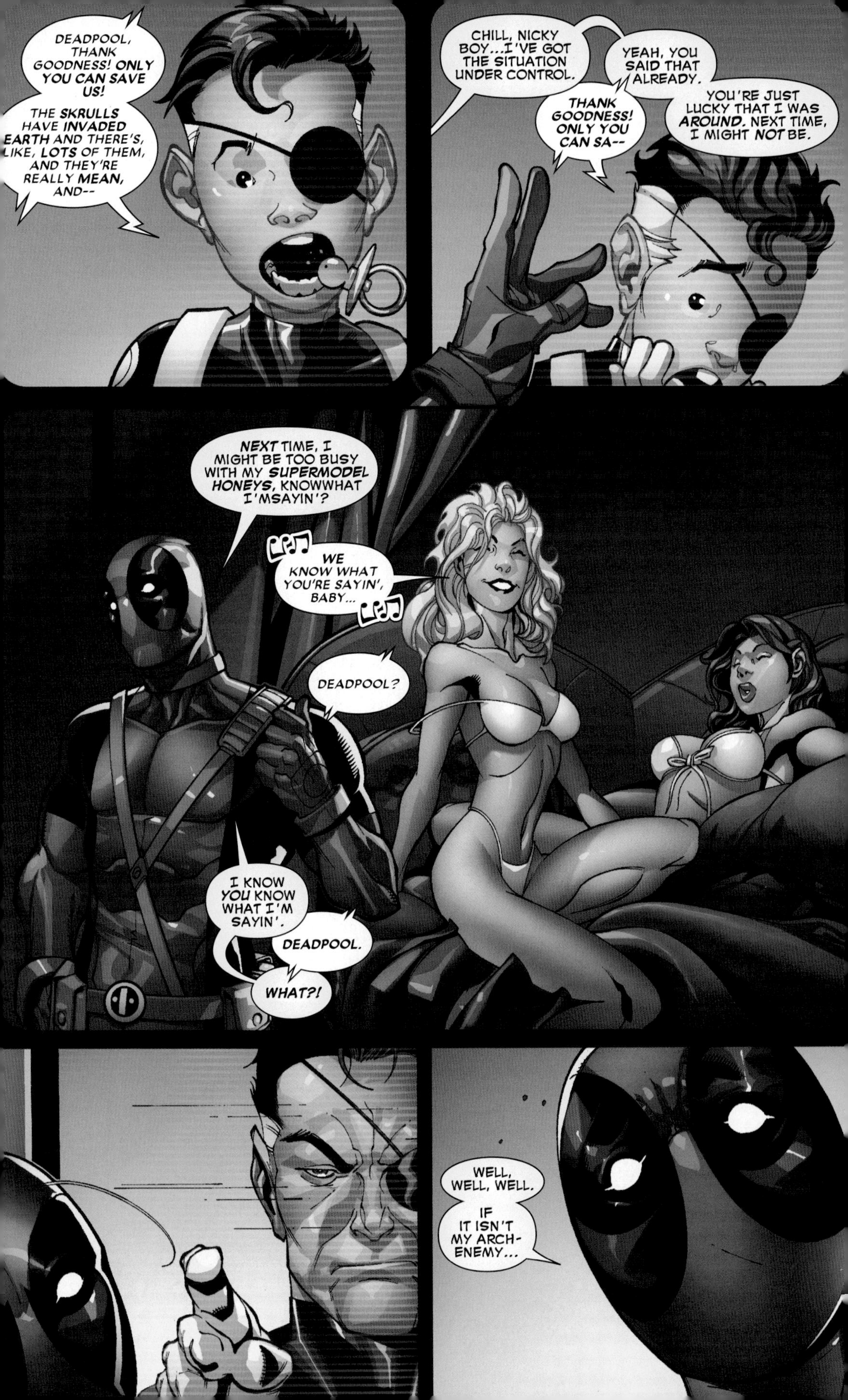
DEADPOOL, THANK GOODNESS! ONLY YOU CAN SAVE US!
THE SKRULLS HAVE INVADED EARTH AND THERE'S, LIKE, LOTS OF THEM, AND THEY'RE REALLY MEAN, AND--
CHILL, NICKY BOY...I'VE GOT THE SITUATION UNDER CONTROL.
THANK GOODNESS! ONLY YOU CAN SA--
YEAH, YOU SAID THAT ALREADY.
YOU'RE JUST LUCKY THAT I WAS AROUND. NEXT TIME, I MIGHT NOT BE.
NEXT TIME, I MIGHT BE TOO BUSY WITH MY SUPERMODEL HONEYS, KNOWWHAT I'MSAYIN'?
WE KNOW WHAT YOU'RE SAYIN', BABY...
DEADPOOL?
I KNOW YOU KNOW WHAT I'M SAYIN'.
DEADPOOL.
WHAT?!
WELL, WELL, WELL.
IF IT ISN'T MY ARCH-ENEMY...

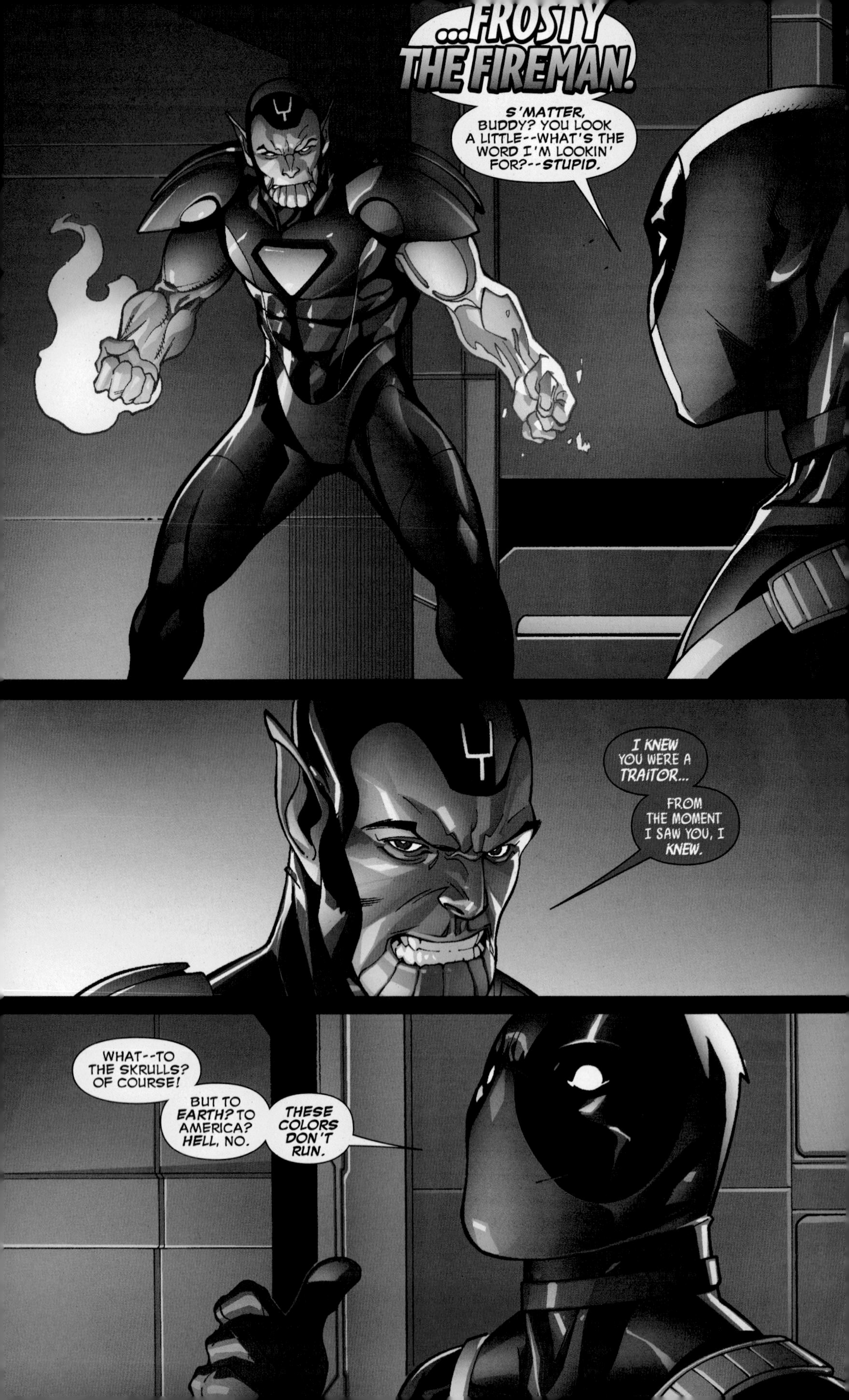
...FROSTY THE FIREMAN!
S'MATTER, BUDDY? YOU LOOK A LITTLE--WHAT'S THE WORD I'M LOOKIN' FOR?--STUPID.
I KNEW YOU WERE A TRAITOR...
FROM THE MOMENT I SAW YOU, I KNEW.
WHAT--TO THE SKRULLS? OF COURSE!
BUT TO EARTH? TO AMERICA? HELL, NO.
THESE COLORS DON'T RUN.

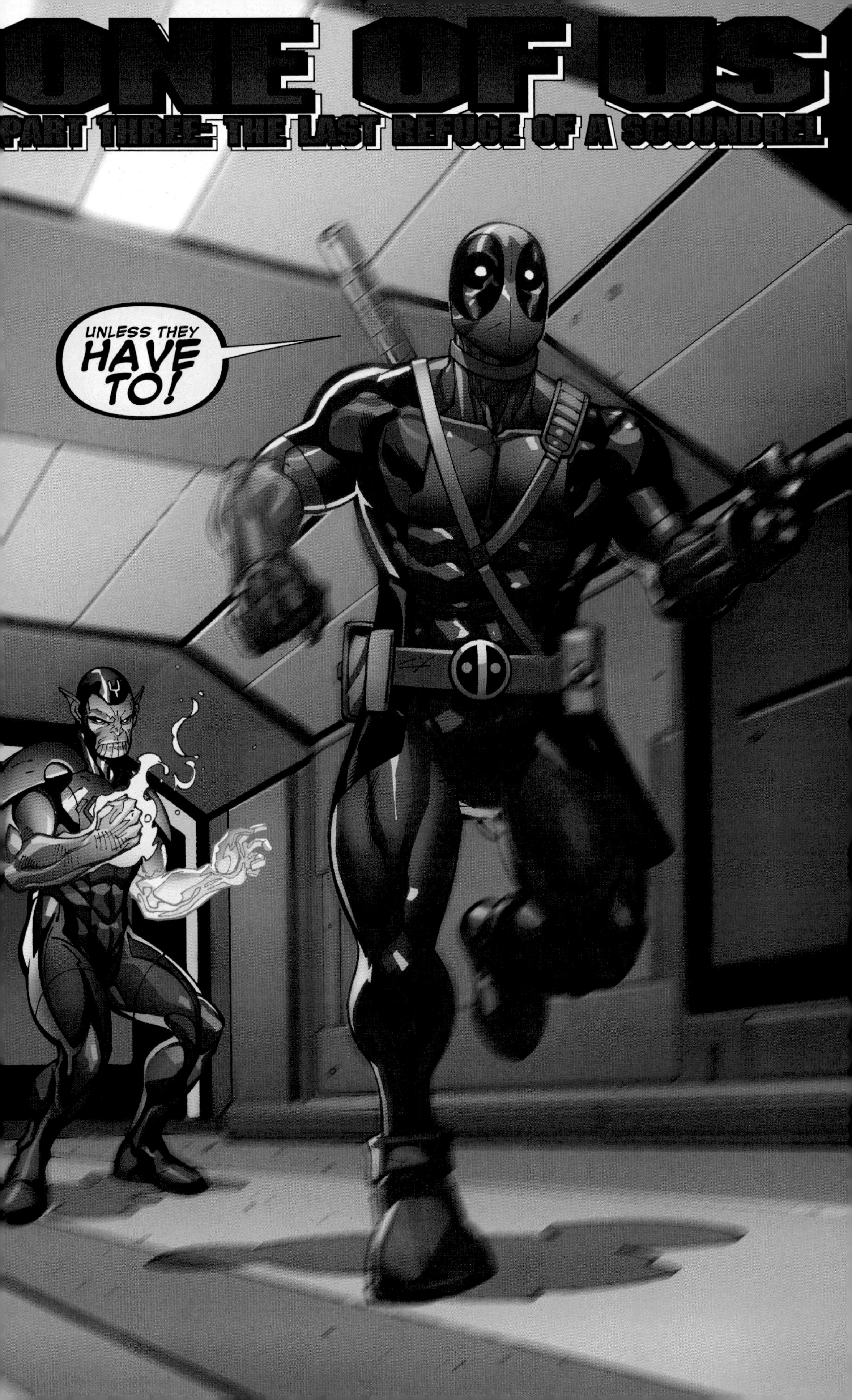
ONE OF US
PART THREE: THE LAST REFUGE OF A SCOUNDREL
UNLESS THEY HAVE TO!

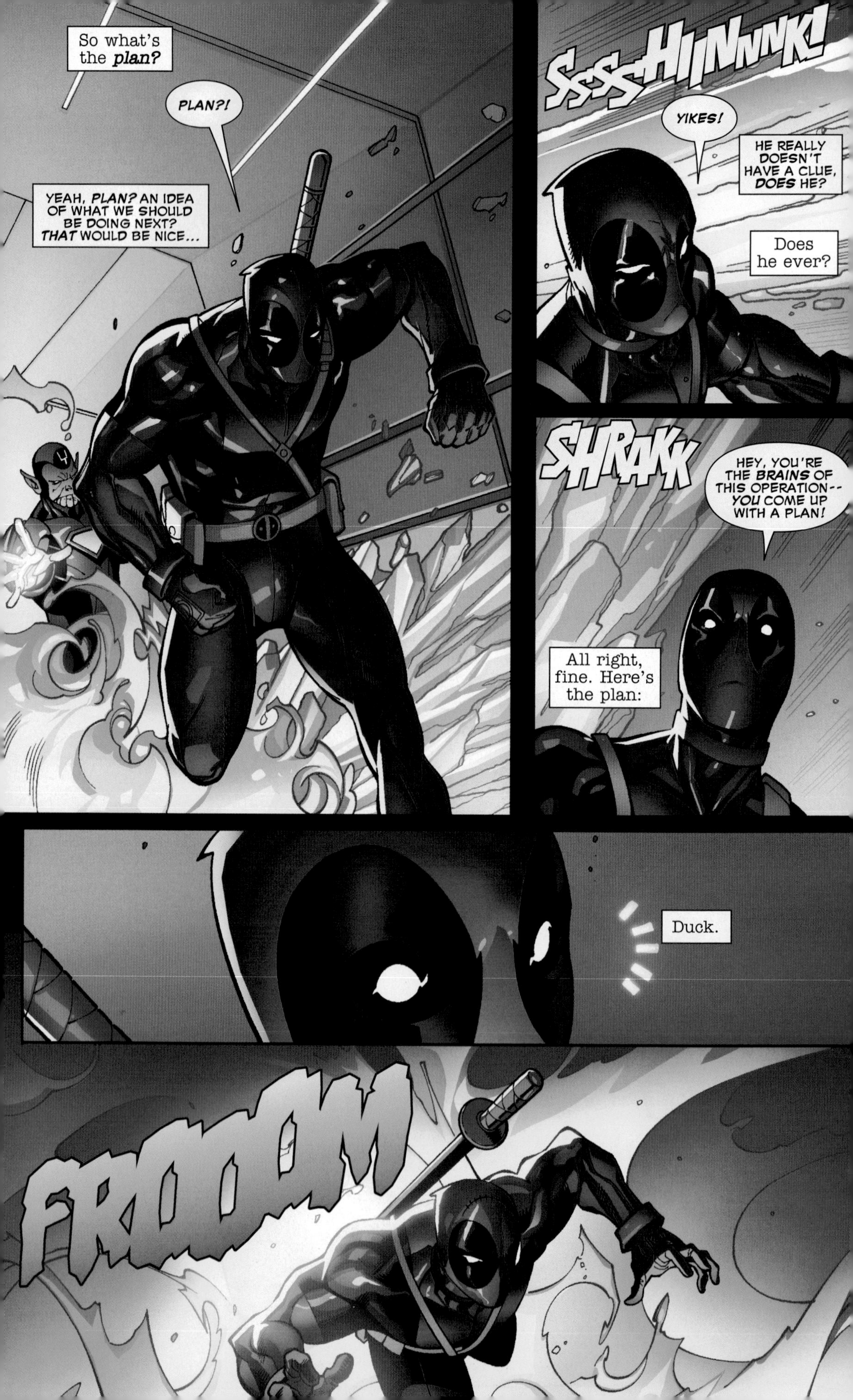

So what's the *plan?*
PLAN?!
YEAH, *PLAN?* AN IDEA OF WHAT WE SHOULD BE DOING NEXT? *THAT* WOULD BE NICE...
SSSS-HIINNNK!
YIKES!
HE REALLY *DOESN'T* HAVE A CLUE, *DOES* HE?
Does he ever?
SHRAKK
HEY, YOU'RE THE *BRAINS* OF THIS OPERATION-- *YOU* COME UP WITH A PLAN!
All right, fine. Here's the plan:
Duck.
FROOOM

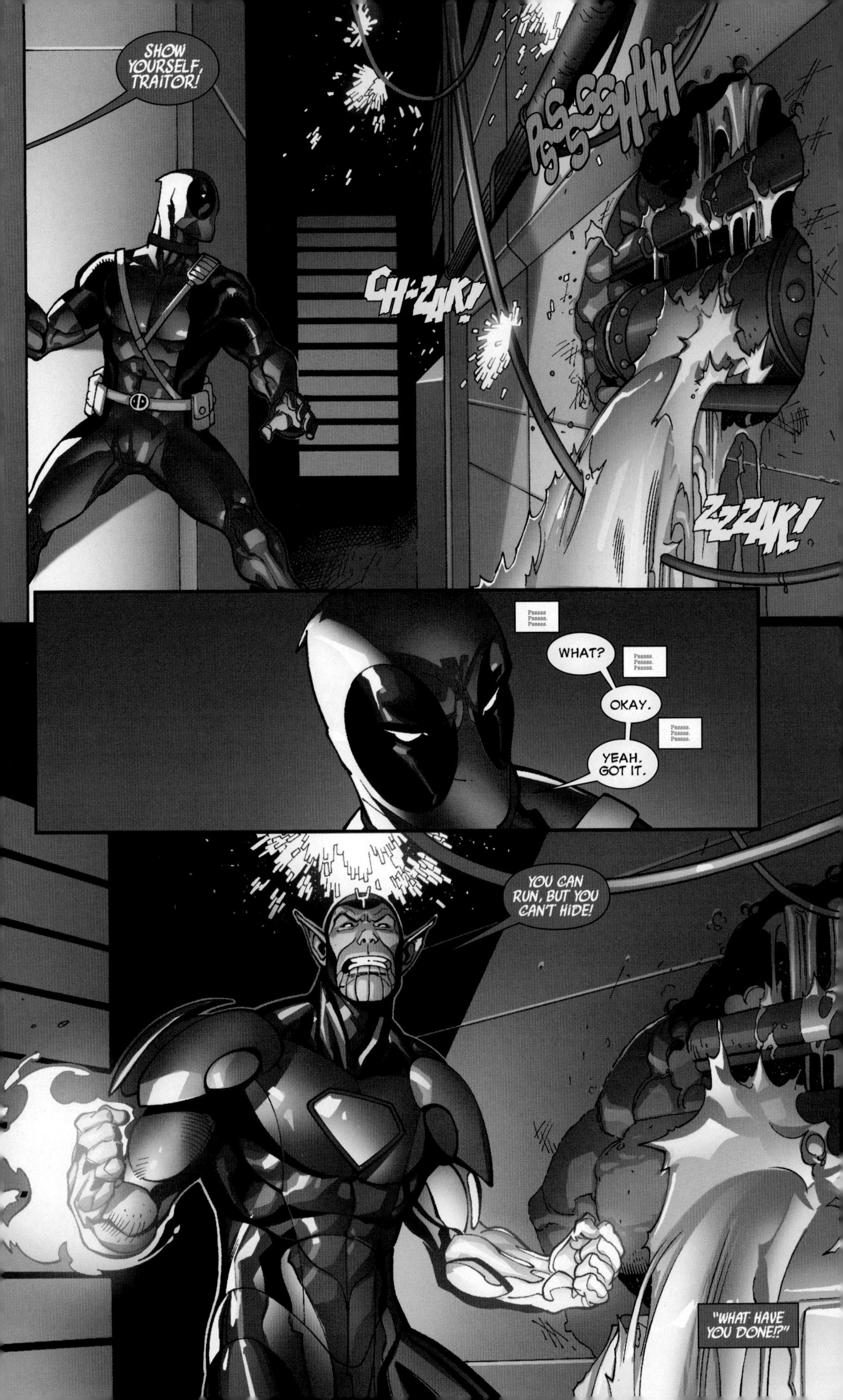
SHOW YOURSELF, TRAITOR!
PSSSSHHH
CH-ZAK!
ZZZAK!
Psssss. Psssss. Psssss.
WHAT?
Psssss. Psssss. Psssss.
OKAY.
Psssss. Psssss. Psssss.
YEAH. GOT IT.
YOU CAN RUN, BUT YOU CAN'T HIDE!
"WHAT HAVE YOU DONE!?"

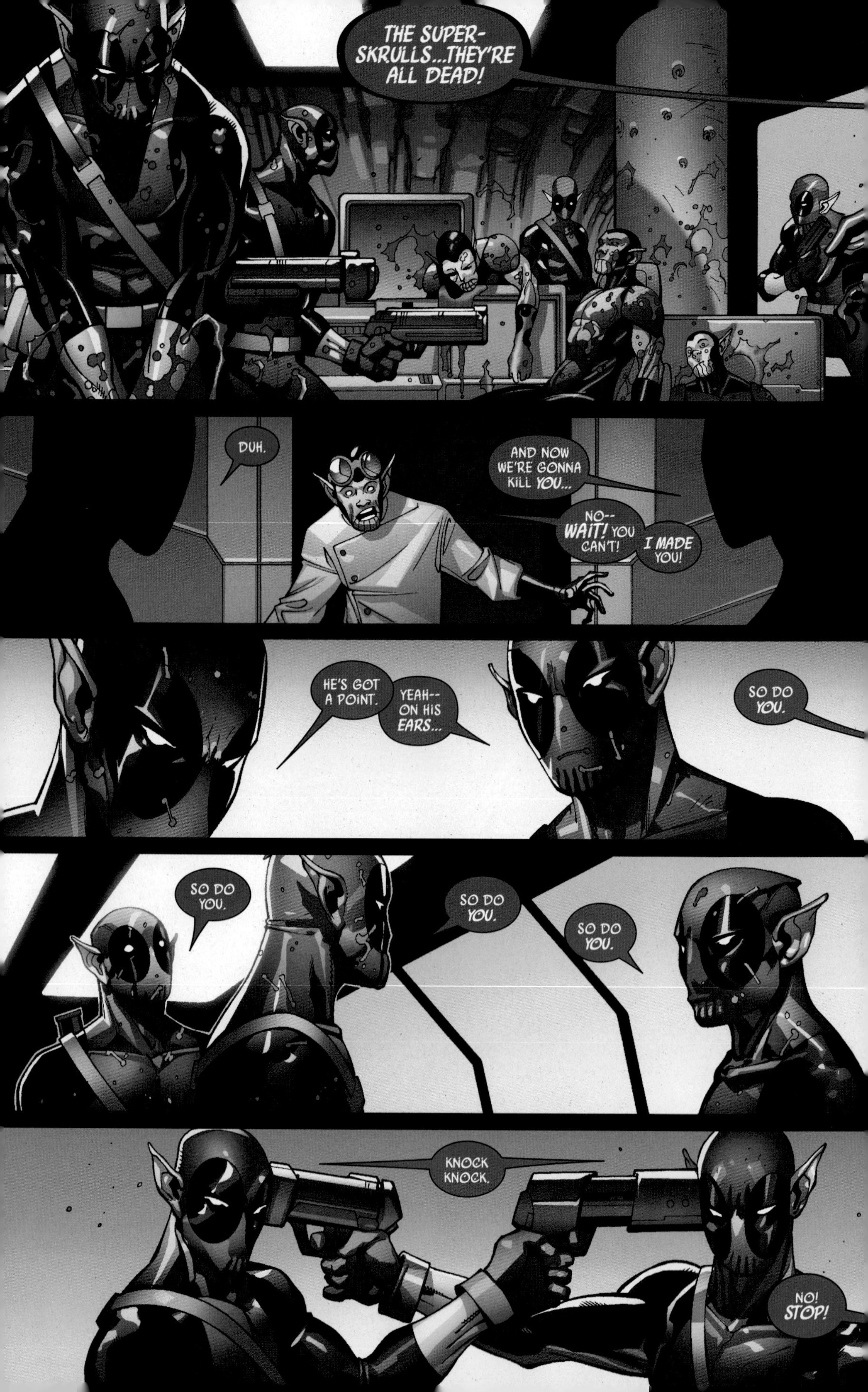
THE SUPER-SKRULLS...THEY'RE ALL DEAD!
DUH.
AND NOW WE'RE GONNA KILL YOU...
NO--WAIT! YOU CAN'T!
I MADE YOU!
HE'S GOT A POINT.
YEAH--ON HIS EARS...
SO DO YOU.
SO DO YOU.
SO DO YOU.
SO DO YOU.
KNOCK KNOCK.
NO! STOP!

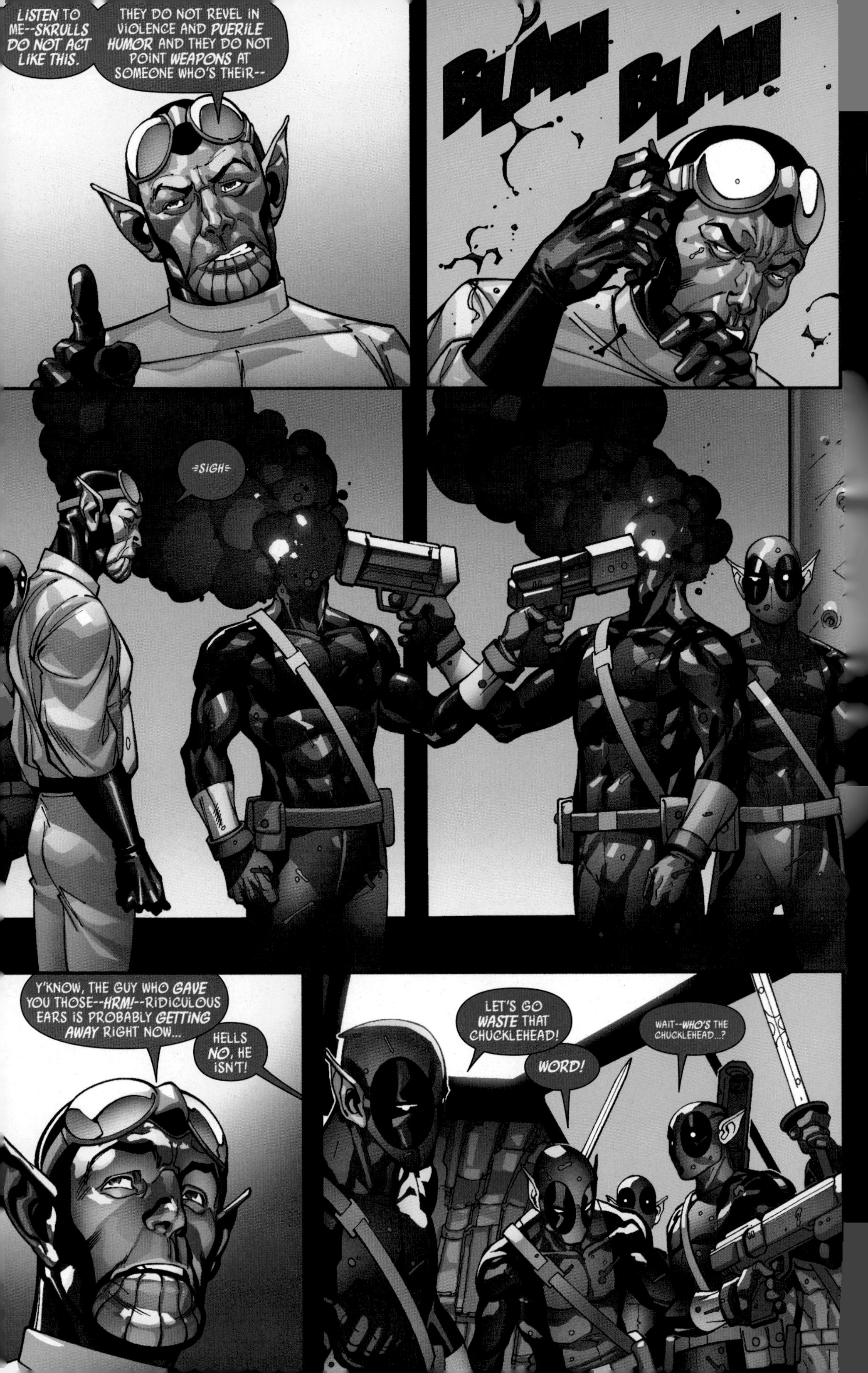
LISTEN TO ME--SKRULLS DO NOT ACT LIKE THIS.
THEY DO NOT REVEL IN VIOLENCE AND PUERILE HUMOR AND THEY DO NOT POINT WEAPONS AT SOMEONE WHO'S THEIR--
BLAM BLAM
=SIGH=
Y'KNOW, THE GUY WHO GAVE YOU THOSE--HRM!--RIDICULOUS EARS IS PROBABLY GETTING AWAY RIGHT NOW...
HELLS NO, HE ISN'T!
LET'S GO WASTE THAT CHUCKLEHEAD!
WORD!
WAIT--WHO'S THE CHUCKLEHEAD...?

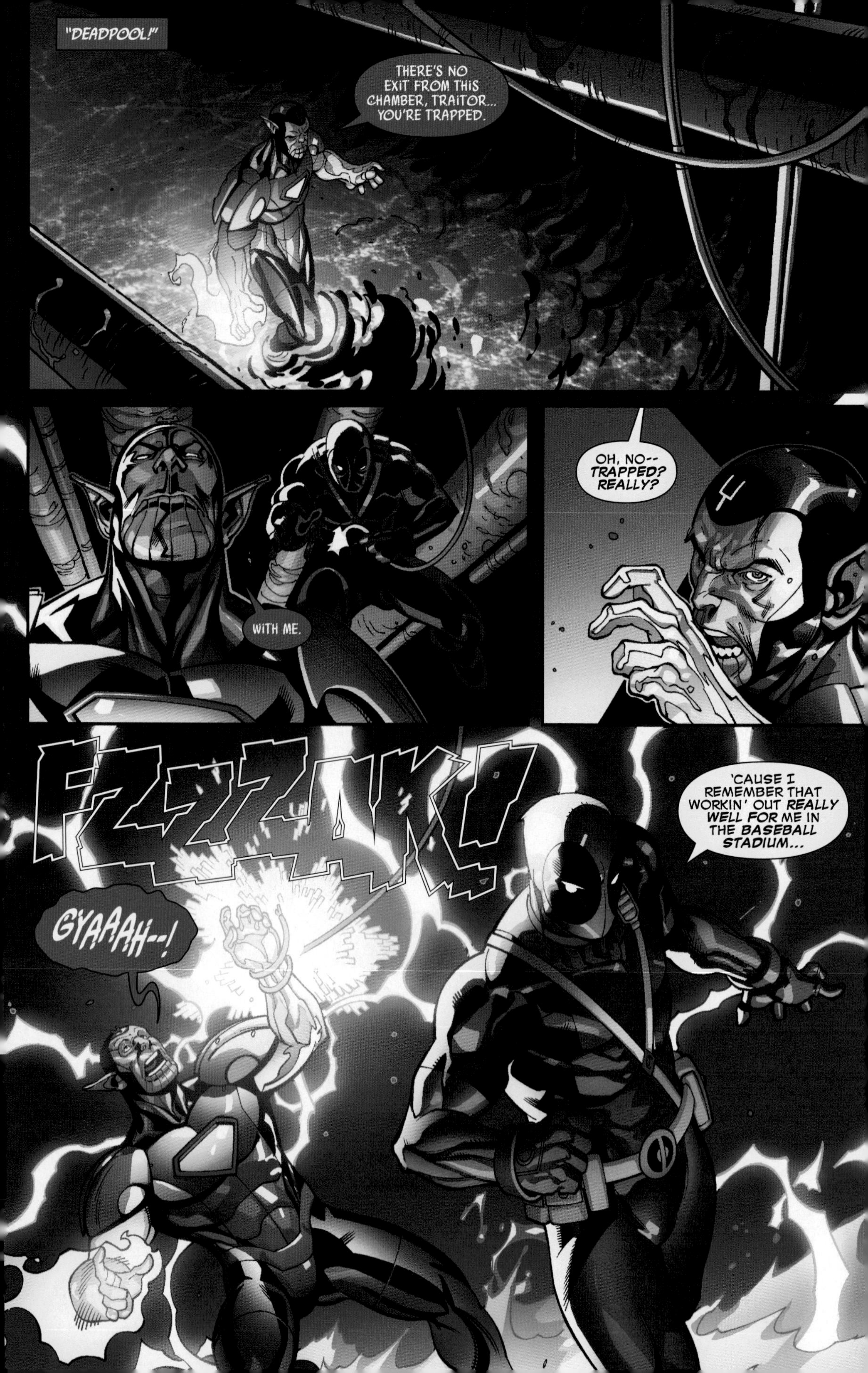
"DEADPOOL!"
THERE'S NO EXIT FROM THIS CHAMBER, TRAITOR... YOU'RE TRAPPED.
WITH ME.
OH, NO-- TRAPPED? REALLY?
FZZZAKK!
'CAUSE I REMEMBER THAT WORKIN' OUT REALLY WELL FOR ME IN THE BASEBALL STADIUM...
GYAAAH--!

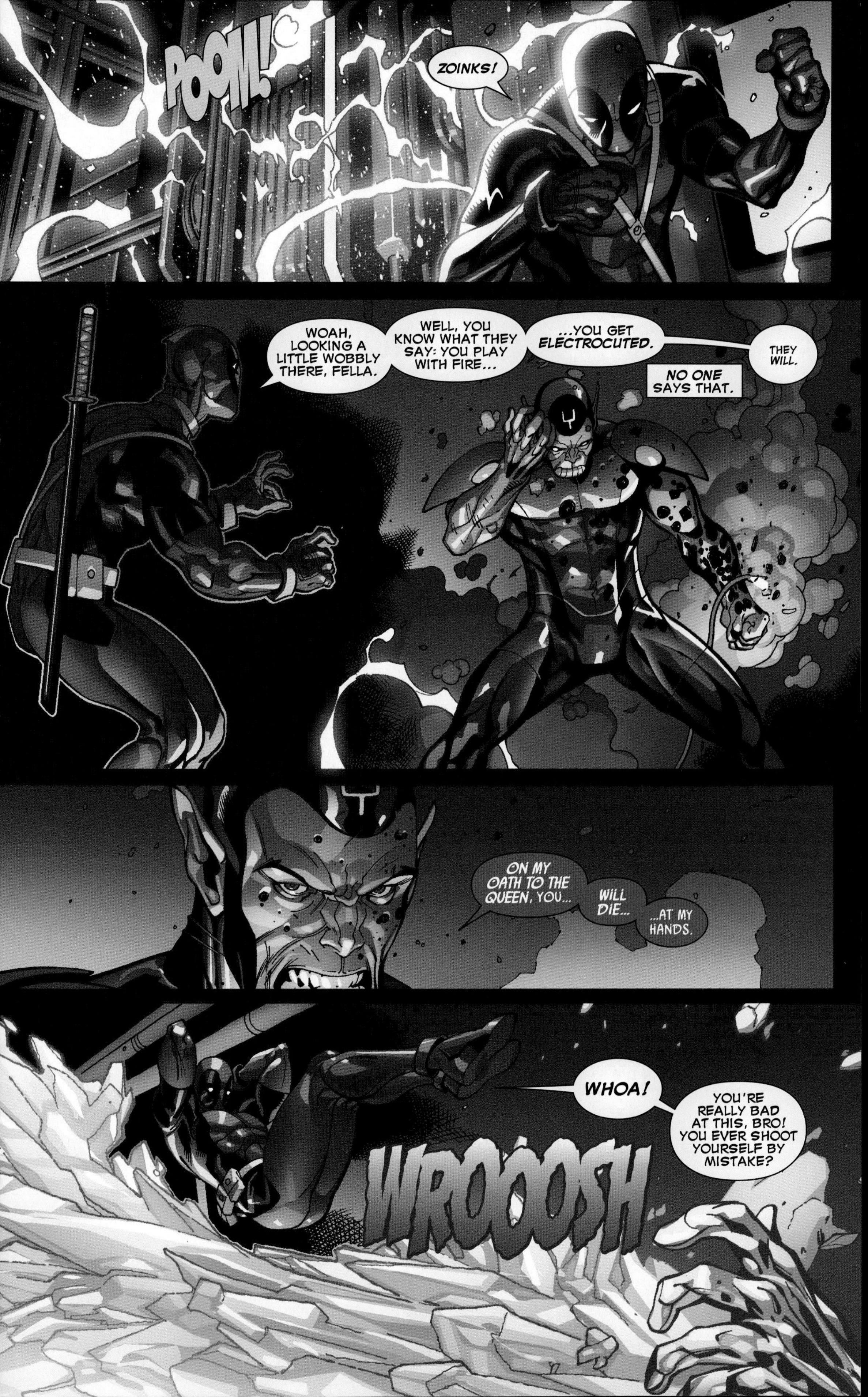
POOM!
ZOINKS!
WOAH, LOOKING A LITTLE WOBBLY THERE, FELLA.
WELL, YOU KNOW WHAT THEY SAY: YOU PLAY WITH FIRE...
...YOU GET ELECTROCUTED.
NO ONE SAYS THAT.
THEY WILL.
ON MY OATH TO THE QUEEN, YOU...
WILL DIE...
...AT MY HANDS.
WHOA!
YOU'RE REALLY BAD AT THIS, BRO! YOU EVER SHOOT YOURSELF BY MISTAKE?
WROOOSH

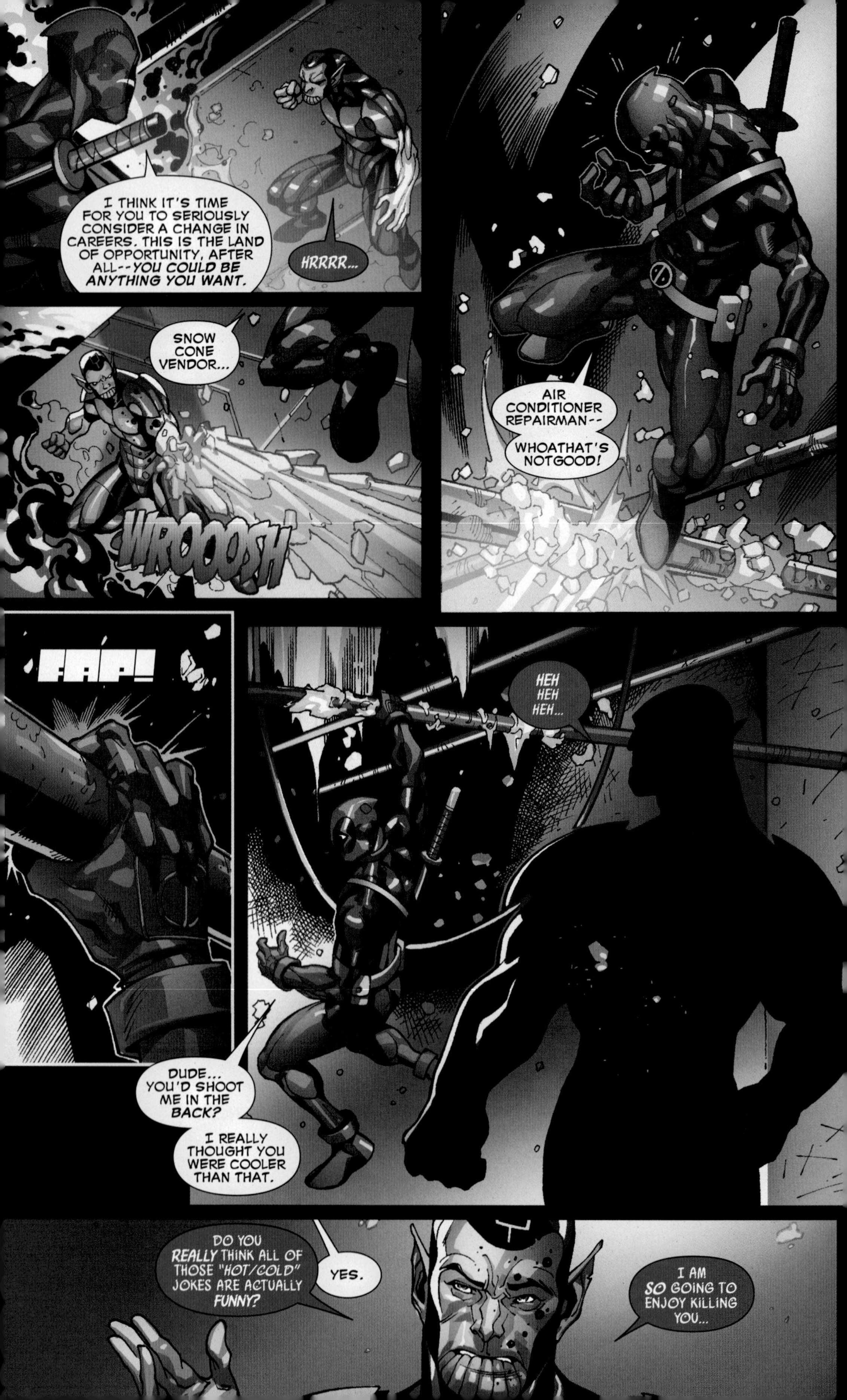
I THINK IT'S TIME FOR YOU TO SERIOUSLY CONSIDER A CHANGE IN CAREERS. THIS IS THE LAND OF OPPORTUNITY, AFTER ALL--*YOU COULD BE ANYTHING YOU WANT.*
*HRRRR...*
SNOW CONE VENDOR...
WROOOSH
AIR CONDITIONER REPAIRMAN--
WHOATHAT'S NOTGOOD!
FAP!
*HEH HEH HEH...*
DUDE... YOU'D SHOOT ME IN THE *BACK?*
I REALLY THOUGHT YOU WERE COOLER THAN THAT.
DO YOU *REALLY* THINK ALL OF THOSE "*HOT/COLD*" JOKES ARE ACTUALLY *FUNNY?*
YES.
I AM *SO* GOING TO ENJOY KILLING YOU...

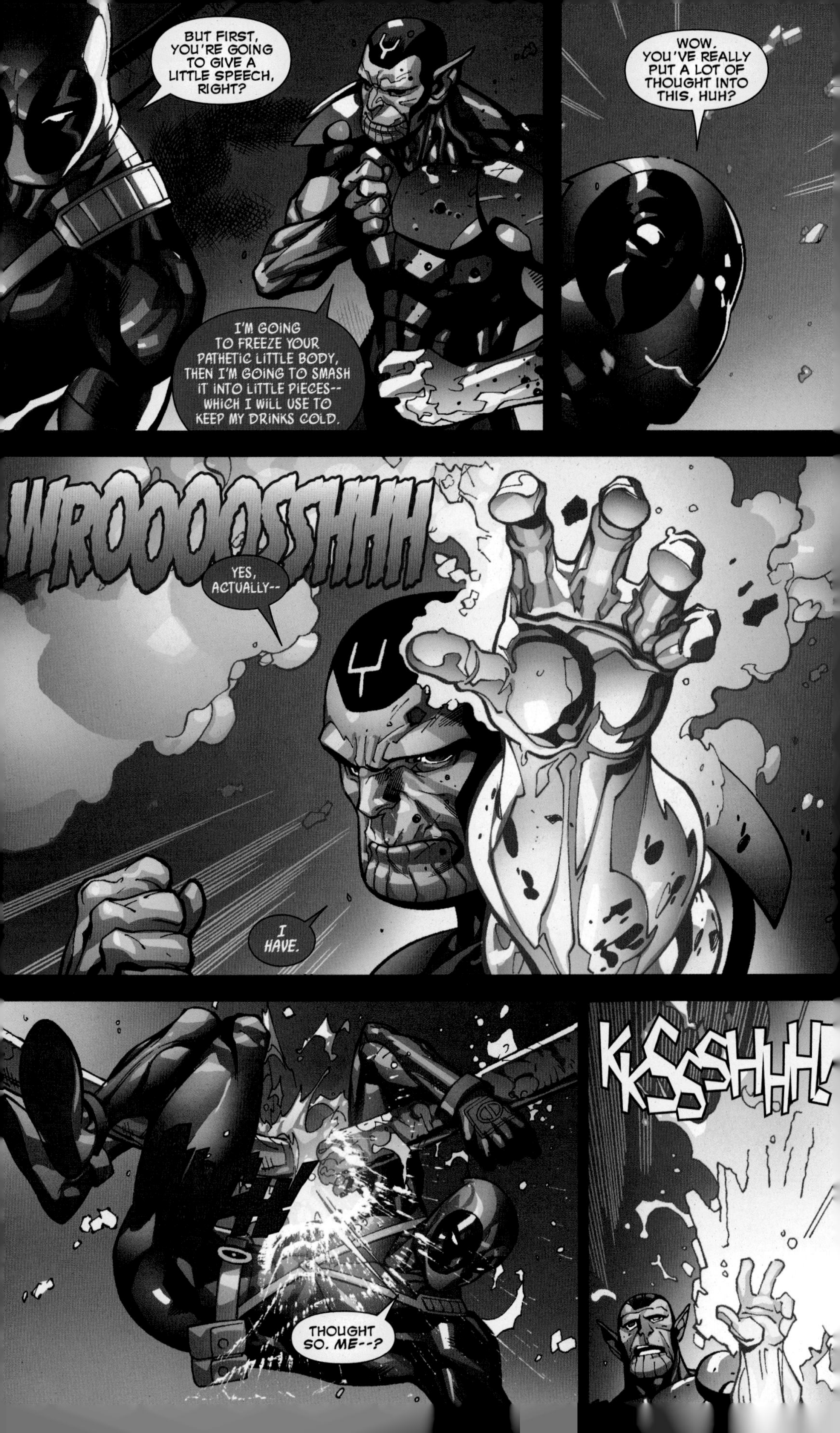
BUT FIRST, YOU'RE GOING TO GIVE A LITTLE SPEECH, RIGHT?
I'M GOING TO FREEZE YOUR PATHETIC LITTLE BODY, THEN I'M GOING TO SMASH IT INTO LITTLE PIECES-- WHICH I WILL USE TO KEEP MY DRINKS COLD.
WOW. YOU'VE REALLY PUT A LOT OF THOUGHT INTO THIS, HUH?
WROOOOSHHH
YES, ACTUALLY--
I HAVE.
THOUGHT SO. ME--?
KKSSSHHH!

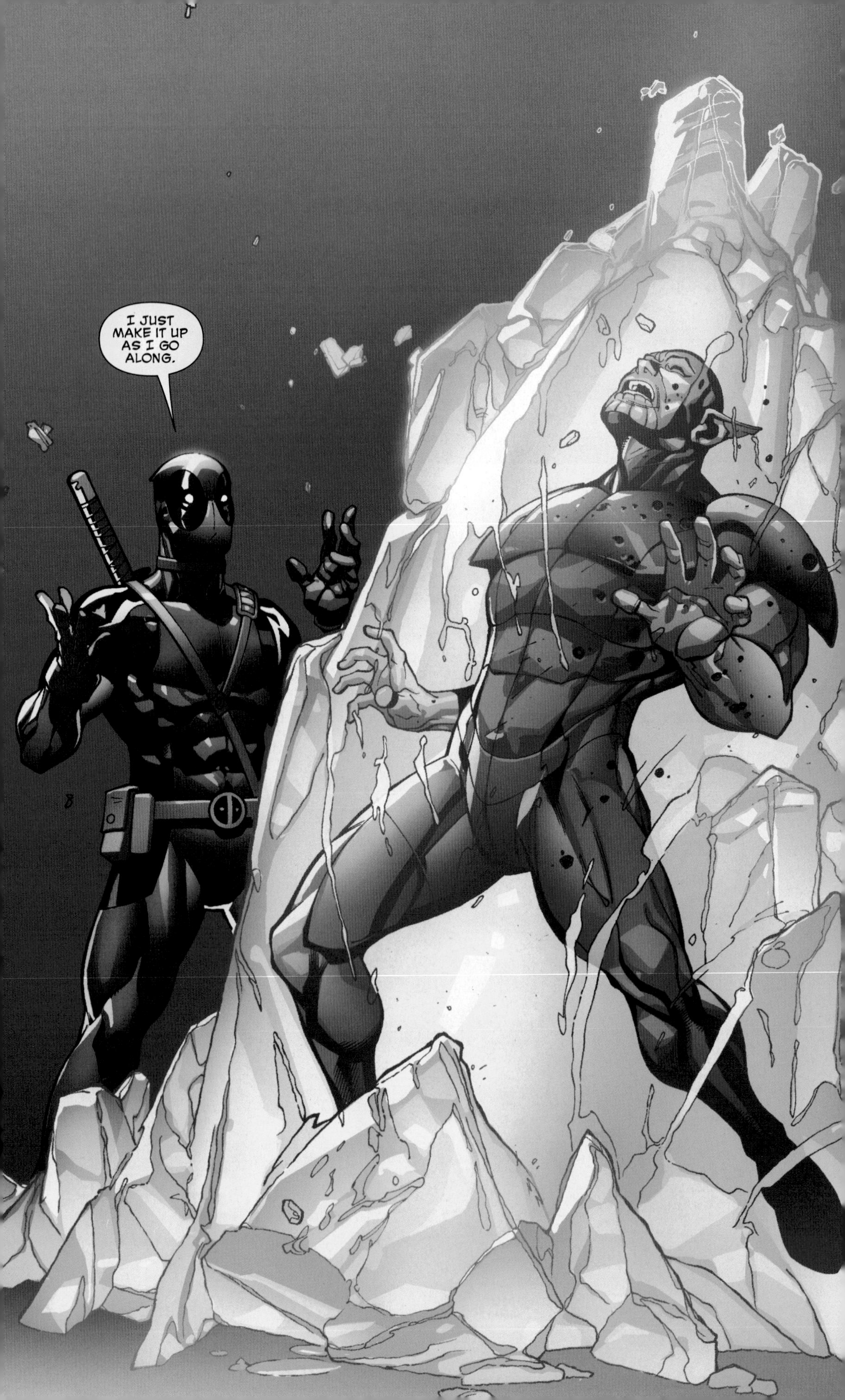
I JUST MAKE IT UP AS I GO ALONG.

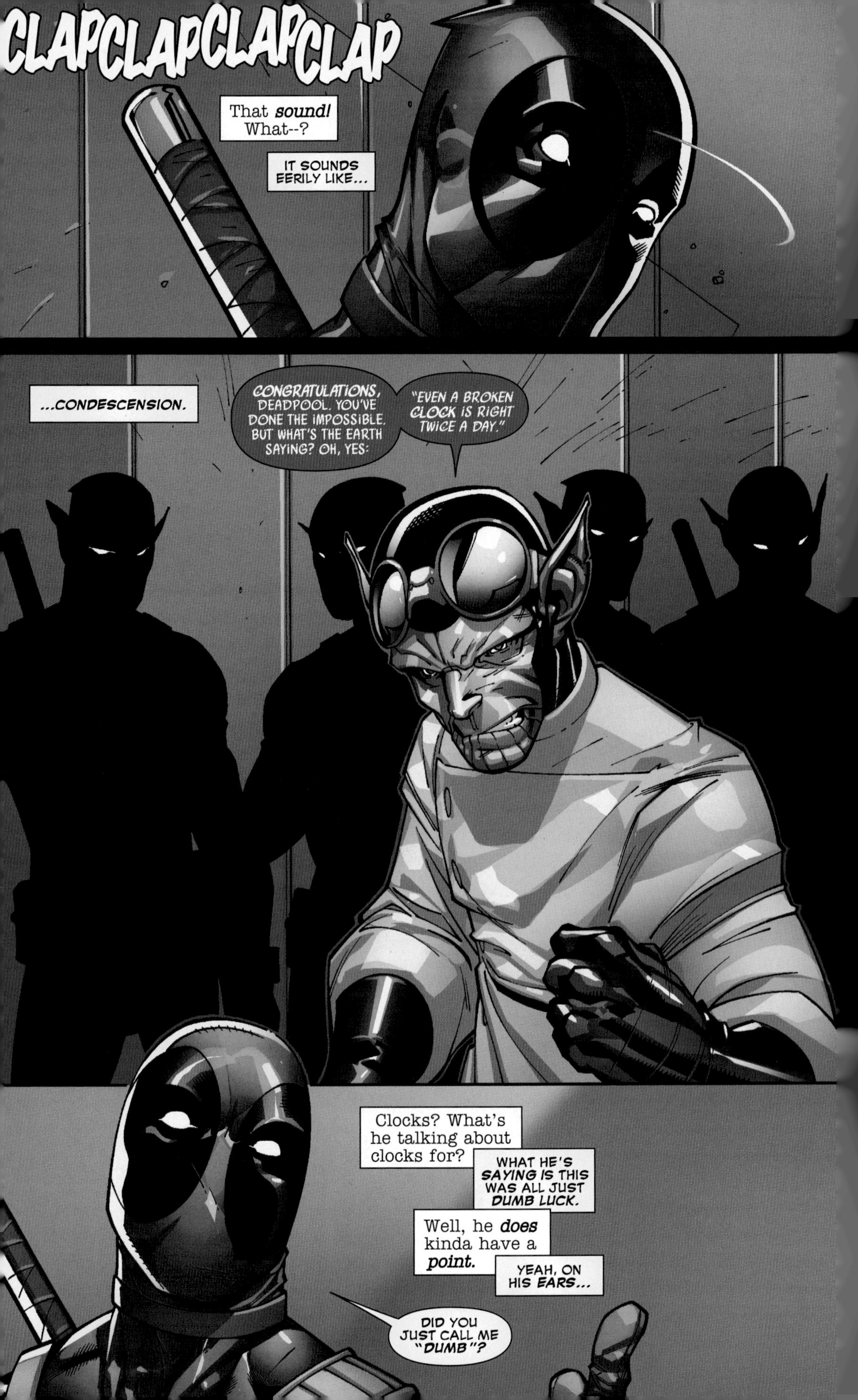
CLAPCLAPCLAPCLAP
That sound! What--?
IT SOUNDS EERILY LIKE...
...CONDESCENSION.
CONGRATULATIONS, DEADPOOL. YOU'VE DONE THE IMPOSSIBLE. BUT WHAT'S THE EARTH SAYING? OH, YES:
"EVEN A BROKEN CLOCK IS RIGHT TWICE A DAY."
Clocks? What's he talking about clocks for?
WHAT HE'S SAYING IS THIS WAS ALL JUST DUMB LUCK.
Well, he does kinda have a point.
YEAH, ON HIS EARS...
DID YOU JUST CALL ME "DUMB"?

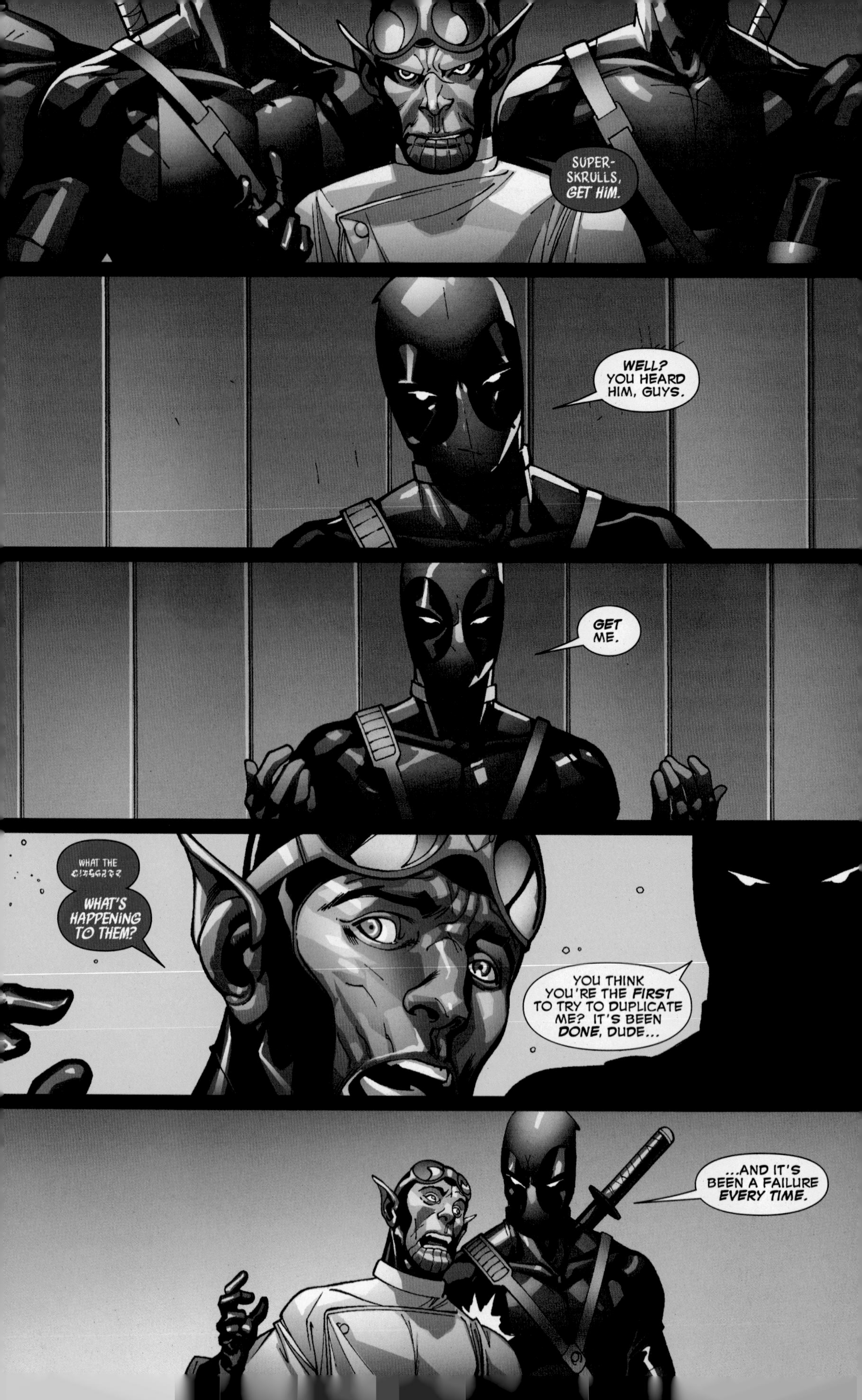
SUPER-SKRULLS, GET HIM.
WELL? YOU HEARD HIM, GUYS.
GET ME.
WHAT THE
WHAT'S HAPPENING TO THEM?
YOU THINK YOU'RE THE FIRST TO TRY TO DUPLICATE ME? IT'S BEEN DONE, DUDE...
...AND IT'S BEEN A FAILURE EVERY TIME.

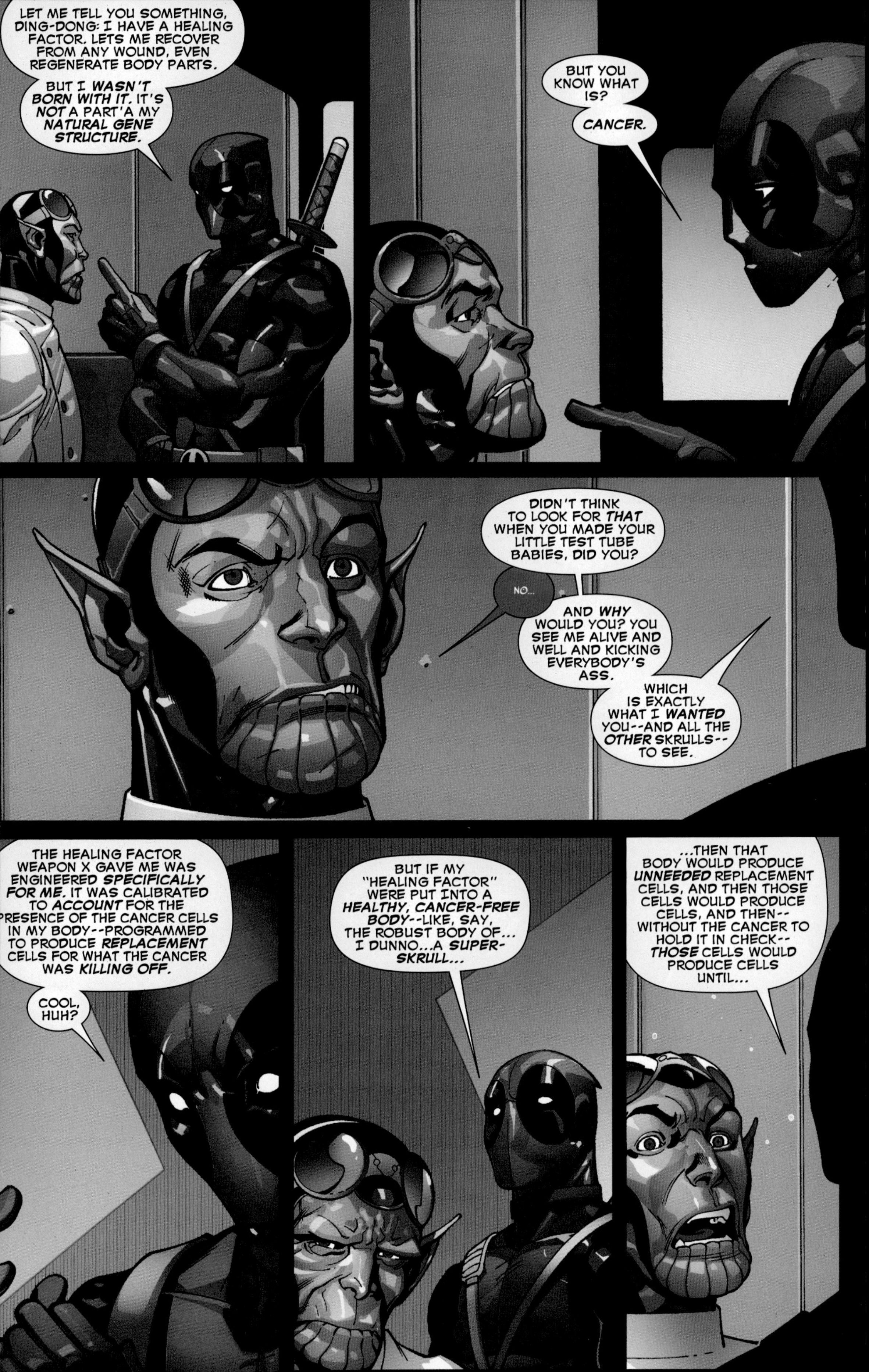
LET ME TELL YOU SOMETHING, DING-DONG: I HAVE A HEALING FACTOR. LETS ME RECOVER FROM ANY WOUND, EVEN REGENERATE BODY PARTS.
BUT I WASN'T BORN WITH IT. IT'S NOT A PART'A MY NATURAL GENE STRUCTURE.
BUT YOU KNOW WHAT IS?
CANCER.
DIDN'T THINK TO LOOK FOR THAT WHEN YOU MADE YOUR LITTLE TEST TUBE BABIES, DID YOU?
NO...
AND WHY WOULD YOU? YOU SEE ME ALIVE AND WELL AND KICKING EVERYBODY'S ASS.
WHICH IS EXACTLY WHAT I WANTED YOU--AND ALL THE OTHER SKRULLS--TO SEE.
THE HEALING FACTOR WEAPON X GAVE ME WAS ENGINEERED SPECIFICALLY FOR ME. IT WAS CALIBRATED TO ACCOUNT FOR THE PRESENCE OF THE CANCER CELLS IN MY BODY--PROGRAMMED TO PRODUCE REPLACEMENT CELLS FOR WHAT THE CANCER WAS KILLING OFF.
COOL, HUH?
BUT IF MY "HEALING FACTOR" WERE PUT INTO A HEALTHY, CANCER-FREE BODY--LIKE, SAY, THE ROBUST BODY OF... I DUNNO...A SUPER-SKRULL...
...THEN THAT BODY WOULD PRODUCE UNNEEDED REPLACEMENT CELLS, AND THEN THOSE CELLS WOULD PRODUCE CELLS, AND THEN--WITHOUT THE CANCER TO HOLD IT IN CHECK--THOSE CELLS WOULD PRODUCE CELLS UNTIL...

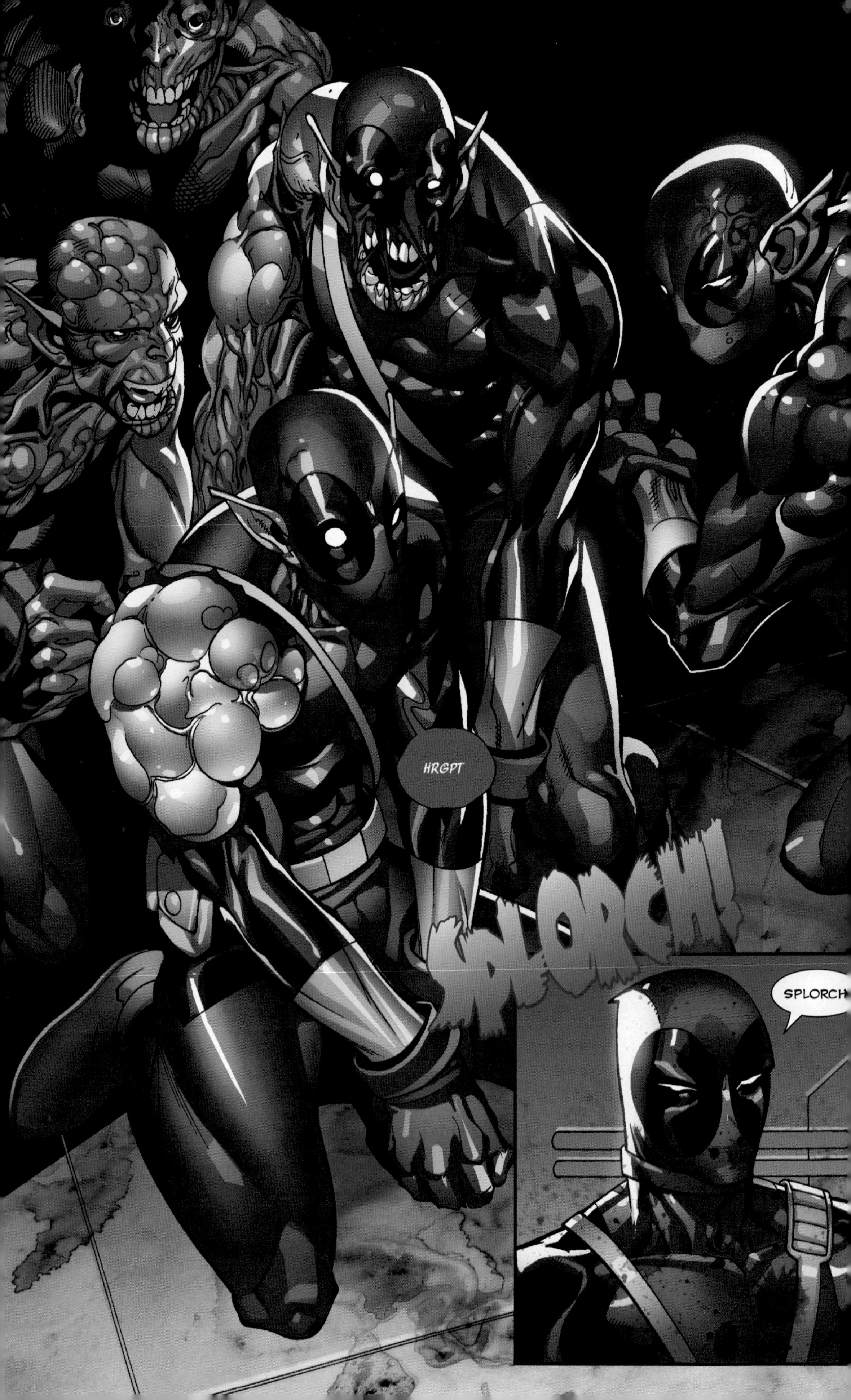
HRGPT
SPLORCH!
SPLORCH

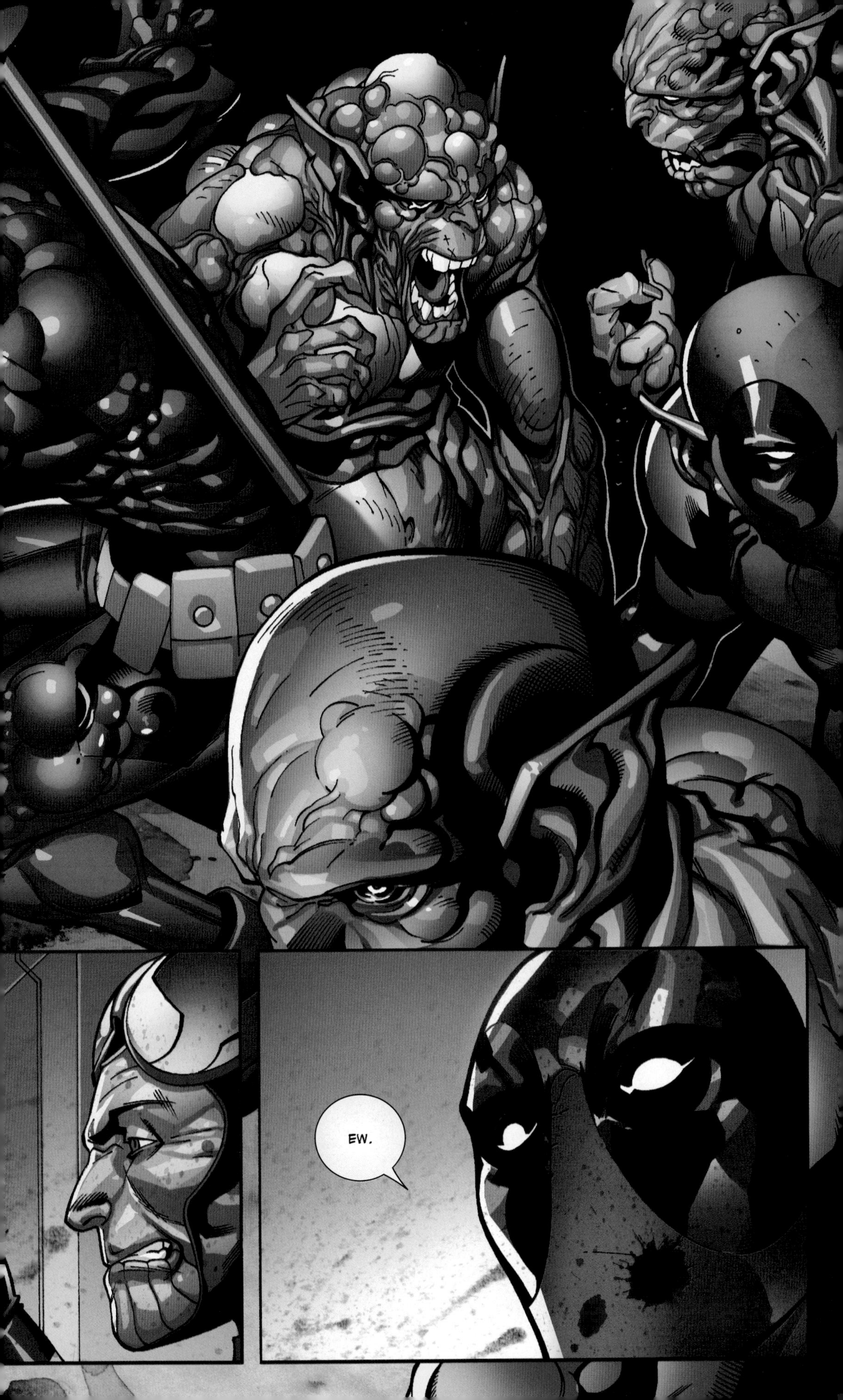
EW.

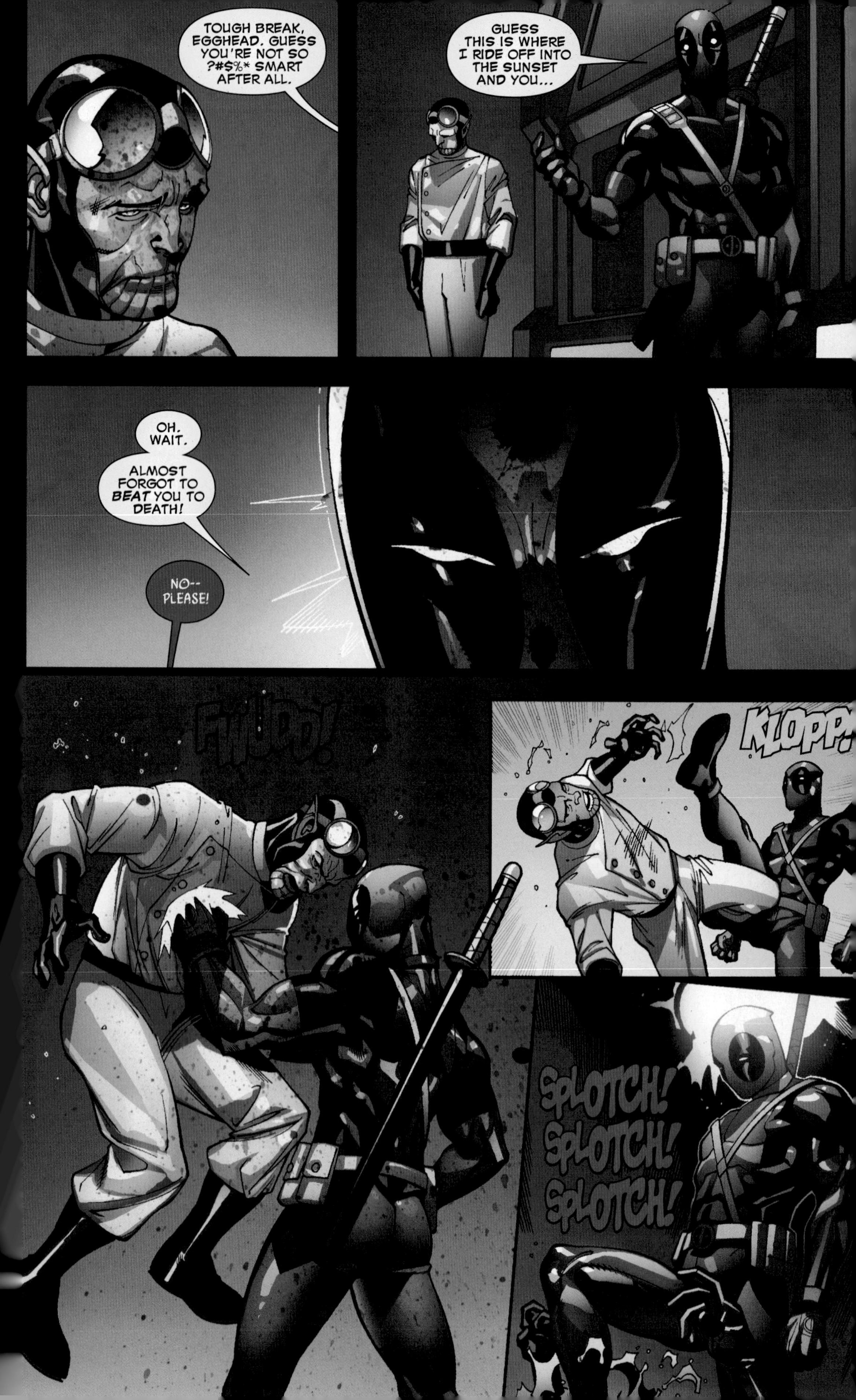
TOUGH BREAK, EGGHEAD. GUESS YOU'RE NOT SO ?#$%* SMART AFTER ALL.
GUESS THIS IS WHERE I RIDE OFF INTO THE SUNSET AND YOU...
OH. WAIT.
ALMOST FORGOT TO *BEAT* YOU TO DEATH!
NO-- PLEASE!
FWUD!
KLOPP!
SPLOTCH! SPLOTCH! SPLOTCH!

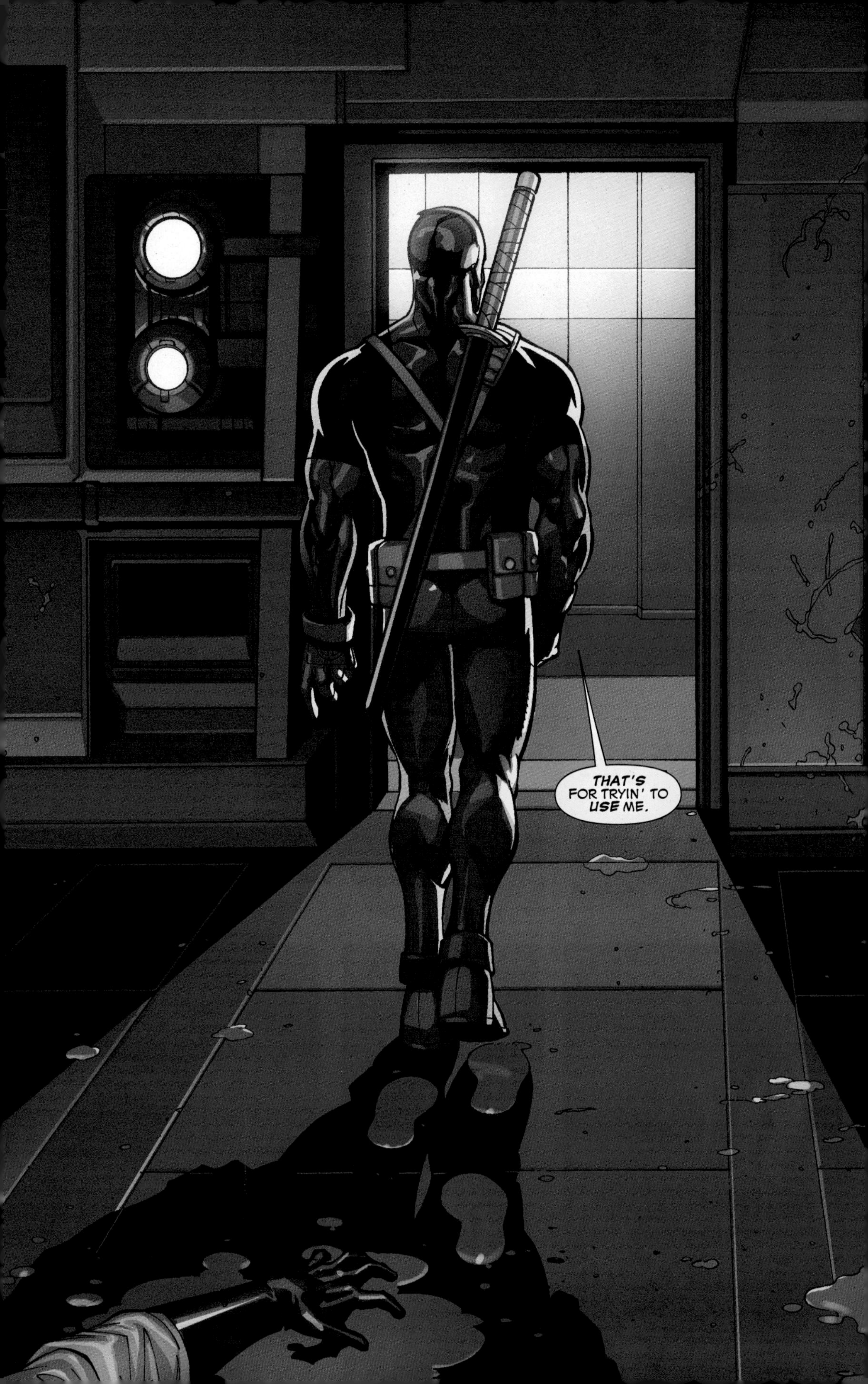
THAT'S FOR TRYIN' TO USE ME.

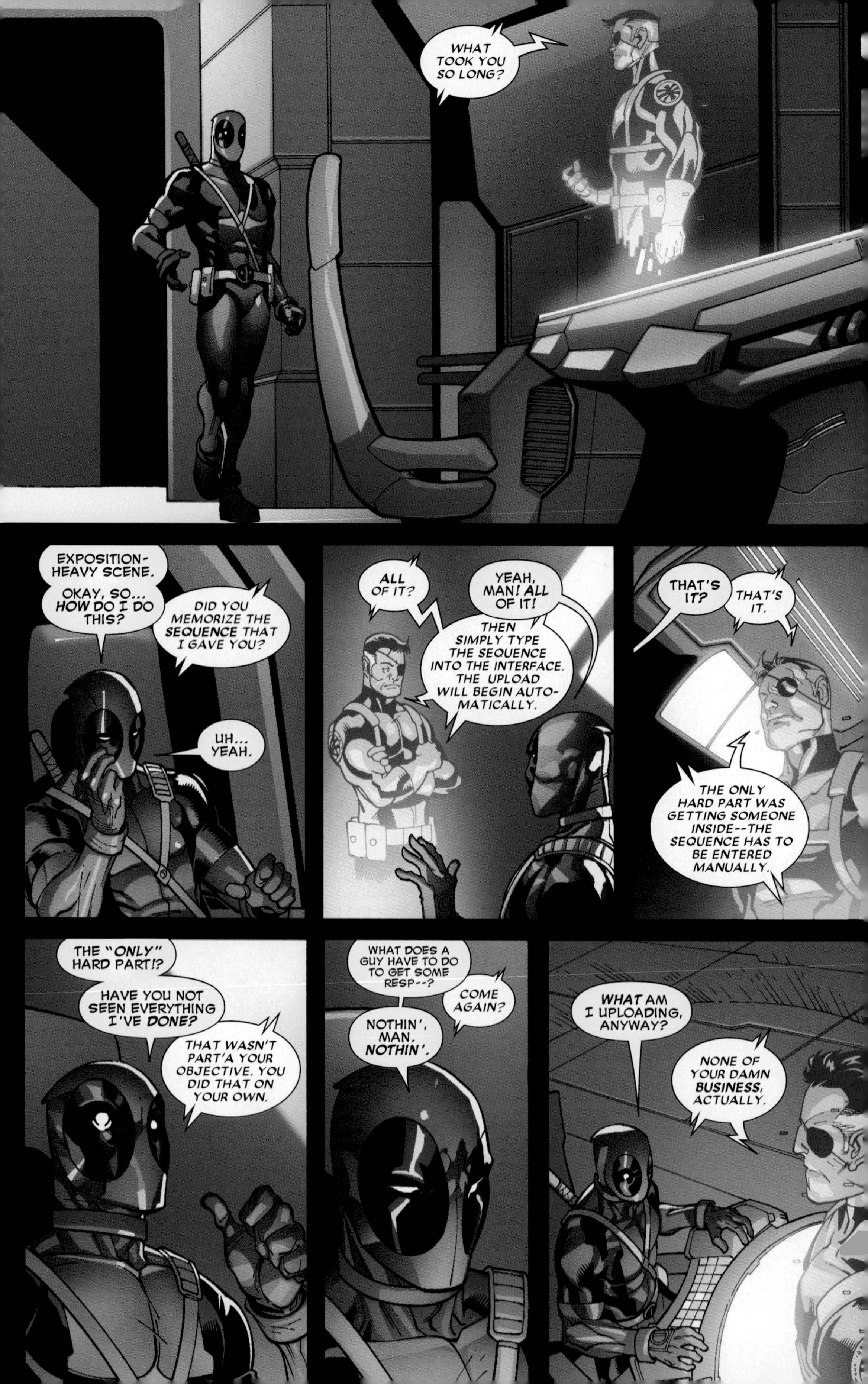
WHAT TOOK YOU SO LONG?
EXPOSITION-HEAVY SCENE.
OKAY, SO... HOW DO I DO THIS?
DID YOU MEMORIZE THE SEQUENCE THAT I GAVE YOU?
UH... YEAH.
ALL OF IT?
YEAH, MAN! ALL OF IT!
THEN SIMPLY TYPE THE SEQUENCE INTO THE INTERFACE. THE UPLOAD WILL BEGIN AUTOMATICALLY.
THAT'S IT?
THAT'S IT.
THE ONLY HARD PART WAS GETTING SOMEONE INSIDE--THE SEQUENCE HAS TO BE ENTERED MANUALLY.
THE "ONLY" HARD PART!?
HAVE YOU NOT SEEN EVERYTHING I'VE DONE?
THAT WASN'T PART'A YOUR OBJECTIVE. YOU DID THAT ON YOUR OWN.
WHAT DOES A GUY HAVE TO DO TO GET SOME RESP--?
COME AGAIN?
NOTHIN', MAN. NOTHIN'.
WHAT AM I UPLOADING, ANYWAY?
NONE OF YOUR DAMN BUSINESS, ACTUALLY.

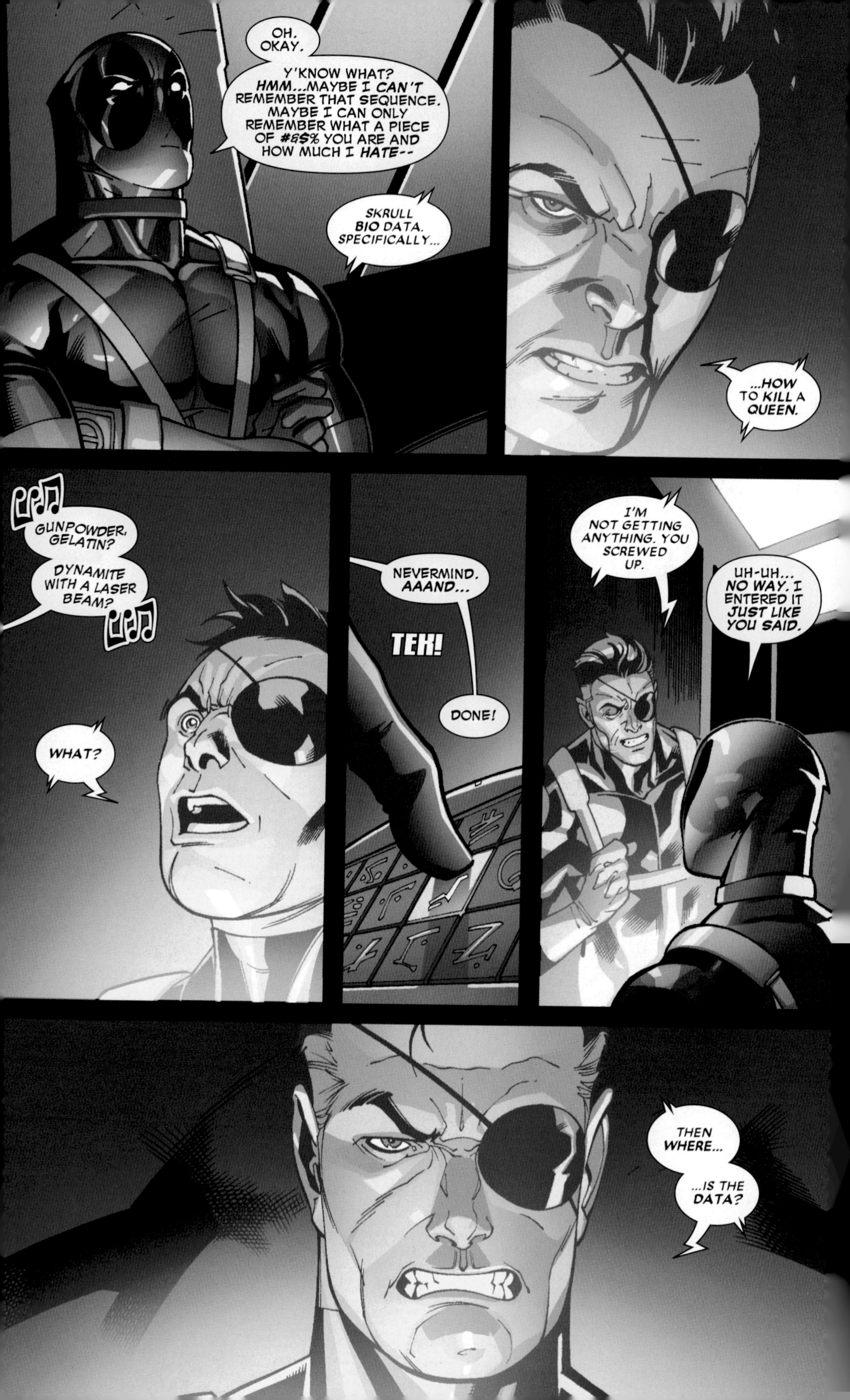
OH. OKAY.
Y'KNOW WHAT? HMM...MAYBE I CAN'T REMEMBER THAT SEQUENCE. MAYBE I CAN ONLY REMEMBER WHAT A PIECE OF #&$% YOU ARE AND HOW MUCH I HATE--
SKRULL BIO DATA. SPECIFICALLY...
...HOW TO KILL A QUEEN.
GUNPOWDER, GELATIN?
DYNAMITE WITH A LASER BEAM?
WHAT?
NEVERMIND. AAAND...
TEK!
DONE!
I'M NOT GETTING ANYTHING. YOU SCREWED UP.
UH-UH... NO WAY. I ENTERED IT JUST LIKE YOU SAID.
THEN WHERE...
...IS THE DATA?

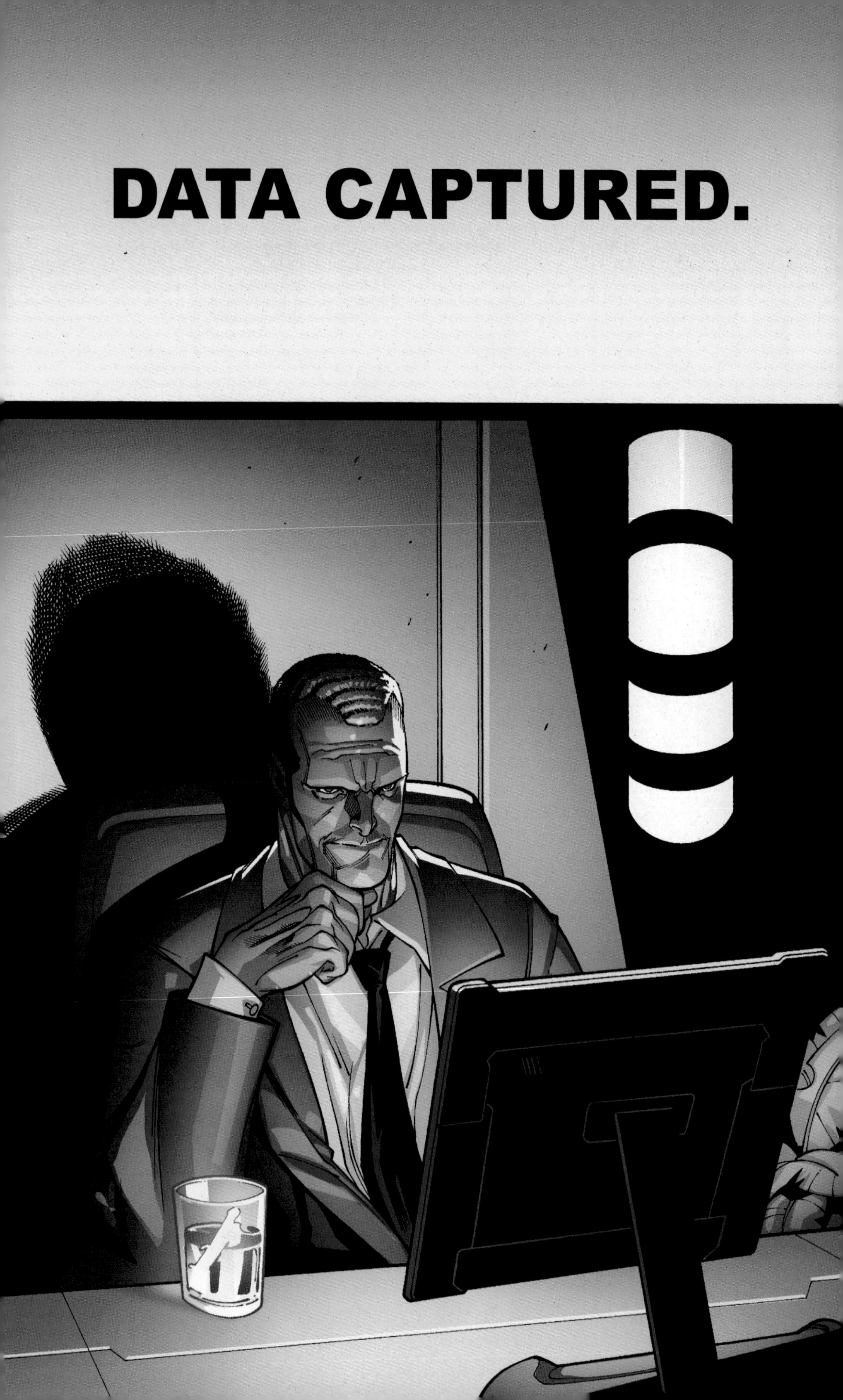
DATA CAPTURED.

# 4

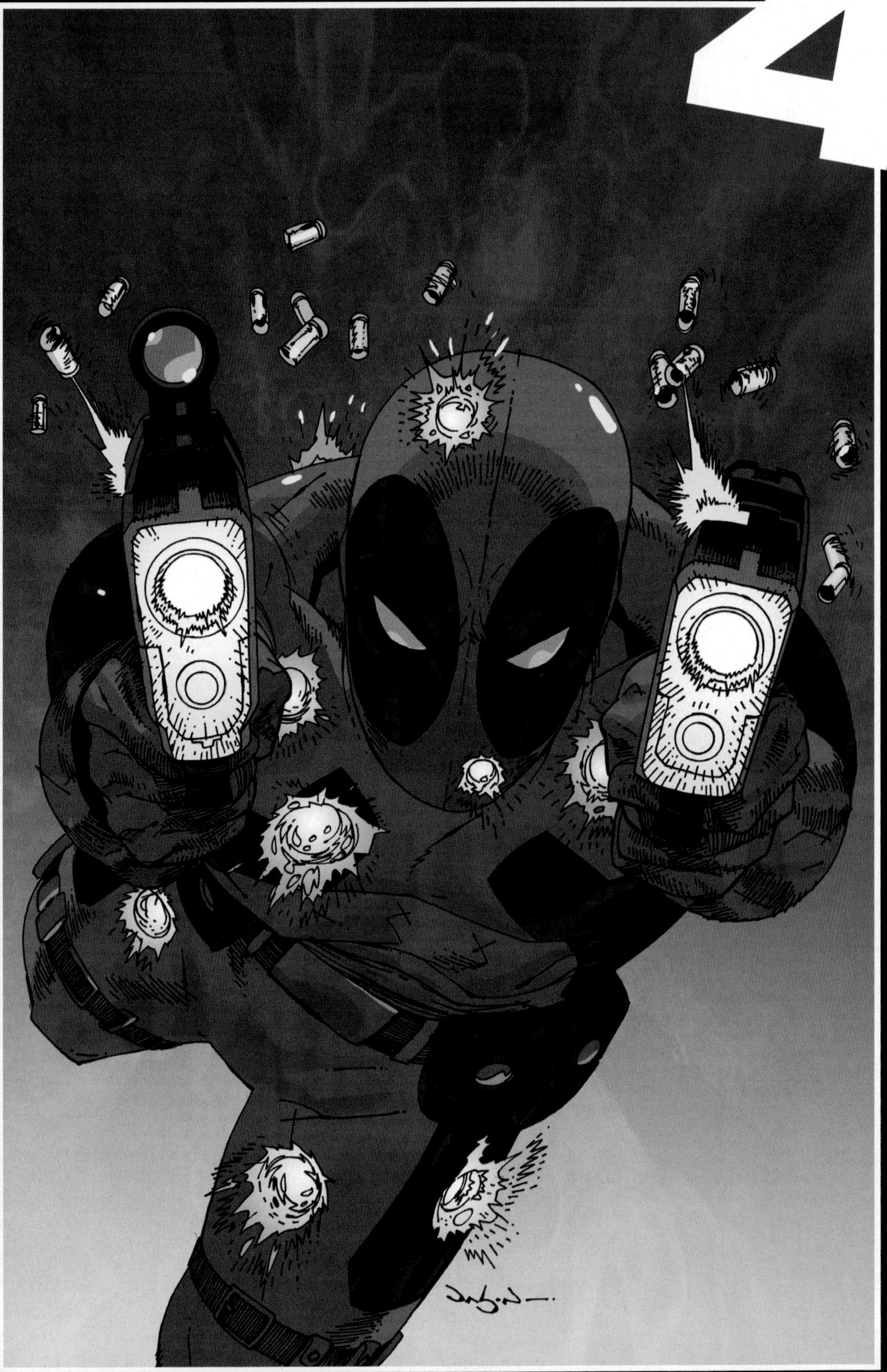

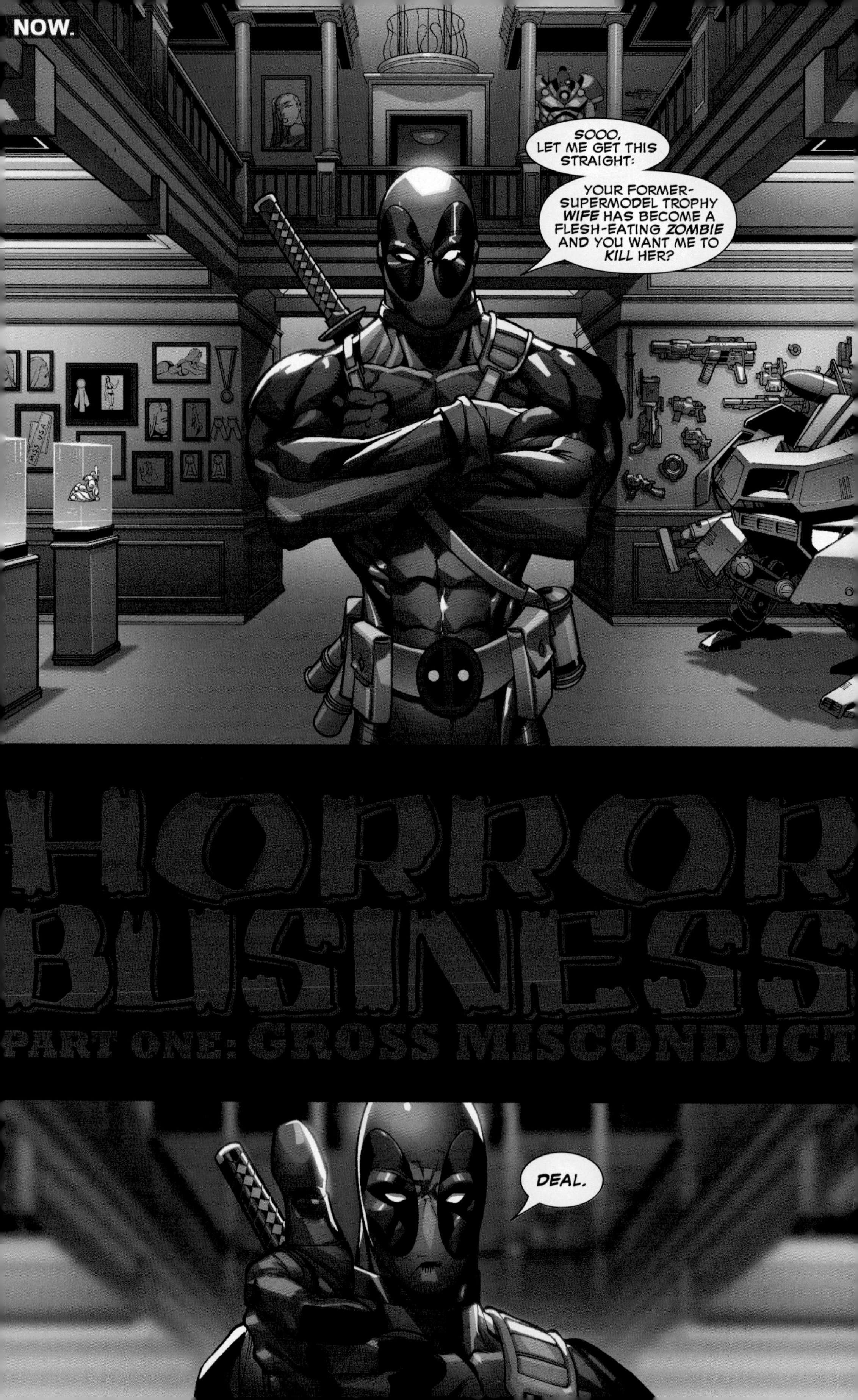
NOW.
SOOO, LET ME GET THIS STRAIGHT:
YOUR FORMER-SUPERMODEL TROPHY WIFE HAS BECOME A FLESH-EATING ZOMBIE AND YOU WANT ME TO KILL HER?
HORROR BUSINESS
PART ONE: GROSS MISCONDUCT
DEAL.

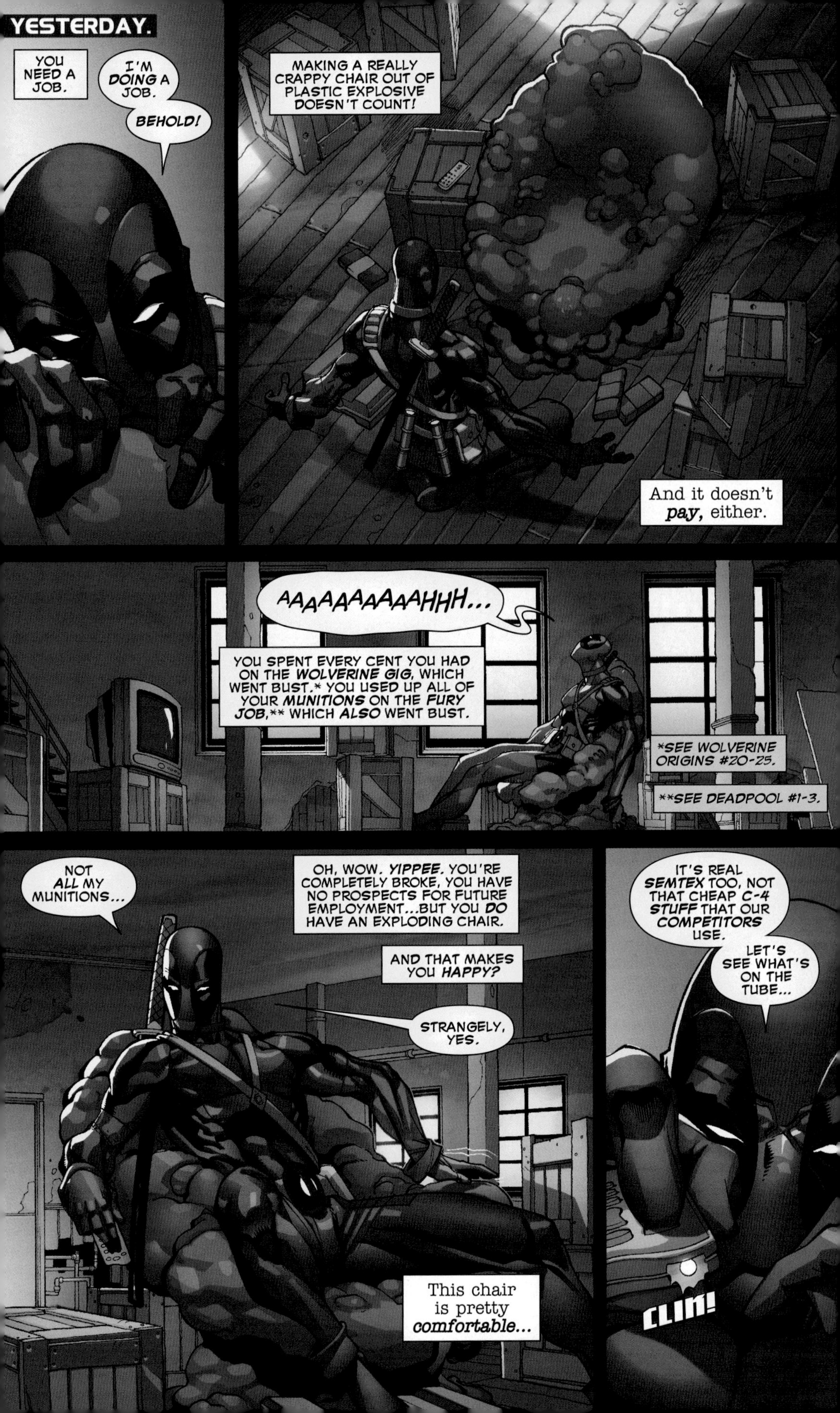
YESTERDAY.
YOU NEED A JOB.
I'M DOING A JOB.
BEHOLD!
MAKING A REALLY CRAPPY CHAIR OUT OF PLASTIC EXPLOSIVE DOESN'T COUNT!
And it doesn't pay, either.
AAAAAAAAAAHHH...
YOU SPENT EVERY CENT YOU HAD ON THE WOLVERINE GIG, WHICH WENT BUST.* YOU USED UP ALL OF YOUR MUNITIONS ON THE FURY JOB,** WHICH ALSO WENT BUST.
*SEE WOLVERINE ORIGINS #20-25.
**SEE DEADPOOL #1-3.
NOT ALL MY MUNITIONS...
OH, WOW. YIPPEE. YOU'RE COMPLETELY BROKE, YOU HAVE NO PROSPECTS FOR FUTURE EMPLOYMENT...BUT YOU DO HAVE AN EXPLODING CHAIR.
AND THAT MAKES YOU HAPPY?
STRANGELY, YES.
This chair is pretty comfortable...
IT'S REAL SEMTEX TOO, NOT THAT CHEAP C-4 STUFF THAT OUR COMPETITORS USE.
LET'S SEE WHAT'S ON THE TUBE...
CLIK!

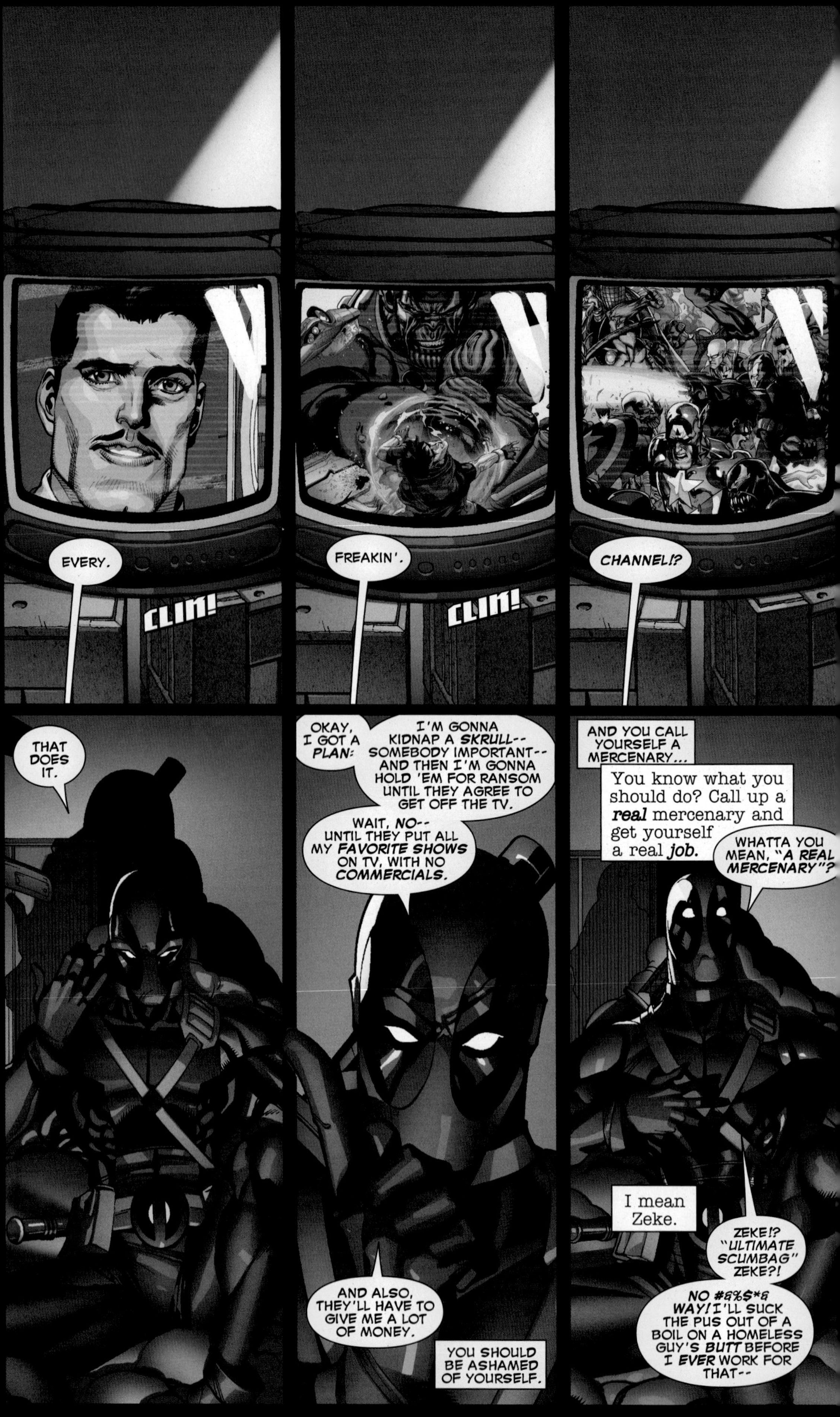
EVERY.
CLIK!
FREAKIN'.
CLIK!
CHANNEL!?
THAT DOES IT.
OKAY, I GOT A PLAN:
I'M GONNA KIDNAP A SKRULL-- SOMEBODY IMPORTANT-- AND THEN I'M GONNA HOLD 'EM FOR RANSOM UNTIL THEY AGREE TO GET OFF THE TV.
WAIT, NO-- UNTIL THEY PUT ALL MY FAVORITE SHOWS ON TV, WITH NO COMMERCIALS.
AND ALSO, THEY'LL HAVE TO GIVE ME A LOT OF MONEY.
YOU SHOULD BE ASHAMED OF YOURSELF.
AND YOU CALL YOURSELF A MERCENARY...
You know what you should do? Call up a real mercenary and get yourself a real job.
WHATTA YOU MEAN, "A REAL MERCENARY"?
I mean Zeke.
ZEKE!? "ULTIMATE SCUMBAG" ZEKE?!
NO #&%$*& WAY! I'LL SUCK THE PUS OUT OF A BOIL ON A HOMELESS GUY'S BUTT BEFORE I EVER WORK FOR THAT--

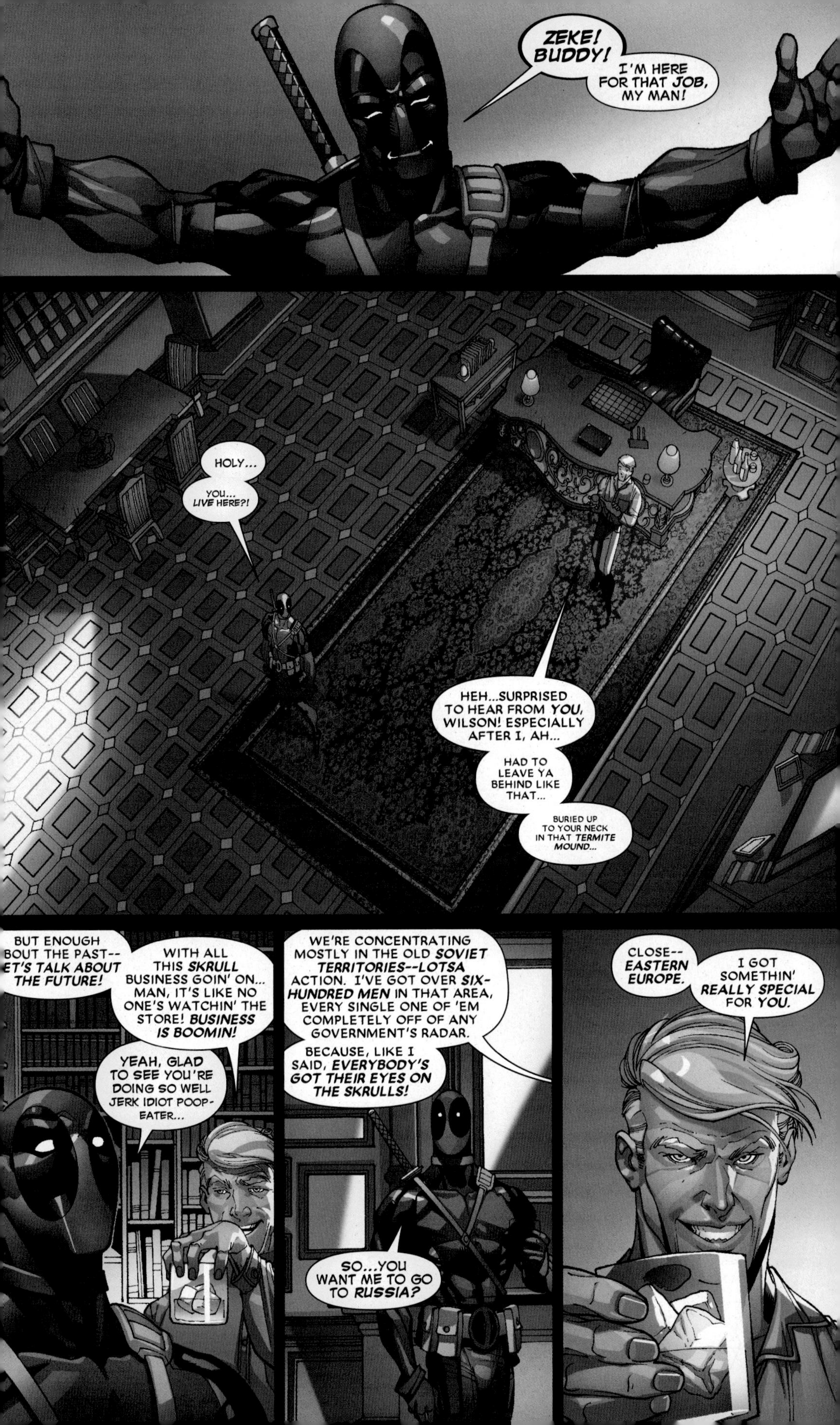

ZEKE! BUDDY!
I'M HERE FOR THAT JOB, MY MAN!
HOLY...
YOU... LIVE HERE?!
HEH...SURPRISED TO HEAR FROM YOU, WILSON! ESPECIALLY AFTER I, AH...
HAD TO LEAVE YA BEHIND LIKE THAT...
BURIED UP TO YOUR NECK IN THAT TERMITE MOUND...
BUT ENOUGH BOUT THE PAST-- ET'S TALK ABOUT THE FUTURE!
WITH ALL THIS SKRULL BUSINESS GOIN' ON... MAN, IT'S LIKE NO ONE'S WATCHIN' THE STORE! BUSINESS IS BOOMIN!
YEAH, GLAD TO SEE YOU'RE DOING SO WELL JERK IDIOT POOP-EATER...
WE'RE CONCENTRATING MOSTLY IN THE OLD SOVIET TERRITORIES--LOTSA ACTION. I'VE GOT OVER SIX-HUNDRED MEN IN THAT AREA, EVERY SINGLE ONE OF 'EM COMPLETELY OFF OF ANY GOVERNMENT'S RADAR.
BECAUSE, LIKE I SAID, EVERYBODY'S GOT THEIR EYES ON THE SKRULLS!
SO...YOU WANT ME TO GO TO RUSSIA?
CLOSE-- EASTERN EUROPE.
I GOT SOMETHIN' REALLY SPECIAL FOR YOU.

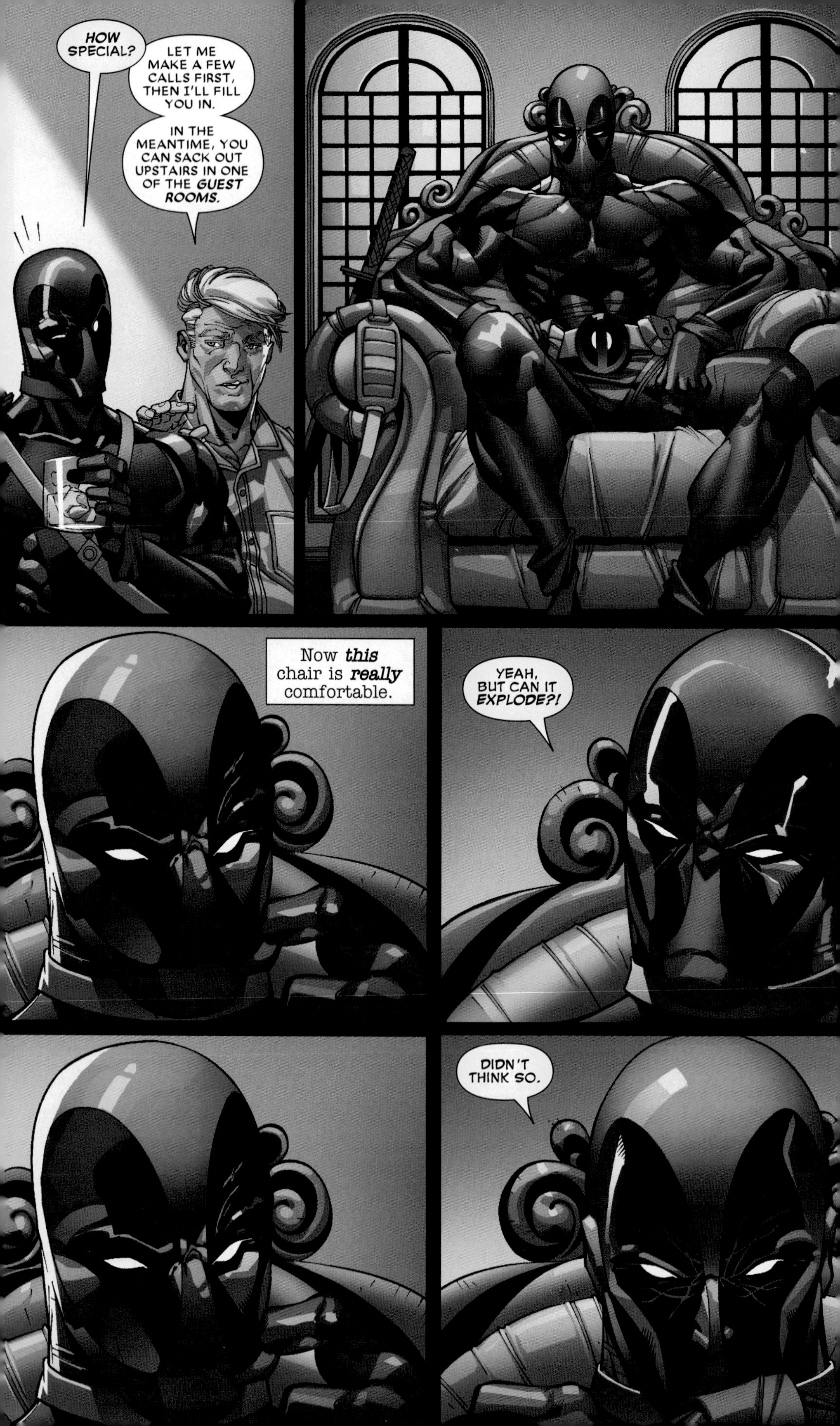
HOW SPECIAL?
LET ME MAKE A FEW CALLS FIRST, THEN I'LL FILL YOU IN.
IN THE MEANTIME, YOU CAN SACK OUT UPSTAIRS IN ONE OF THE GUEST ROOMS.
Now this chair is really comfortable.
YEAH, BUT CAN IT EXPLODE?!
DIDN'T THINK SO.

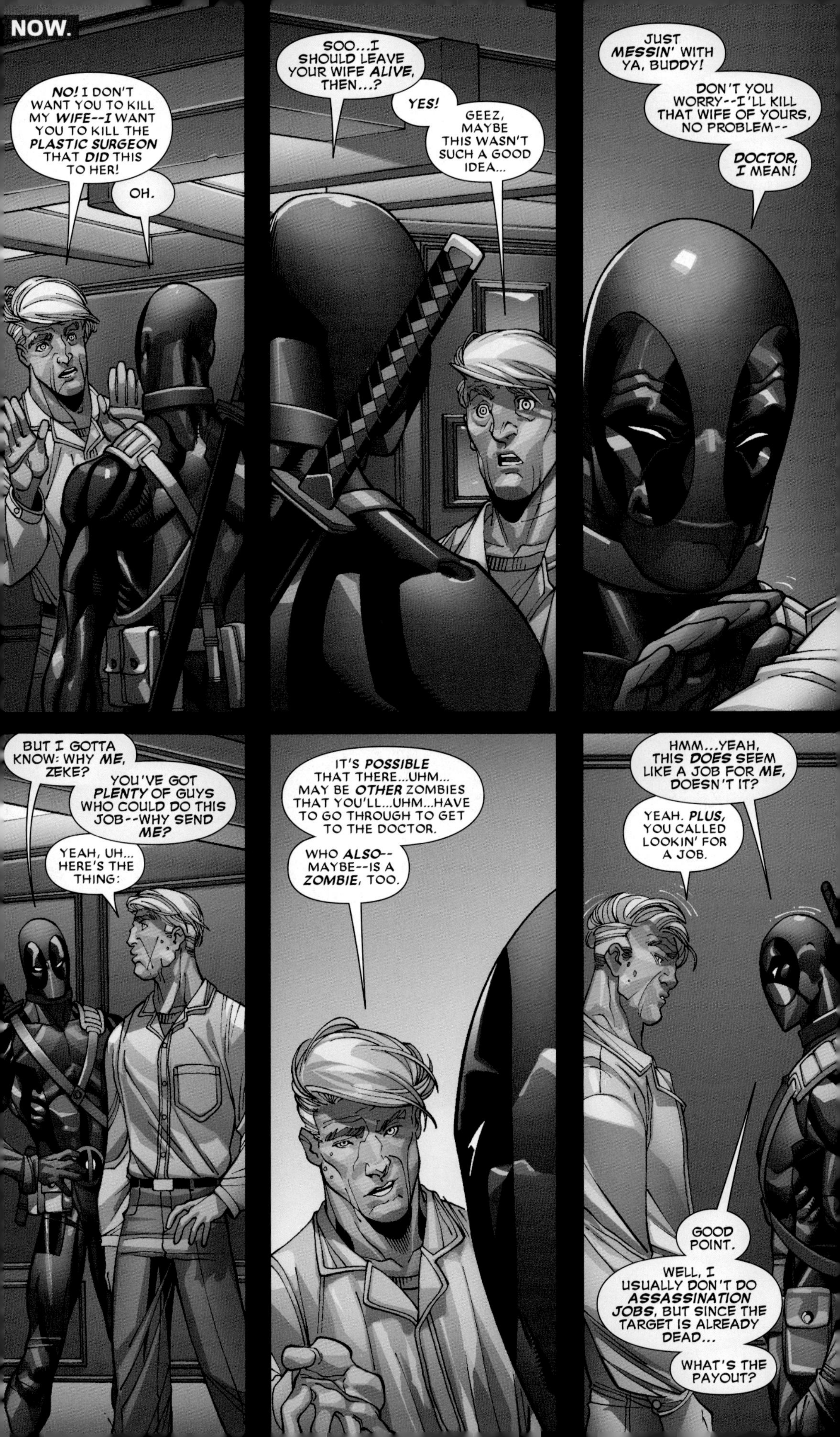
NOW.
NO! I DON'T WANT YOU TO KILL MY WIFE--I WANT YOU TO KILL THE PLASTIC SURGEON THAT DID THIS TO HER!
OH.
SOO...I SHOULD LEAVE YOUR WIFE ALIVE, THEN...?
YES!
GEEZ, MAYBE THIS WASN'T SUCH A GOOD IDEA...
JUST MESSIN' WITH YA, BUDDY!
DON'T YOU WORRY--I'LL KILL THAT WIFE OF YOURS, NO PROBLEM--
DOCTOR, I MEAN!
BUT I GOTTA KNOW: WHY ME, ZEKE?
YOU'VE GOT PLENTY OF GUYS WHO COULD DO THIS JOB--WHY SEND ME?
YEAH, UH... HERE'S THE THING:
IT'S POSSIBLE THAT THERE...UHM... MAY BE OTHER ZOMBIES THAT YOU'LL...UHM...HAVE TO GO THROUGH TO GET TO THE DOCTOR.
WHO ALSO-- MAYBE--IS A ZOMBIE, TOO.
HMM...YEAH, THIS DOES SEEM LIKE A JOB FOR ME, DOESN'T IT?
YEAH. PLUS, YOU CALLED LOOKIN' FOR A JOB.
GOOD POINT.
WELL, I USUALLY DON'T DO ASSASSINATION JOBS, BUT SINCE THE TARGET IS ALREADY DEAD...
WHAT'S THE PAYOUT?

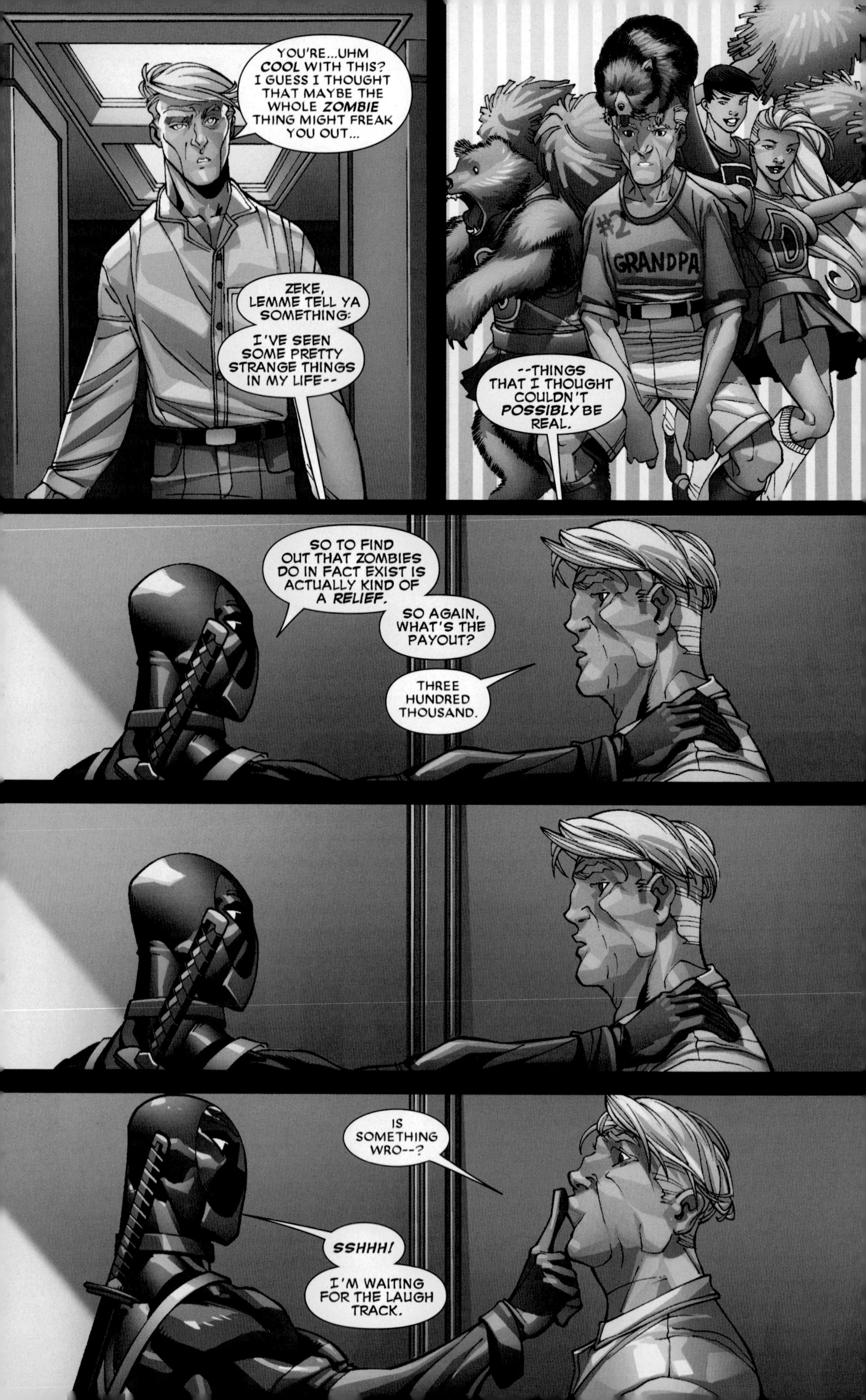
YOU'RE...UHM COOL WITH THIS? I GUESS I THOUGHT THAT MAYBE THE WHOLE ZOMBIE THING MIGHT FREAK YOU OUT...
ZEKE, LEMME TELL YA SOMETHING:
I'VE SEEN SOME PRETTY STRANGE THINGS IN MY LIFE--
#2
GRANDPA
--THINGS THAT I THOUGHT COULDN'T POSSIBLY BE REAL.
SO TO FIND OUT THAT ZOMBIES DO IN FACT EXIST IS ACTUALLY KIND OF A RELIEF.
SO AGAIN, WHAT'S THE PAYOUT?
THREE HUNDRED THOUSAND.
IS SOMETHING WRO--?
SSHHH!
I'M WAITING FOR THE LAUGH TRACK.

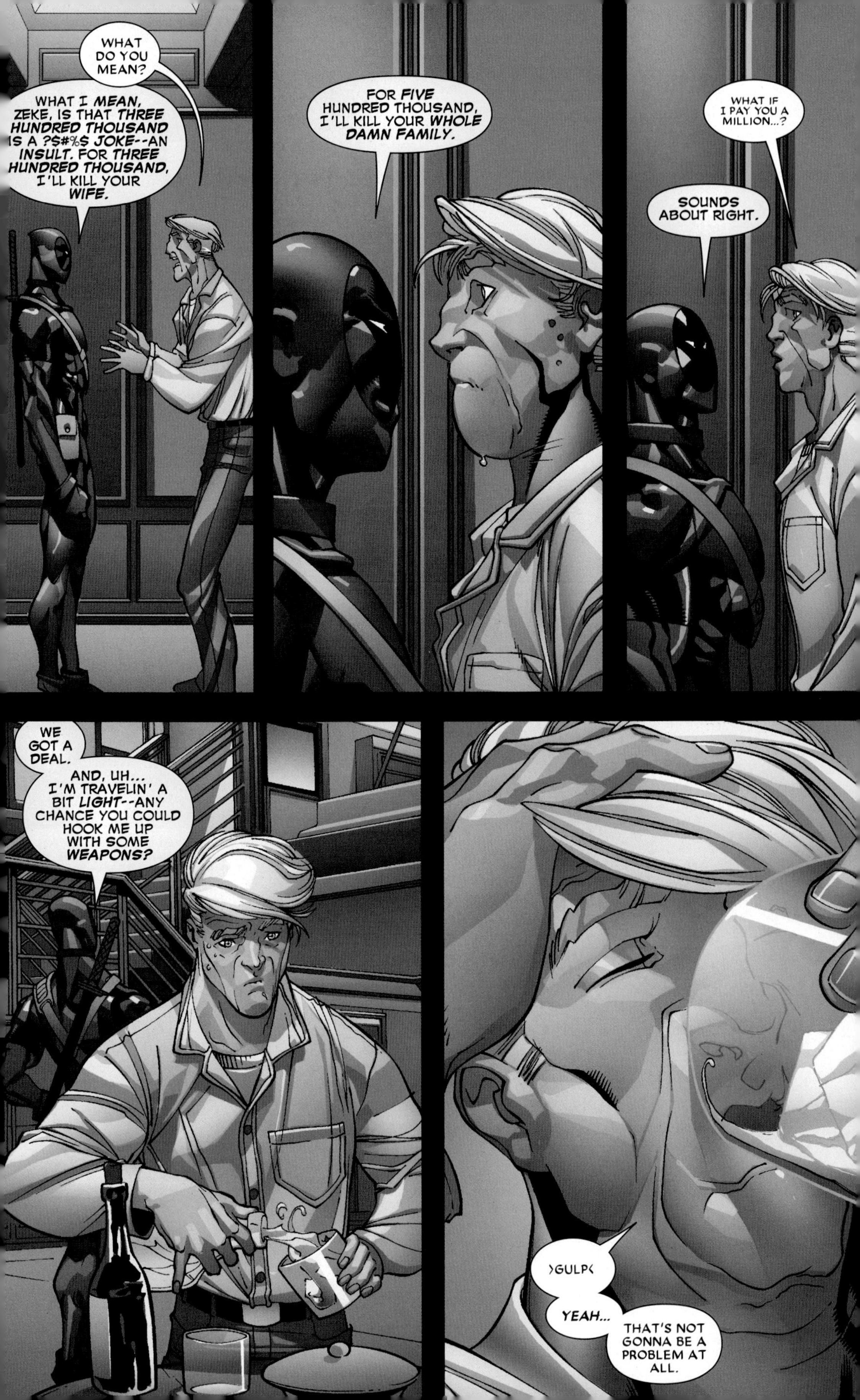

WHAT DO YOU MEAN?
WHAT I MEAN, ZEKE, IS THAT THREE HUNDRED THOUSAND IS A ?$#%$ JOKE--AN INSULT. FOR THREE HUNDRED THOUSAND, I'LL KILL YOUR WIFE.
FOR FIVE HUNDRED THOUSAND, I'LL KILL YOUR WHOLE DAMN FAMILY.
WHAT IF I PAY YOU A MILLION...?
SOUNDS ABOUT RIGHT.
WE GOT A DEAL.
AND, UH... I'M TRAVELIN' A BIT LIGHT--ANY CHANCE YOU COULD HOOK ME UP WITH SOME WEAPONS?
>GULP<
YEAH...
THAT'S NOT GONNA BE A PROBLEM AT ALL.

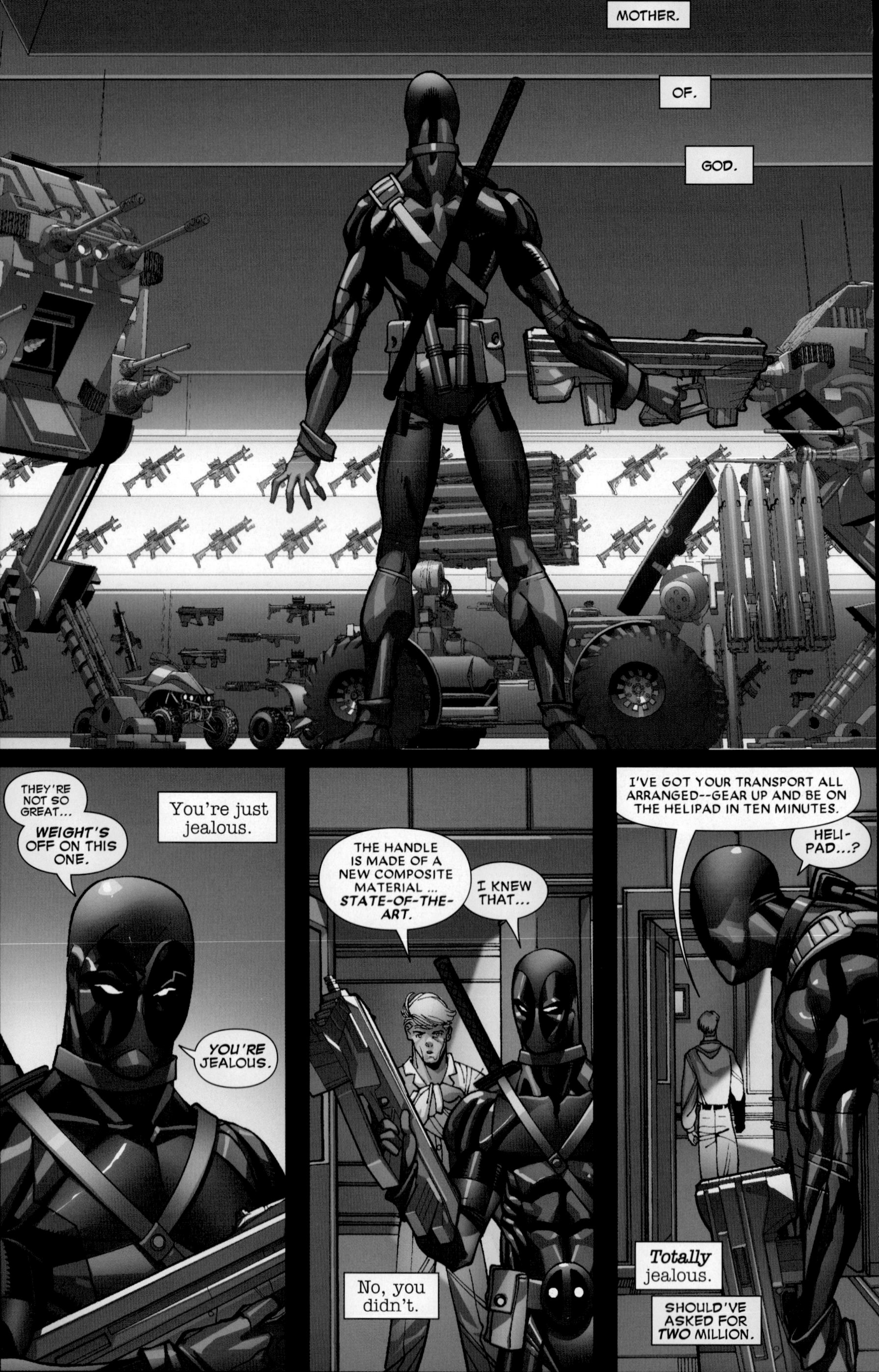
MOTHER.
OF.
GOD.
THEY'RE NOT SO GREAT... WEIGHT'S OFF ON THIS ONE.
You're just jealous.
YOU'RE JEALOUS.
THE HANDLE IS MADE OF A NEW COMPOSITE MATERIAL ... STATE-OF-THE-ART.
I KNEW THAT...
No, you didn't.
I'VE GOT YOUR TRANSPORT ALL ARRANGED--GEAR UP AND BE ON THE HELIPAD IN TEN MINUTES.
HELI-PAD...?
Totally jealous.
SHOULD'VE ASKED FOR TWO MILLION.

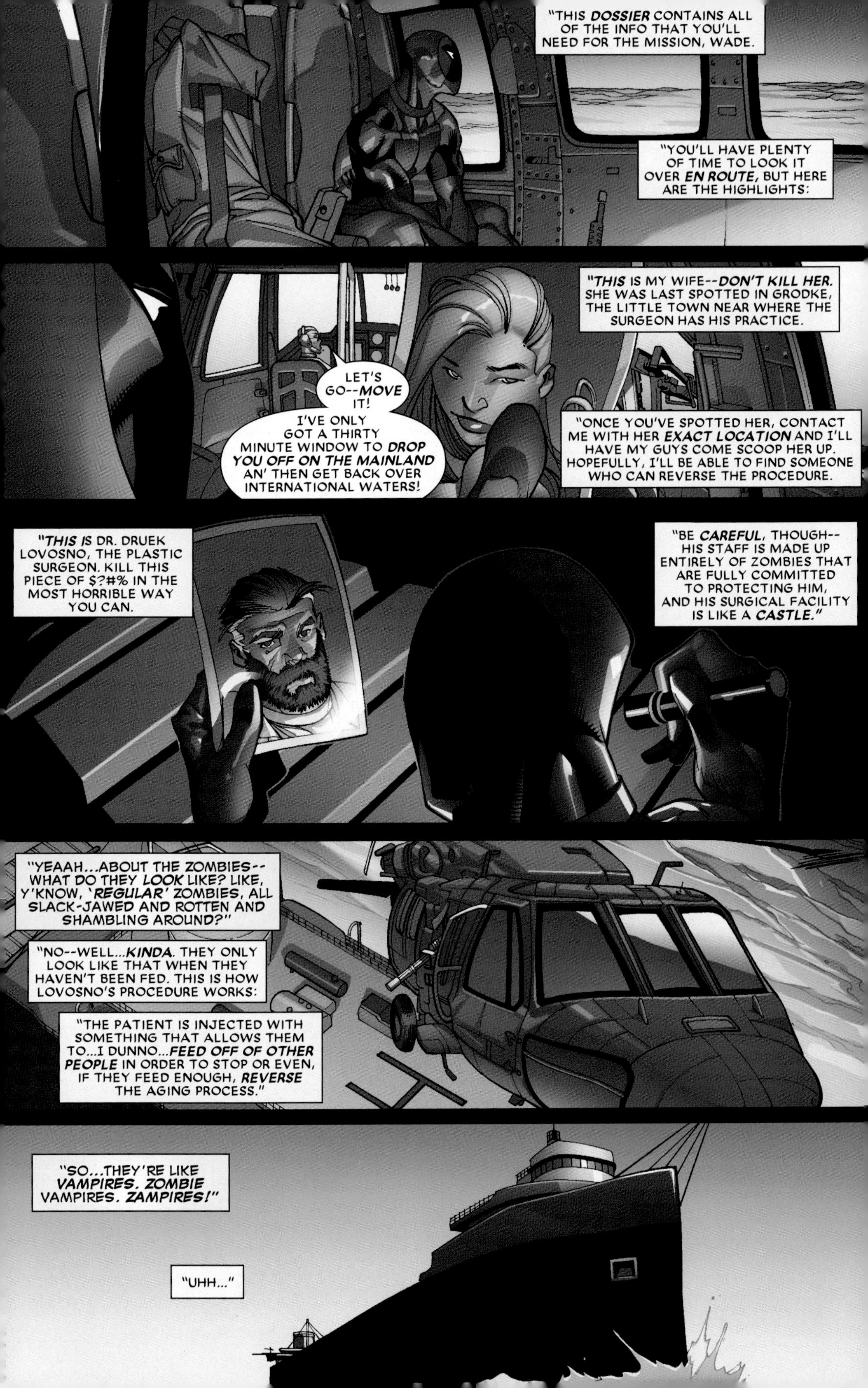
"THIS DOSSIER CONTAINS ALL OF THE INFO THAT YOU'LL NEED FOR THE MISSION, WADE.
"YOU'LL HAVE PLENTY OF TIME TO LOOK IT OVER EN ROUTE, BUT HERE ARE THE HIGHLIGHTS:
"THIS IS MY WIFE--DON'T KILL HER. SHE WAS LAST SPOTTED IN GRODKE, THE LITTLE TOWN NEAR WHERE THE SURGEON HAS HIS PRACTICE.
LET'S GO--MOVE IT!
I'VE ONLY GOT A THIRTY MINUTE WINDOW TO DROP YOU OFF ON THE MAINLAND AN' THEN GET BACK OVER INTERNATIONAL WATERS!
"ONCE YOU'VE SPOTTED HER, CONTACT ME WITH HER EXACT LOCATION AND I'LL HAVE MY GUYS COME SCOOP HER UP. HOPEFULLY, I'LL BE ABLE TO FIND SOMEONE WHO CAN REVERSE THE PROCEDURE.
"THIS IS DR. DRUEK LOVOSNO, THE PLASTIC SURGEON. KILL THIS PIECE OF $?#% IN THE MOST HORRIBLE WAY YOU CAN.
"BE CAREFUL, THOUGH--HIS STAFF IS MADE UP ENTIRELY OF ZOMBIES THAT ARE FULLY COMMITTED TO PROTECTING HIM, AND HIS SURGICAL FACILITY IS LIKE A CASTLE."
"YEAAH...ABOUT THE ZOMBIES--WHAT DO THEY LOOK LIKE? LIKE, Y'KNOW, 'REGULAR' ZOMBIES, ALL SLACK-JAWED AND ROTTEN AND SHAMBLING AROUND?"
"NO--WELL...KINDA. THEY ONLY LOOK LIKE THAT WHEN THEY HAVEN'T BEEN FED. THIS IS HOW LOVOSNO'S PROCEDURE WORKS:
"THE PATIENT IS INJECTED WITH SOMETHING THAT ALLOWS THEM TO...I DUNNO...FEED OFF OF OTHER PEOPLE IN ORDER TO STOP OR EVEN, IF THEY FEED ENOUGH, REVERSE THE AGING PROCESS."
"SO...THEY'RE LIKE VAMPIRES. ZOMBIE VAMPIRES. ZAMPIRES!"
"UHH..."

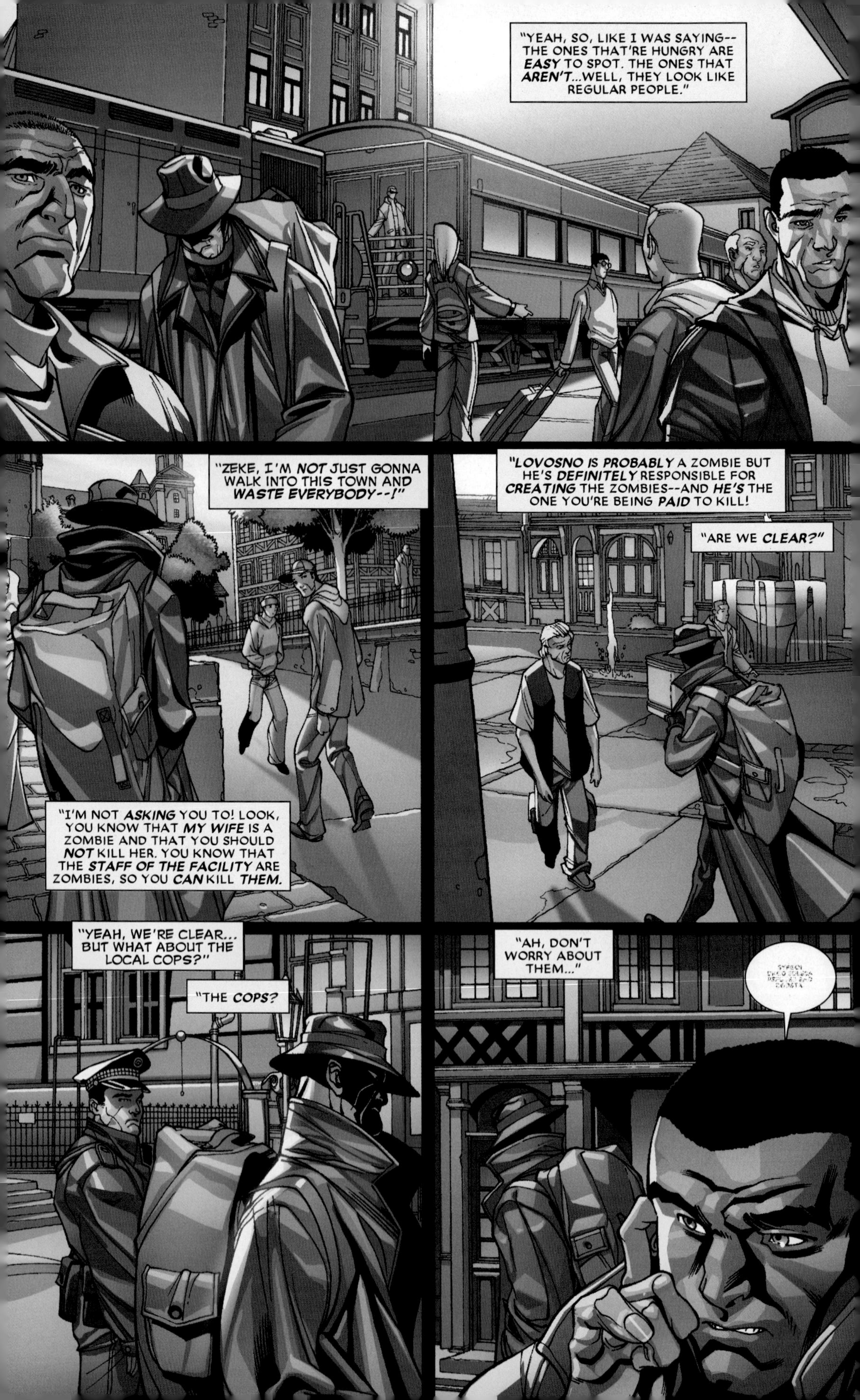
"YEAH, SO, LIKE I WAS SAYING-- THE ONES THAT'RE HUNGRY ARE EASY TO SPOT. THE ONES THAT AREN'T...WELL, THEY LOOK LIKE REGULAR PEOPLE."
"ZEKE, I'M NOT JUST GONNA WALK INTO THIS TOWN AND WASTE EVERYBODY--!"
"I'M NOT ASKING YOU TO! LOOK, YOU KNOW THAT MY WIFE IS A ZOMBIE AND THAT YOU SHOULD NOT KILL HER. YOU KNOW THAT THE STAFF OF THE FACILITY ARE ZOMBIES, SO YOU CAN KILL THEM.
"LOVOSNO IS PROBABLY A ZOMBIE BUT HE'S DEFINITELY RESPONSIBLE FOR CREATING THE ZOMBIES--AND HE'S THE ONE YOU'RE BEING PAID TO KILL!
"ARE WE CLEAR?"
"YEAH, WE'RE CLEAR... BUT WHAT ABOUT THE LOCAL COPS?"
"THE COPS?
"AH, DON'T WORRY ABOUT THEM..."

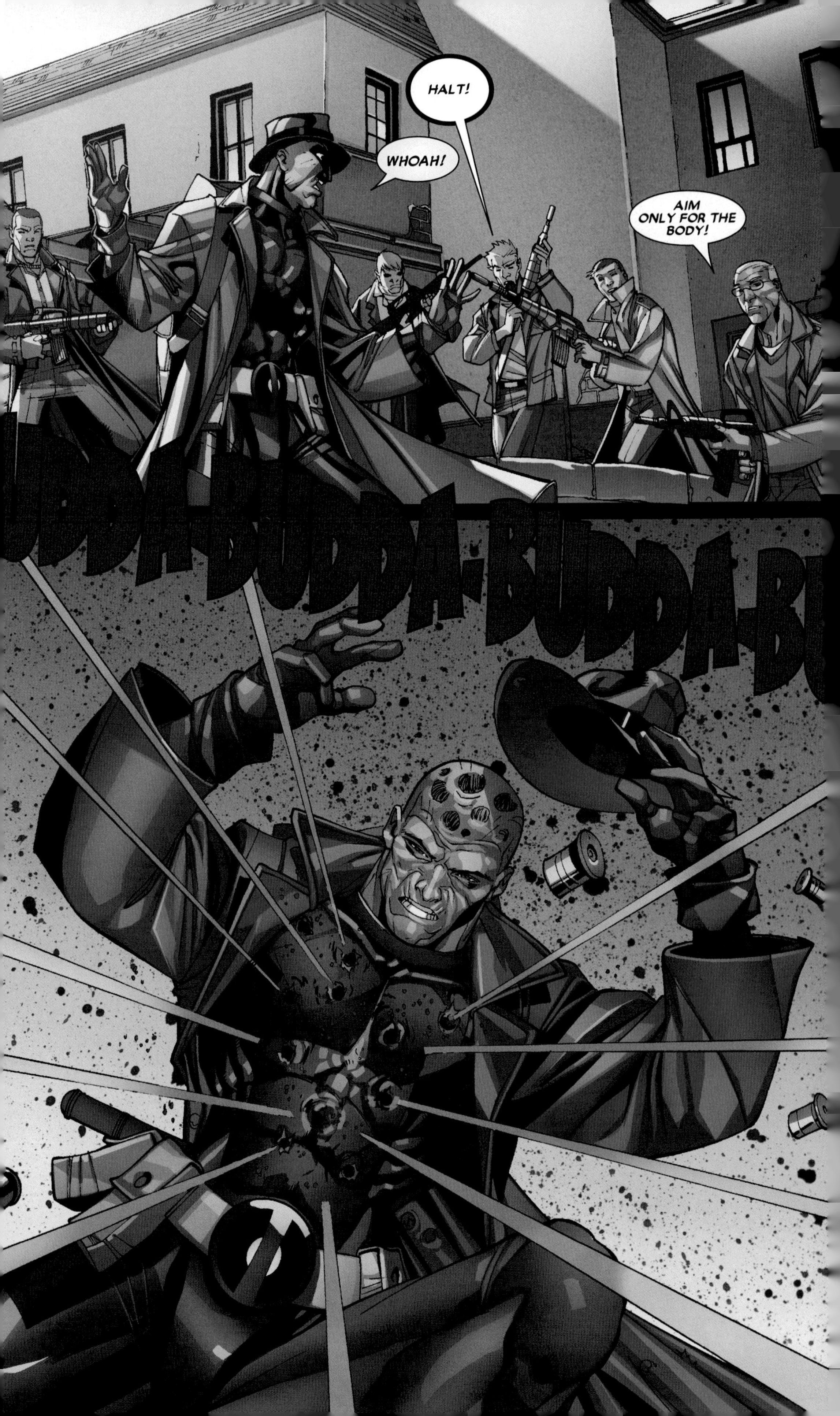
HALT!
WHOAH!
AIM ONLY FOR THE BODY!
BUDDA-BUDDA-BUDDA-BU

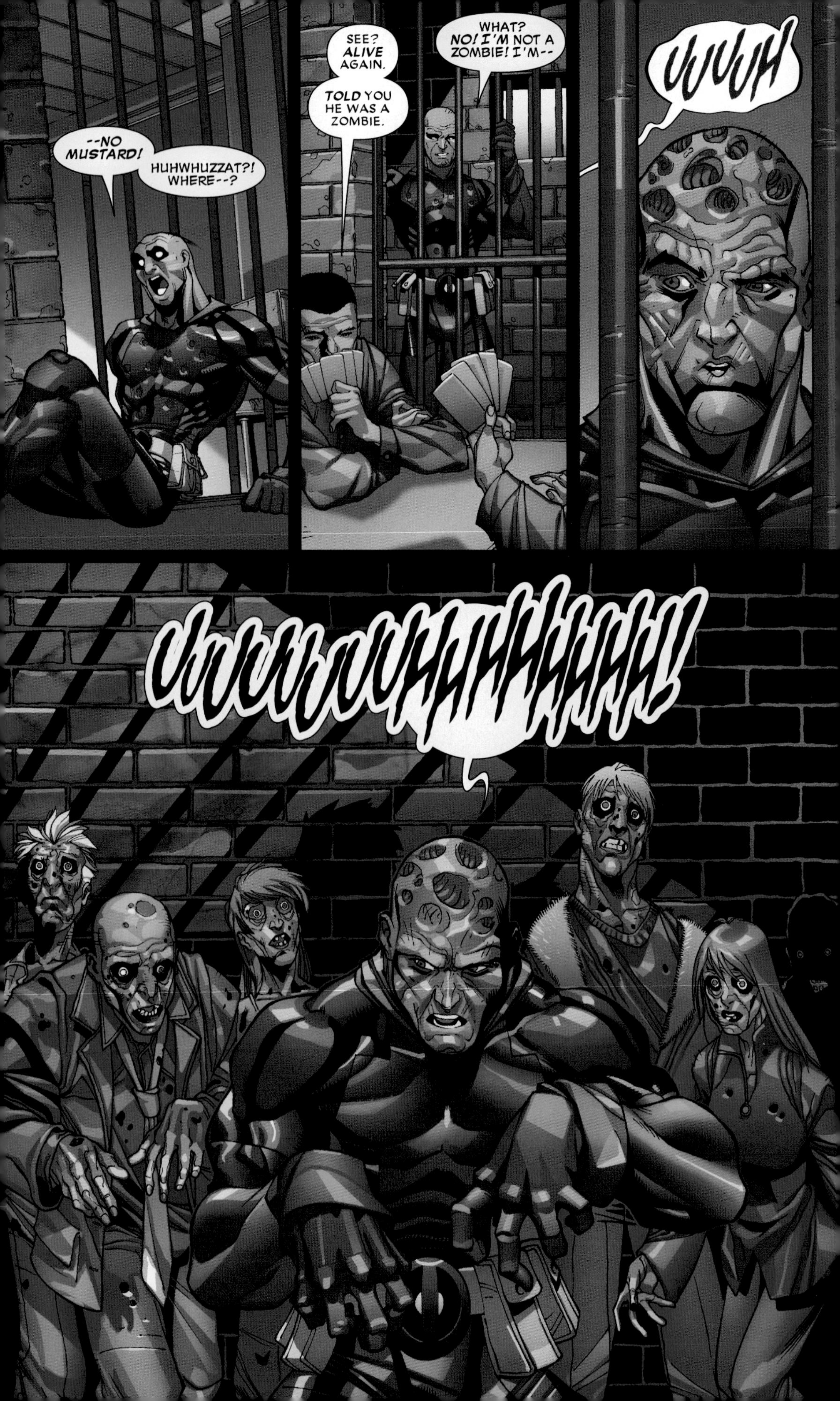
--NO MUSTARD!
HUHWHUZZAT?! WHERE--?
SEE? ALIVE AGAIN.
TOLD YOU HE WAS A ZOMBIE.
WHAT? NO! I'M NOT A ZOMBIE! I'M--
UUUUH
UUUUUUUHHHHHHHH!

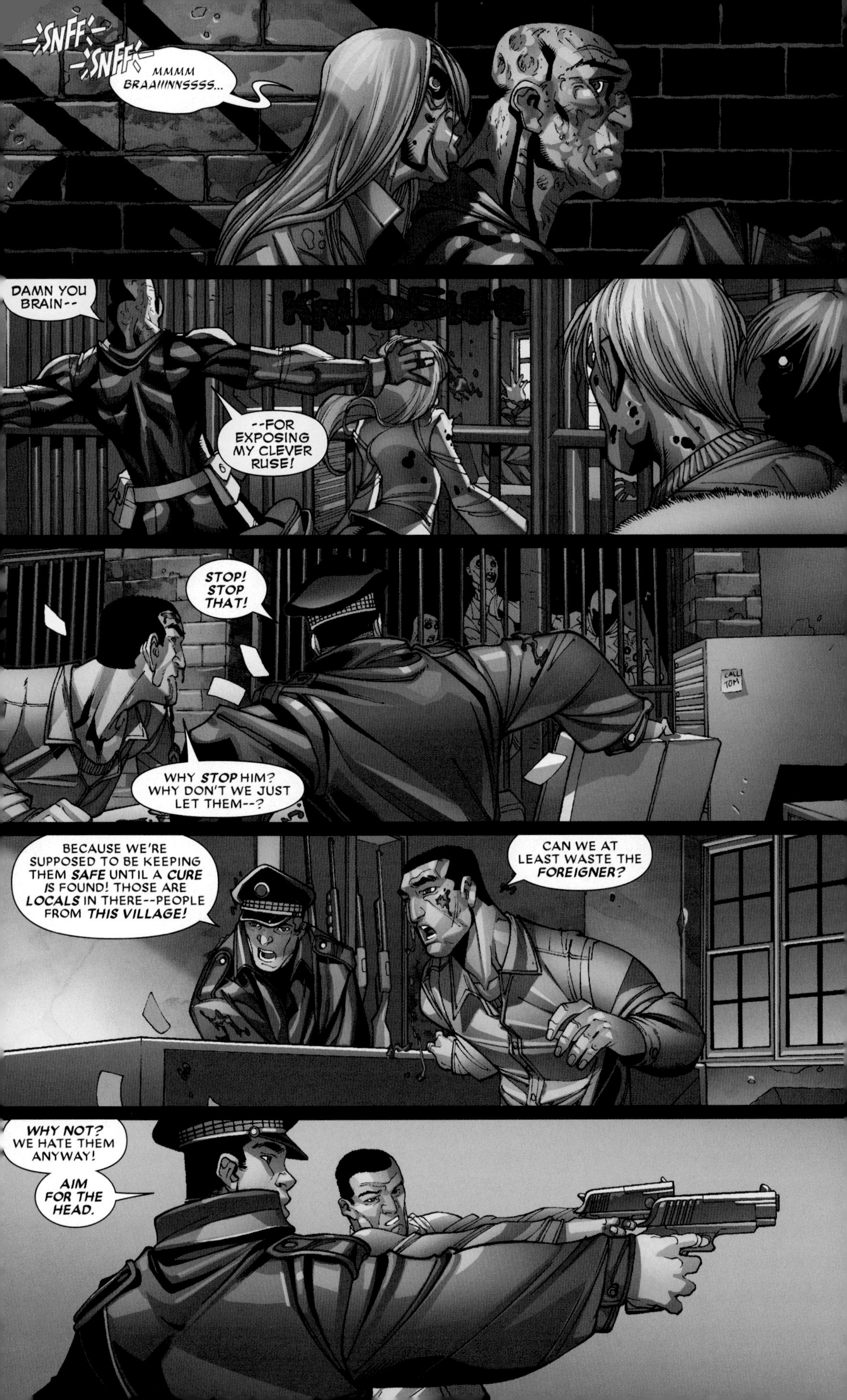
SNFF
SNFF
MMMM BRAAIIINNSSSS...
DAMN YOU BRAIN--
KRUDSHH
--FOR EXPOSING MY CLEVER RUSE!
STOP! STOP THAT!
CALL TOM
WHY STOP HIM? WHY DON'T WE JUST LET THEM--?
BECAUSE WE'RE SUPPOSED TO BE KEEPING THEM SAFE UNTIL A CURE IS FOUND! THOSE ARE LOCALS IN THERE--PEOPLE FROM THIS VILLAGE!
CAN WE AT LEAST WASTE THE FOREIGNER?
WHY NOT? WE HATE THEM ANYWAY!
AIM FOR THE HEAD.

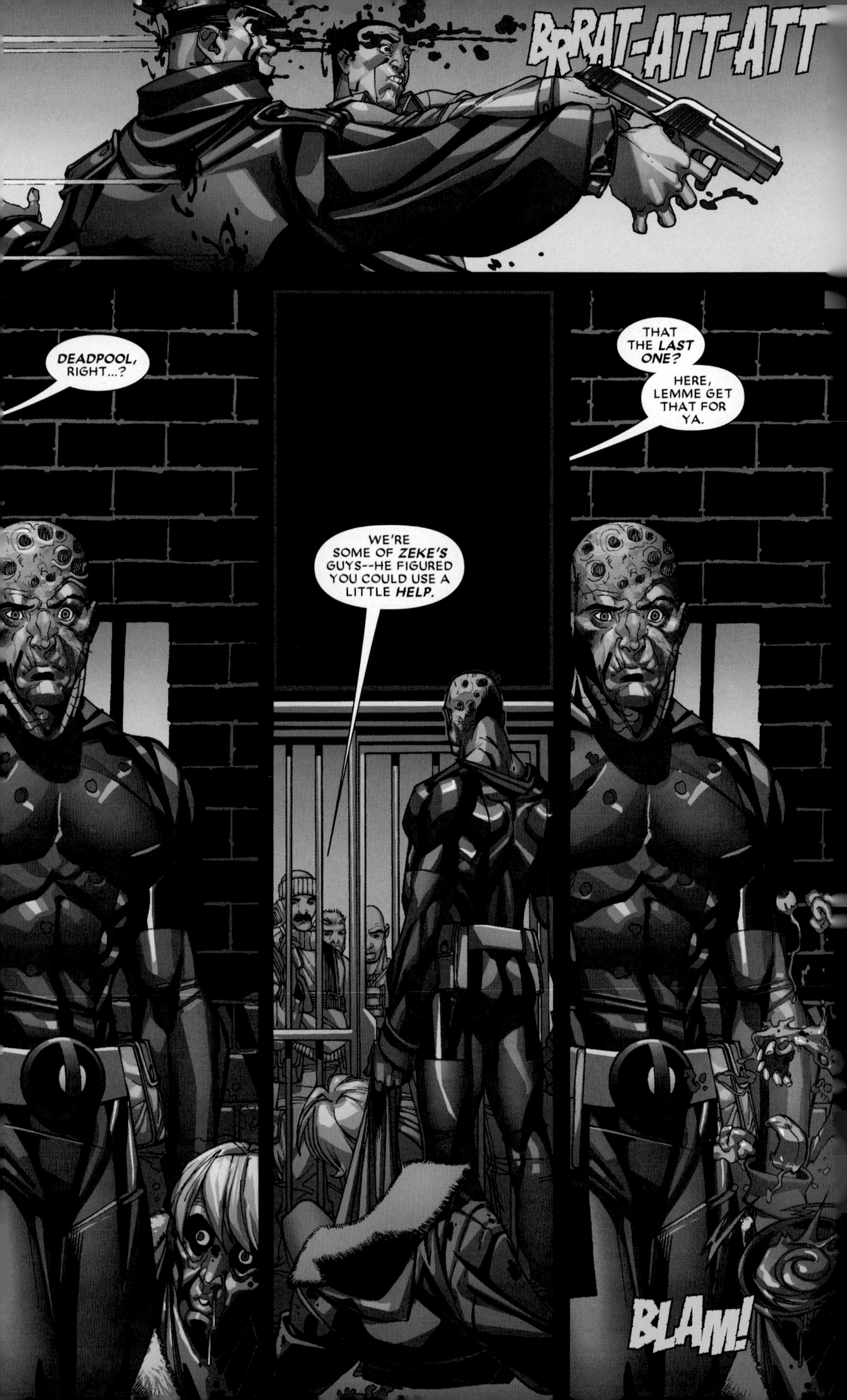
BRRAT-ATT-ATT
DEADPOOL, RIGHT...?
WE'RE SOME OF ZEKE'S GUYS--HE FIGURED YOU COULD USE A LITTLE HELP.
THAT THE LAST ONE?
HERE, LEMME GET THAT FOR YA.
BLAM!

ZEKE SENT YOU...

BECAUSE HE THOUGHT I...

...NEEDED HELP?

FROM YOU.

YEAH.

UHH... YEAH.

I WOULD'A BEEN OUTTA HERE IN LESS'N AN HOUR.

AN' I WOULD'A DONE IT WITHOUT KILLIN' ANYBODY THAT WASN'T ALREADY DEAD.

HEY, IT AIN'T LIKE THEY WERE CIVILIANS-- THEY WERE COPS!

YEAH--COPS THAT WERE JUST TRYING TO PROTECT THE PEOPLE OF THEIR TOWN.

$#%?!%# TRIGGER-HAPPY AMATEURS...

WAITASEC.

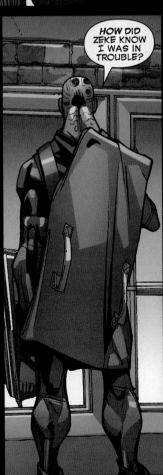

HOW DID ZEKE KNOW I WAS IN TROUBLE?

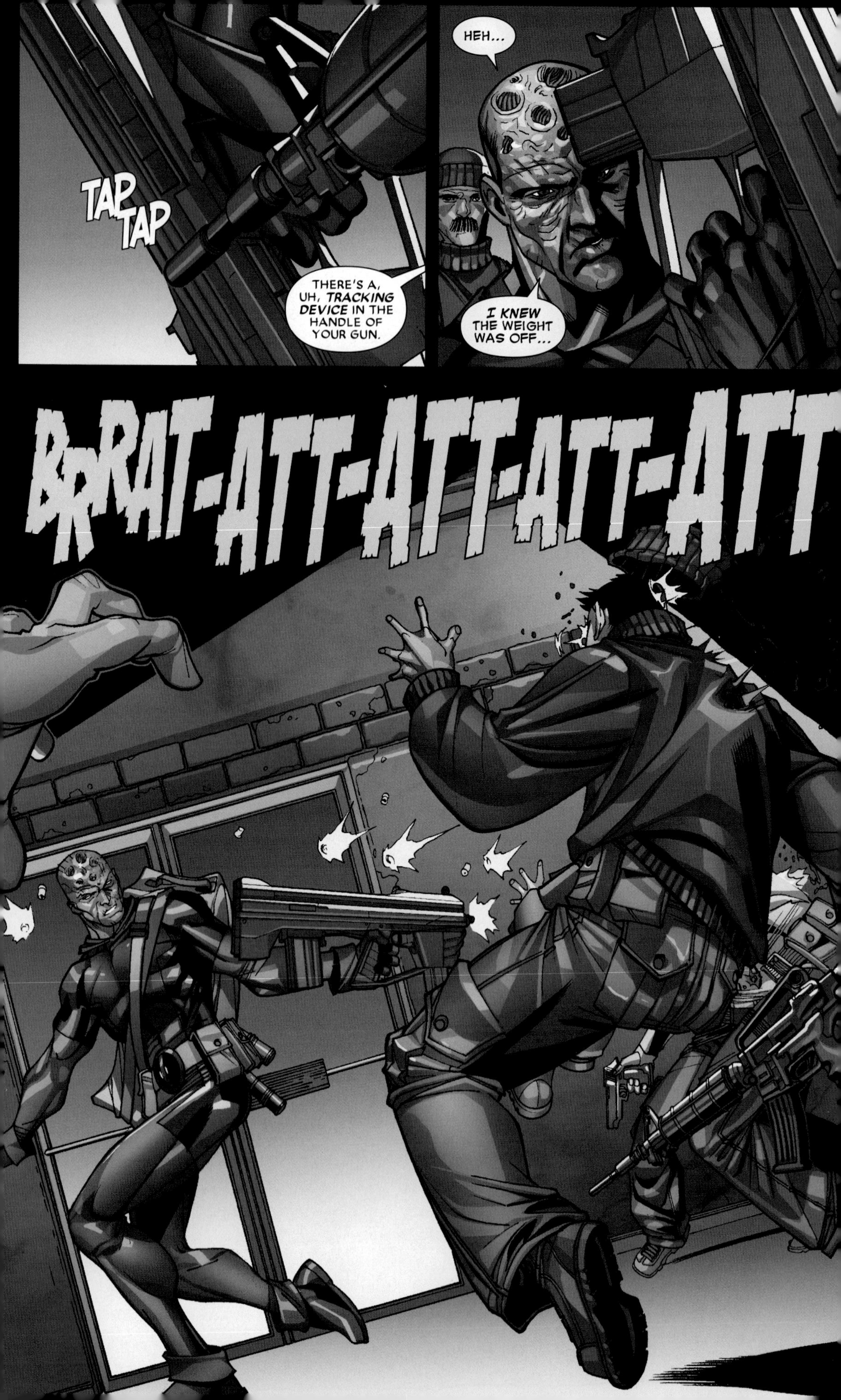
TAP TAP
THERE'S A, UH, TRACKING DEVICE IN THE HANDLE OF YOUR GUN.
HEH...
I KNEW THE WEIGHT WAS OFF...
BRRAT-ATT-ATT-ATT-ATT

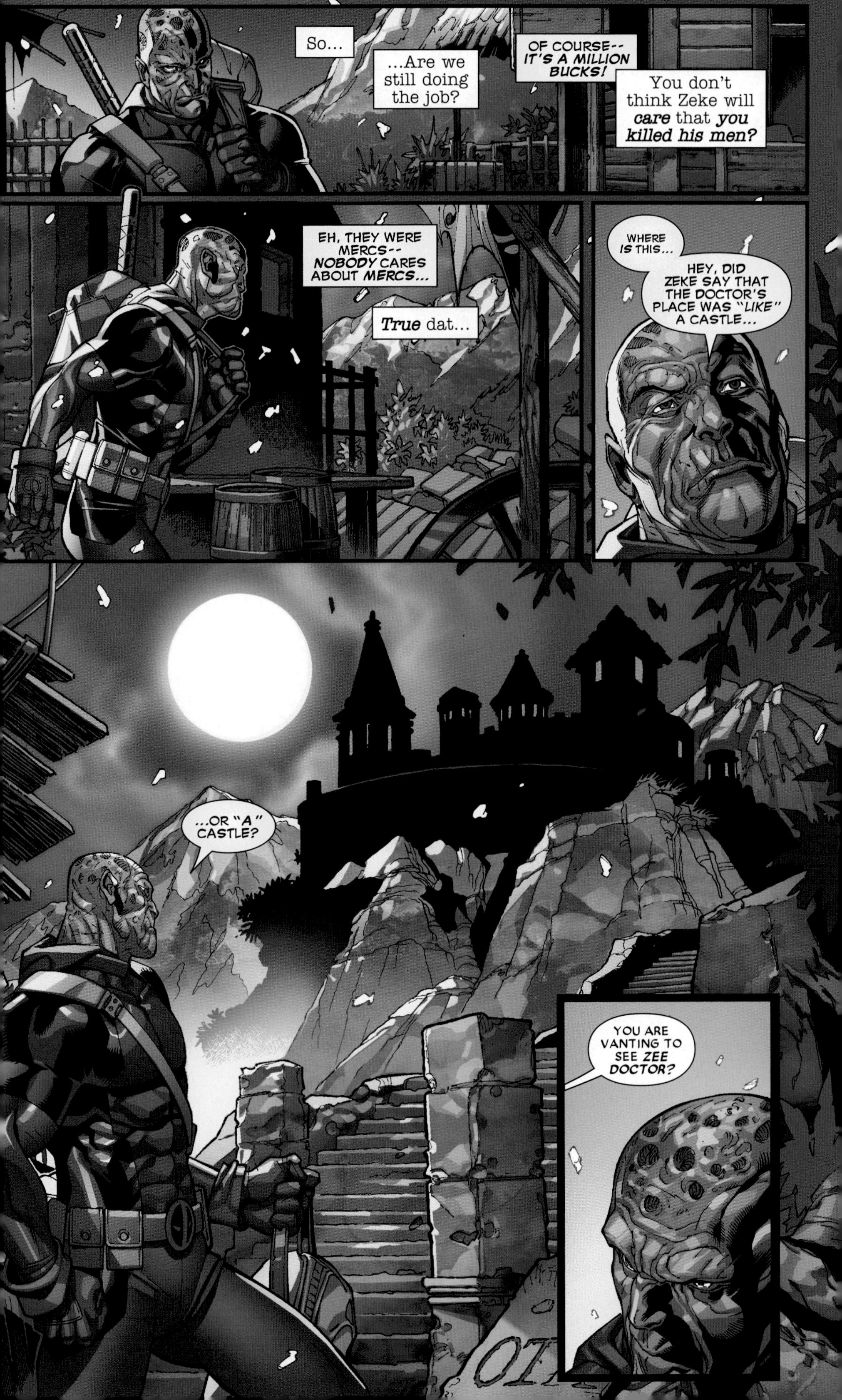
So...
...Are we still doing the job?
OF COURSE-- IT'S A MILLION BUCKS!
You don't think Zeke will care that you killed his men?
EH, THEY WERE MERCS-- NOBODY CARES ABOUT MERCS...
True dat...
WHERE IS THIS...
HEY, DID ZEKE SAY THAT THE DOCTOR'S PLACE WAS "LIKE" A CASTLE...
...OR "A" CASTLE?
YOU ARE VANTING TO SEE ZEE DOCTOR?

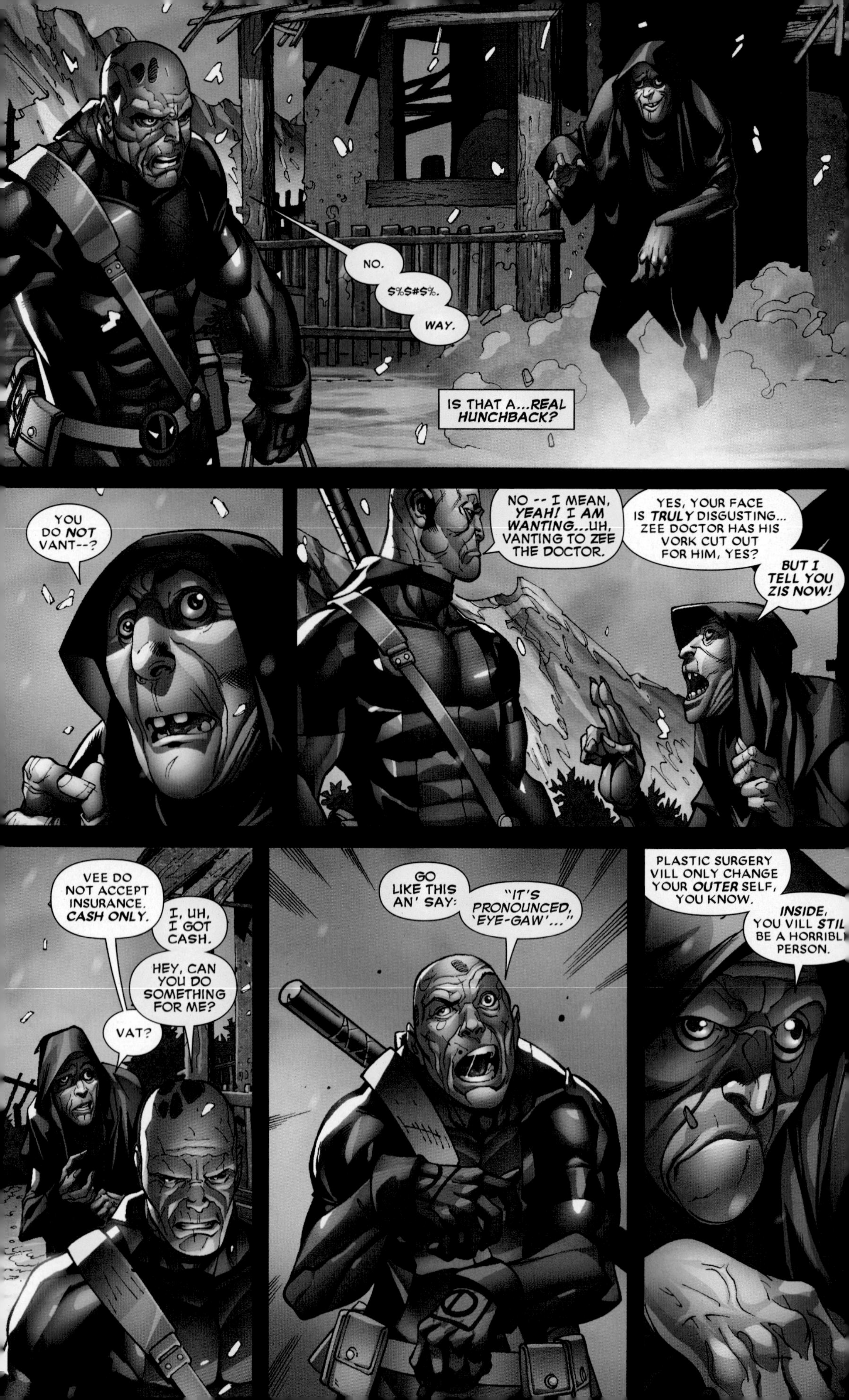
NO.
$%$#$%.
WAY.
IS THAT A...REAL HUNCHBACK?
YOU DO NOT VANT--?
NO -- I MEAN, YEAH! I AM WANTING...UH, VANTING TO ZEE THE DOCTOR.
YES, YOUR FACE IS TRULY DISGUSTING... ZEE DOCTOR HAS HIS VORK CUT OUT FOR HIM, YES?
BUT I TELL YOU ZIS NOW!
VEE DO NOT ACCEPT INSURANCE. CASH ONLY.
I, UH, I GOT CASH.
HEY, CAN YOU DO SOMETHING FOR ME?
VAT?
GO LIKE THIS AN' SAY:
"IT'S PRONOUNCED, 'EYE-GAW'..."
PLASTIC SURGERY VILL ONLY CHANGE YOUR OUTER SELF, YOU KNOW.
INSIDE, YOU VILL STIL BE A HORRIBL PERSON.

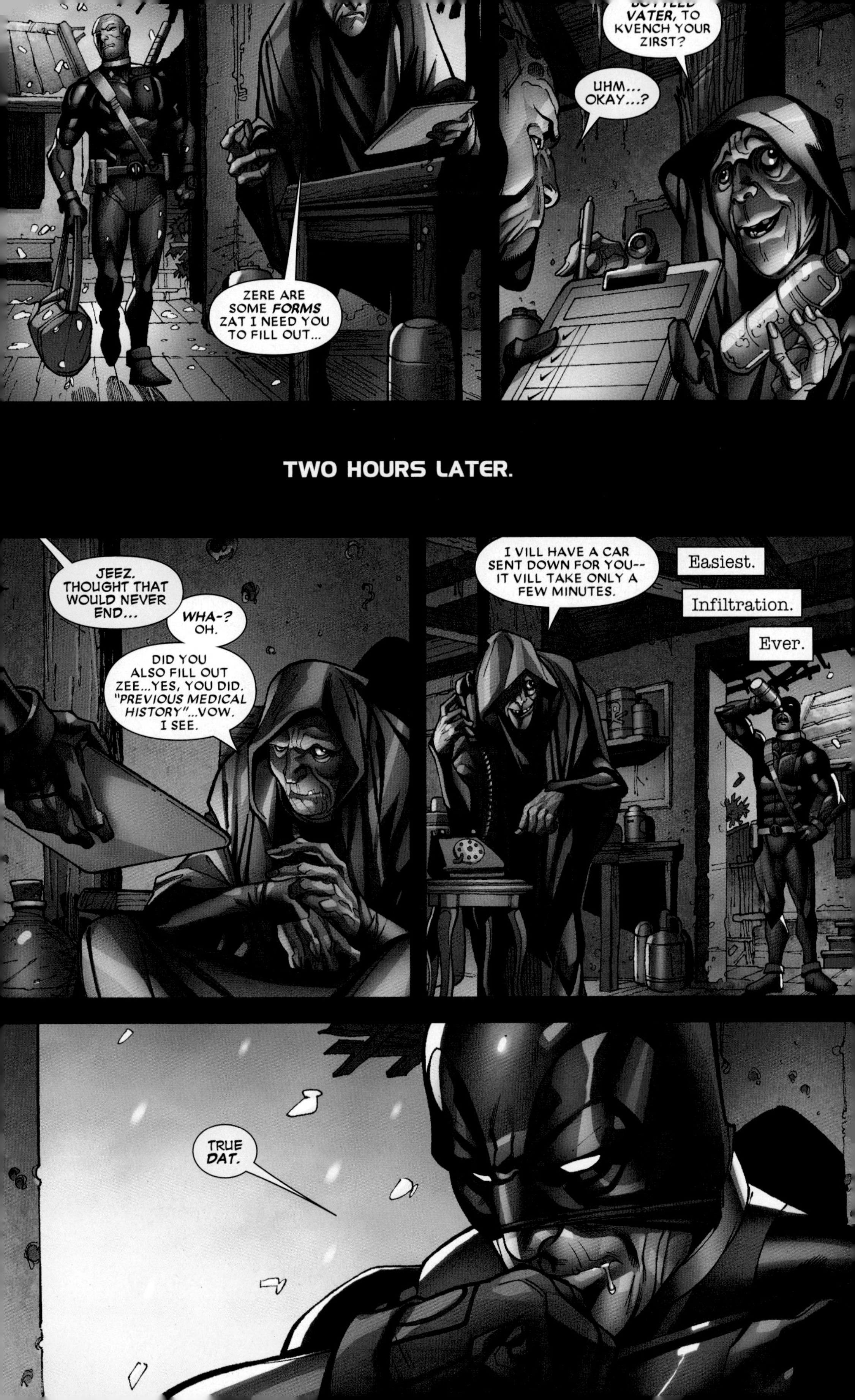
ZERE ARE SOME *FORMS* ZAT I NEED YOU TO FILL OUT...
*VATER,* TO KVENCH YOUR ZIRST?
UHM... OKAY...?
TWO HOURS LATER.
JEEZ. THOUGHT THAT WOULD NEVER END...
*WHA-?* OH.
DID YOU ALSO FILL OUT ZEE...YES, YOU DID. *"PREVIOUS MEDICAL HISTORY"*...VOW. I SEE.
I VILL HAVE A CAR SENT DOWN FOR YOU-- IT VILL TAKE ONLY A FEW MINUTES.
Easiest.
Infiltration.
Ever.
TRUE *DAT.*

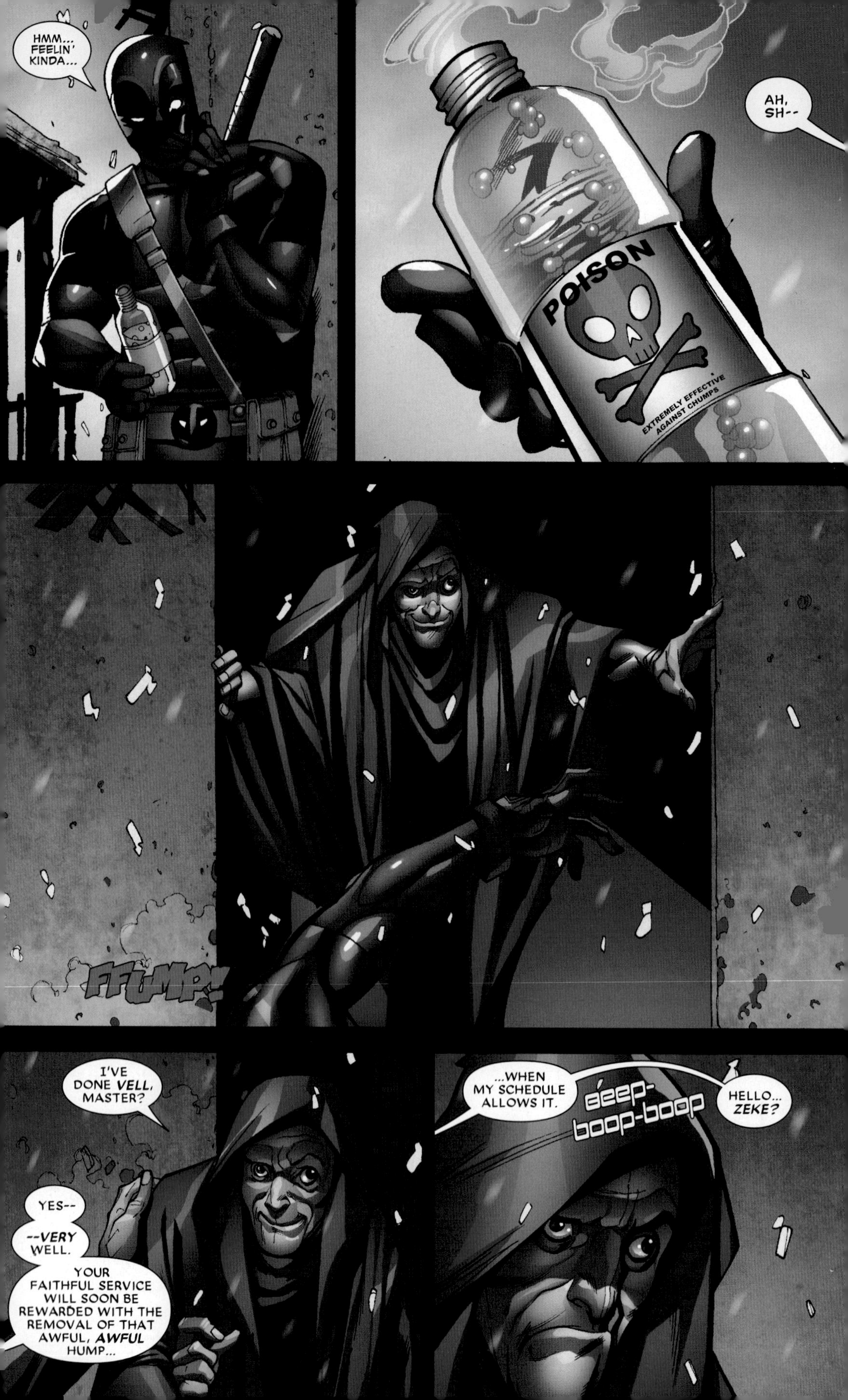
HMM... FEELIN' KINDA...
AH, SH--
POISON
EXTREMELY EFFECTIVE AGAINST CHUMPS
FFUMP!
I'VE DONE *VELL*, MASTER?
YES--
--*VERY* WELL.
YOUR FAITHFUL SERVICE WILL SOON BE REWARDED WITH THE REMOVAL OF THAT AWFUL, *AWFUL* HUMP...
...WHEN MY SCHEDULE ALLOWS IT.
BEEP-BOOP-BOOP
HELLO... *ZEKE?*

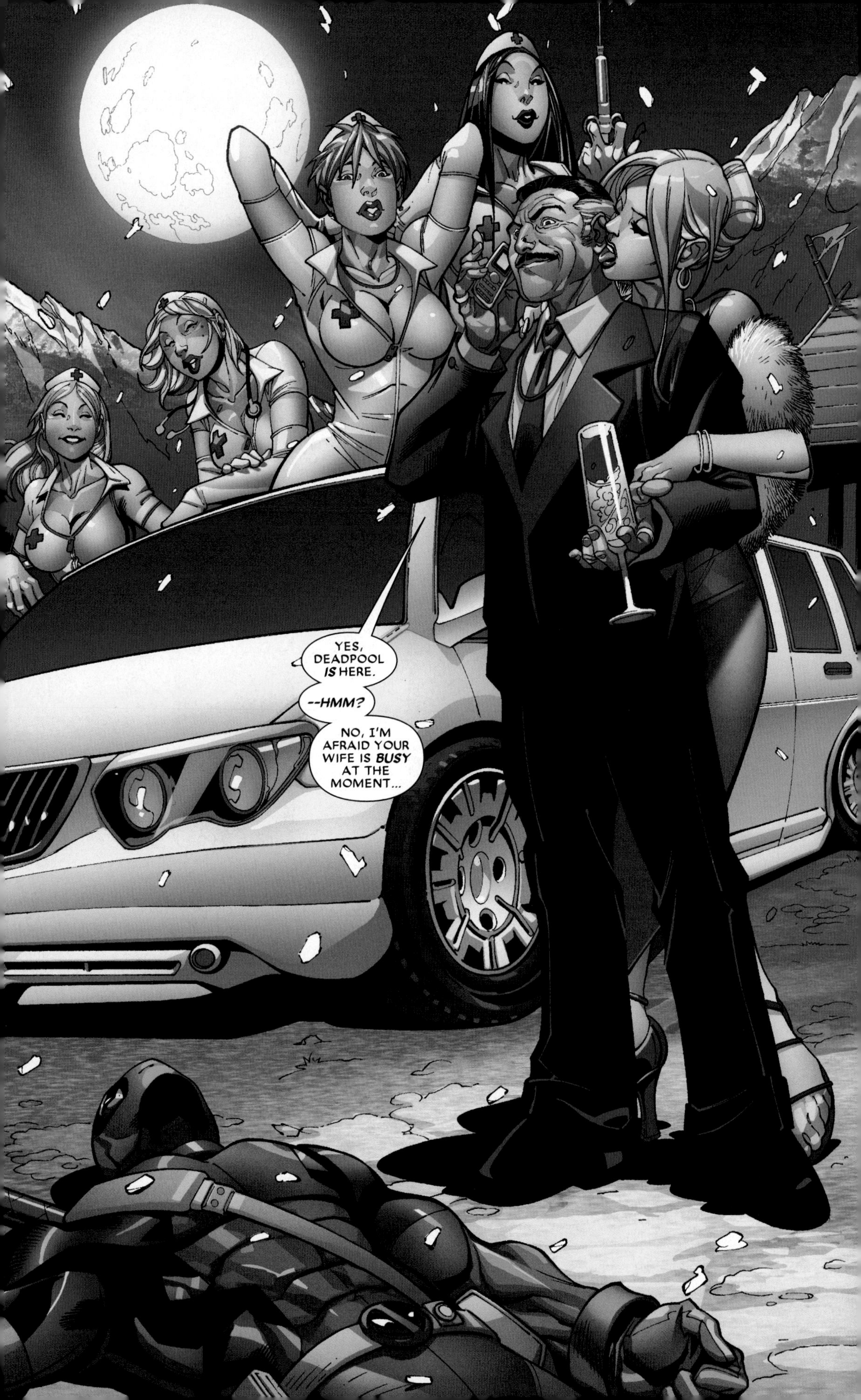
YES, DEADPOOL *IS* HERE.
--*HMM?*
NO, I'M AFRAID YOUR WIFE IS *BUSY* AT THE MOMENT...

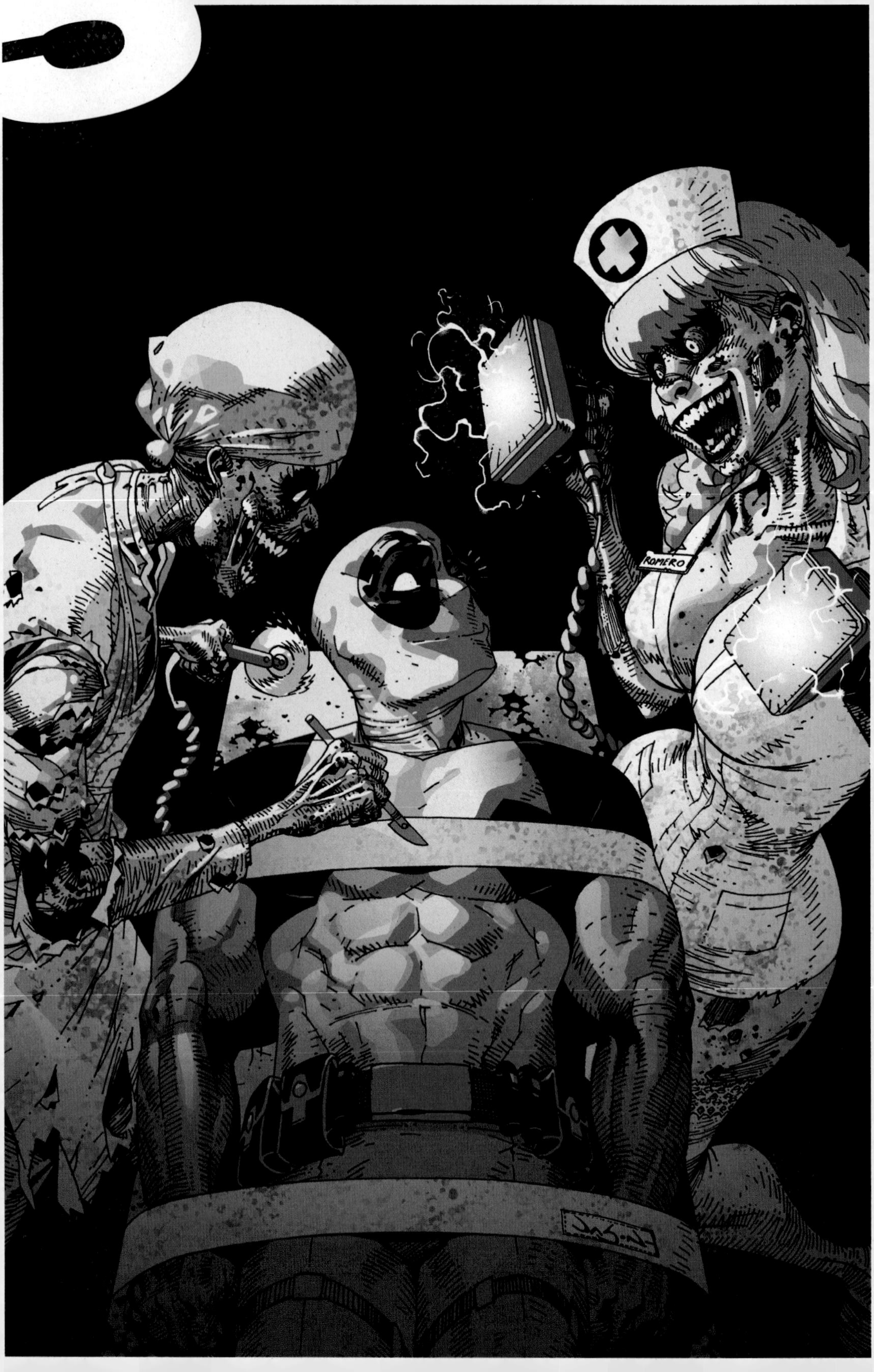
ROMERO

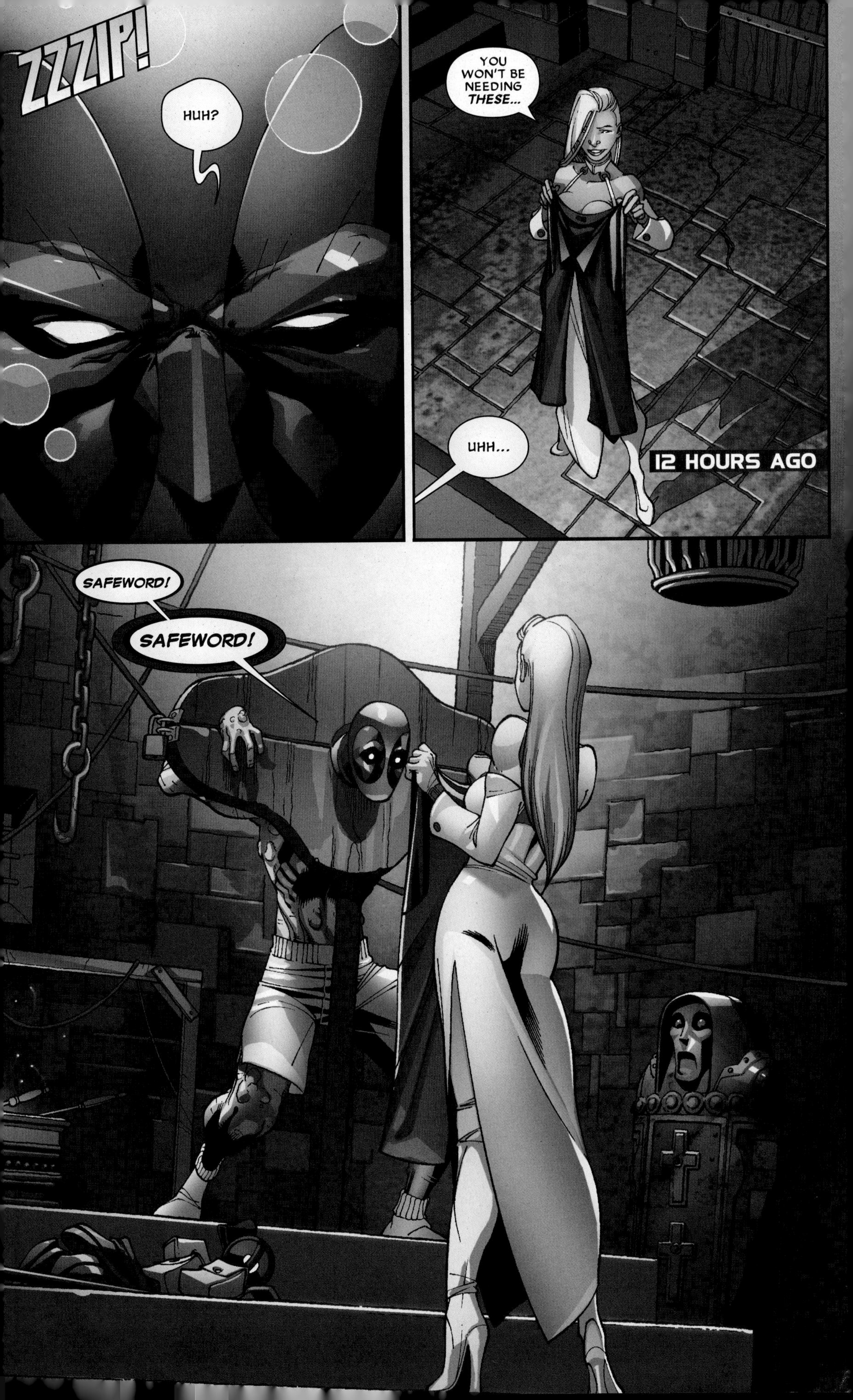
ZZZIP!
HUH?
YOU WON'T BE NEEDING *THESE*...
UHH...
12 HOURS AGO
SAFEWORD!
SAFEWORD!

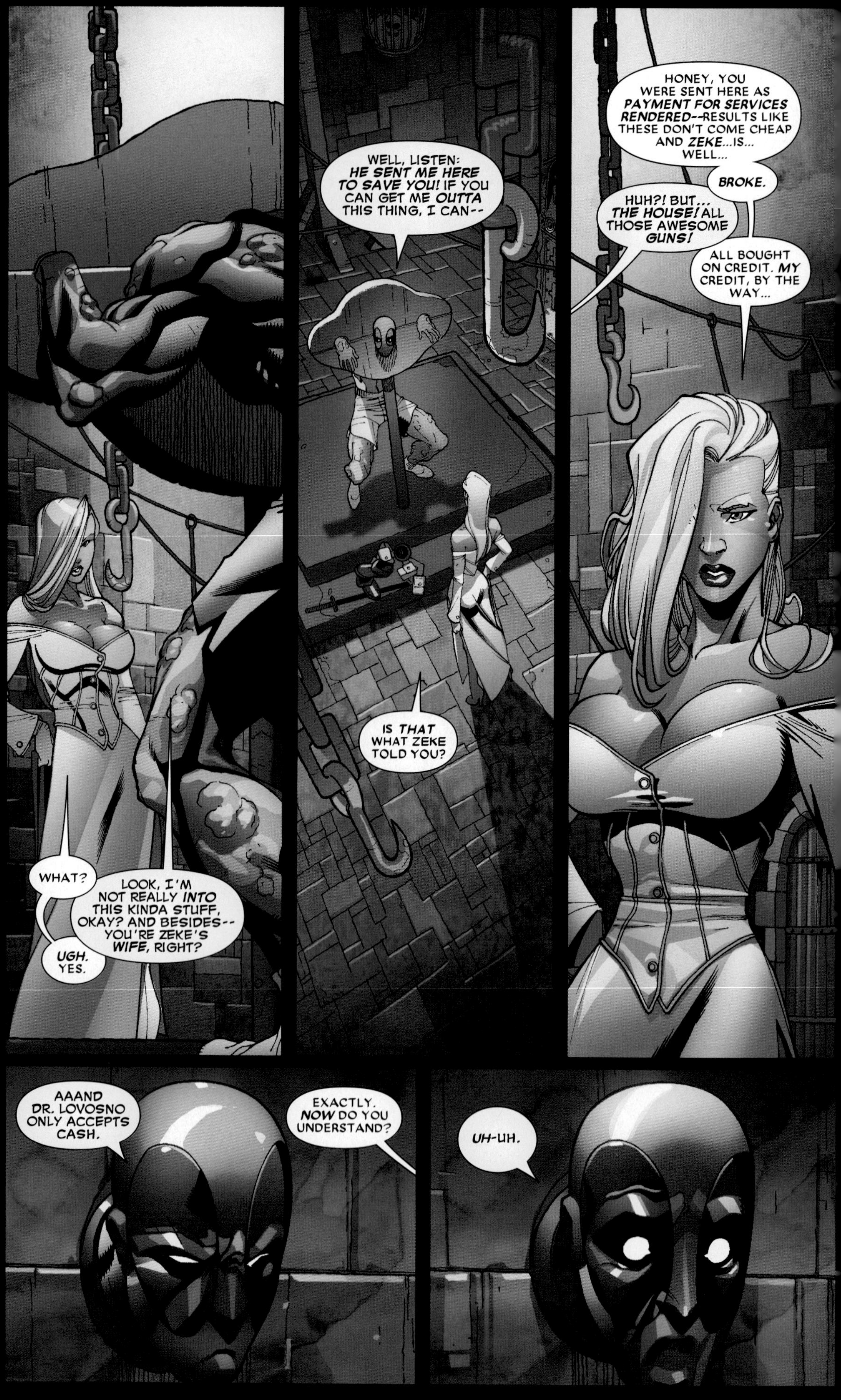

WHAT?
LOOK, I'M NOT REALLY INTO THIS KINDA STUFF, OKAY? AND BESIDES-- YOU'RE ZEKE'S WIFE, RIGHT?
UGH. YES.
WELL, LISTEN: HE SENT ME HERE TO SAVE YOU! IF YOU CAN GET ME OUTTA THIS THING, I CAN--
IS THAT WHAT ZEKE TOLD YOU?
HONEY, YOU WERE SENT HERE AS PAYMENT FOR SERVICES RENDERED--RESULTS LIKE THESE DON'T COME CHEAP AND ZEKE...IS... WELL...
BROKE.
HUH?! BUT... THE HOUSE! ALL THOSE AWESOME GUNS!
ALL BOUGHT ON CREDIT. MY CREDIT, BY THE WAY...
AAAND DR. LOVOSNO ONLY ACCEPTS CASH.
EXACTLY. NOW DO YOU UNDERSTAND?
UH-UH.

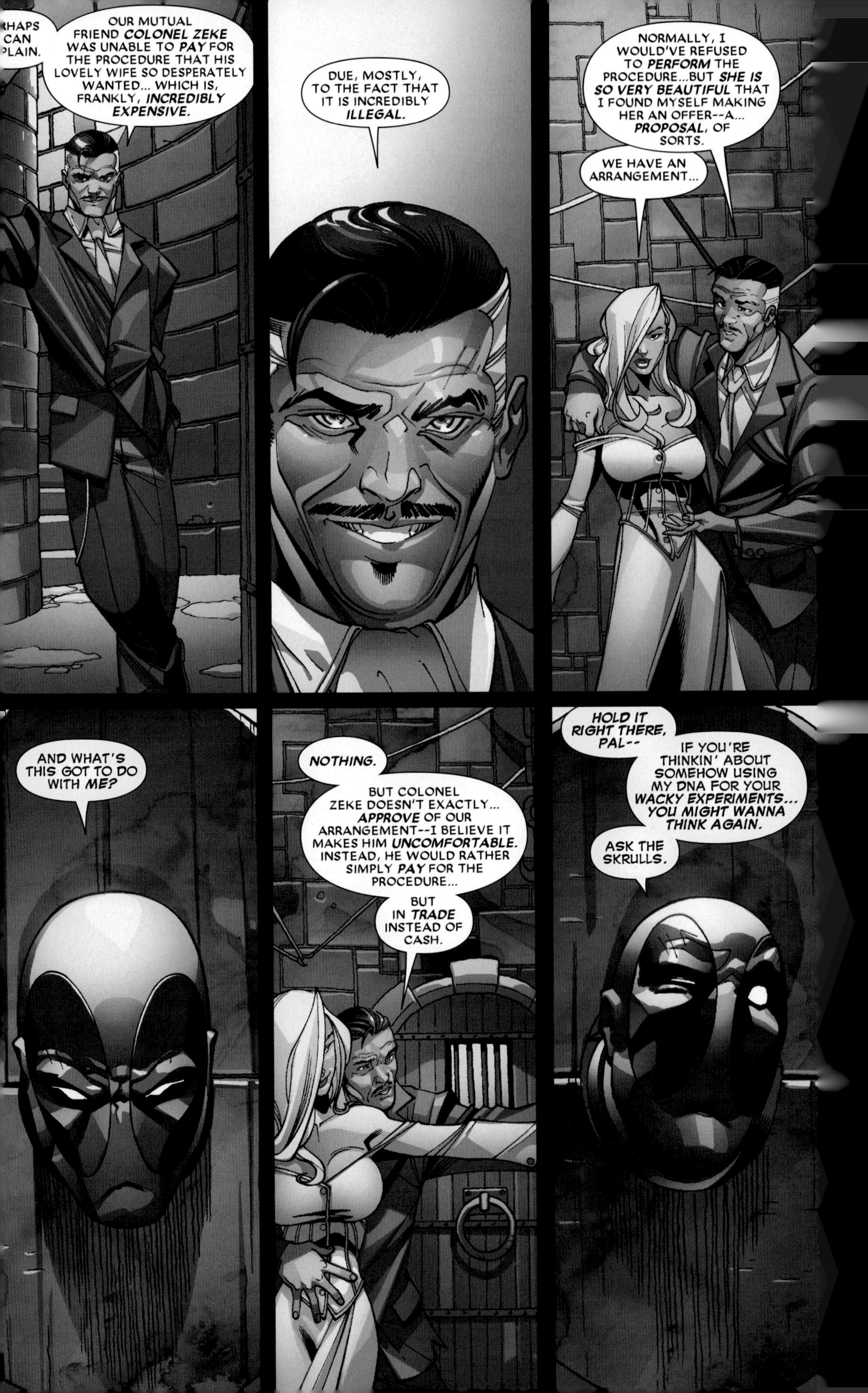

HAPS CAN PLAIN.
OUR MUTUAL FRIEND COLONEL ZEKE WAS UNABLE TO PAY FOR THE PROCEDURE THAT HIS LOVELY WIFE SO DESPERATELY WANTED... WHICH IS, FRANKLY, INCREDIBLY EXPENSIVE.
DUE, MOSTLY, TO THE FACT THAT IT IS INCREDIBLY ILLEGAL.
NORMALLY, I WOULD'VE REFUSED TO PERFORM THE PROCEDURE...BUT SHE IS SO VERY BEAUTIFUL THAT I FOUND MYSELF MAKING HER AN OFFER--A... PROPOSAL, OF SORTS.
WE HAVE AN ARRANGEMENT...
AND WHAT'S THIS GOT TO DO WITH ME?
NOTHING.
BUT COLONEL ZEKE DOESN'T EXACTLY... APPROVE OF OUR ARRANGEMENT--I BELIEVE IT MAKES HIM UNCOMFORTABLE. INSTEAD, HE WOULD RATHER SIMPLY PAY FOR THE PROCEDURE...
BUT IN TRADE INSTEAD OF CASH.
HOLD IT RIGHT THERE, PAL--
IF YOU'RE THINKIN' ABOUT SOMEHOW USING MY DNA FOR YOUR WACKY EXPERIMENTS... YOU MIGHT WANNA THINK AGAIN.
ASK THE SKRULLS.

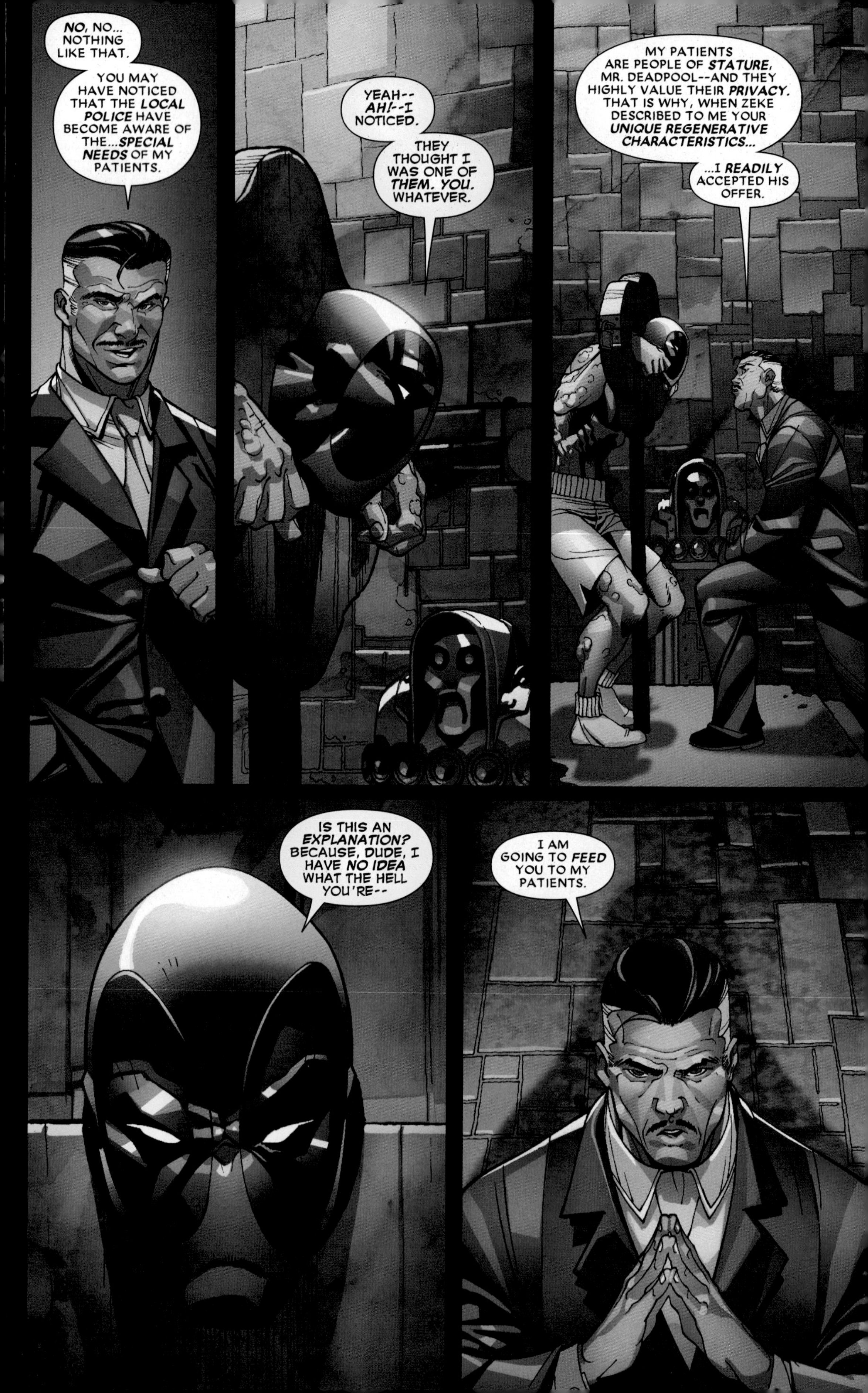
NO, NO... NOTHING LIKE THAT.
YOU MAY HAVE NOTICED THAT THE LOCAL POLICE HAVE BECOME AWARE OF THE...SPECIAL NEEDS OF MY PATIENTS.
YEAH--AH!--I NOTICED.
THEY THOUGHT I WAS ONE OF THEM. YOU. WHATEVER.
MY PATIENTS ARE PEOPLE OF STATURE, MR. DEADPOOL--AND THEY HIGHLY VALUE THEIR PRIVACY. THAT IS WHY, WHEN ZEKE DESCRIBED TO ME YOUR UNIQUE REGENERATIVE CHARACTERISTICS...
...I READILY ACCEPTED HIS OFFER.
IS THIS AN EXPLANATION? BECAUSE, DUDE, I HAVE NO IDEA WHAT THE HELL YOU'RE--
I AM GOING TO FEED YOU TO MY PATIENTS.

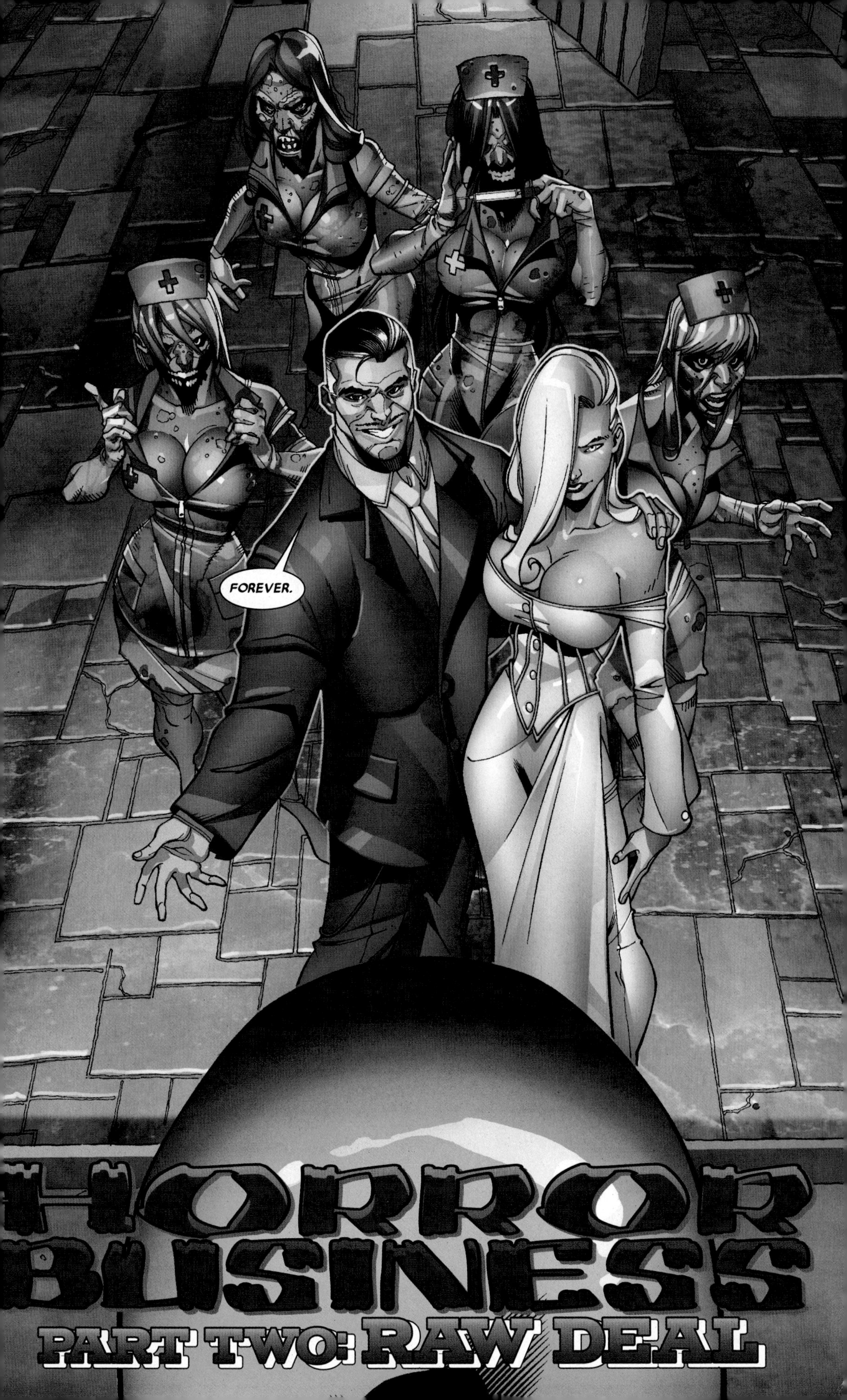
FOREVER.
HORROR BUSINESS
PART TWO: RAW DEAL

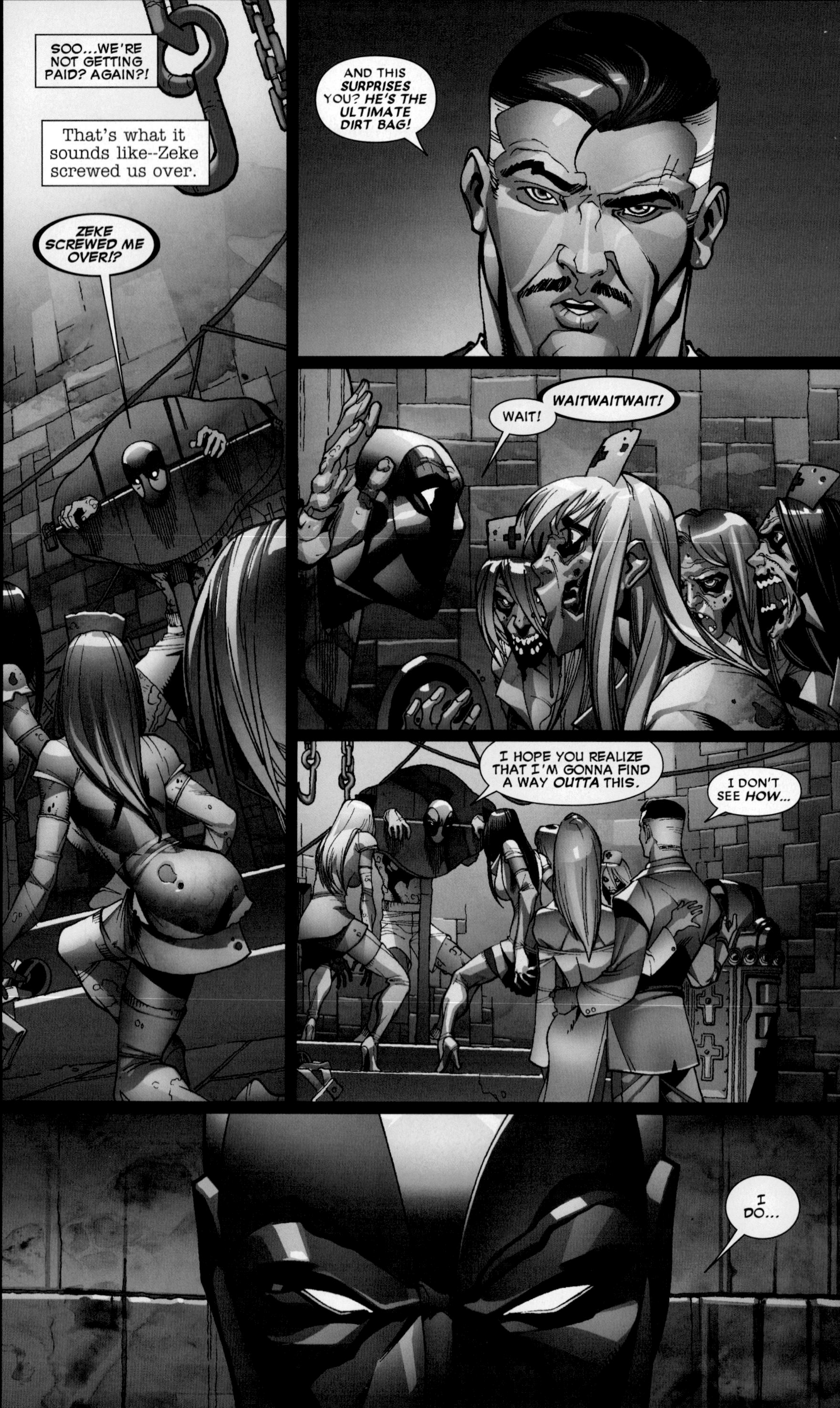
SOO...WE'RE NOT GETTING PAID? AGAIN?!
That's what it sounds like--Zeke screwed us over.
ZEKE SCREWED ME OVER!?
AND THIS SURPRISES YOU? HE'S THE ULTIMATE DIRT BAG!
WAIT!
WAITWAITWAIT!
I HOPE YOU REALIZE THAT I'M GONNA FIND A WAY OUTTA THIS.
I DON'T SEE HOW...
I DO...

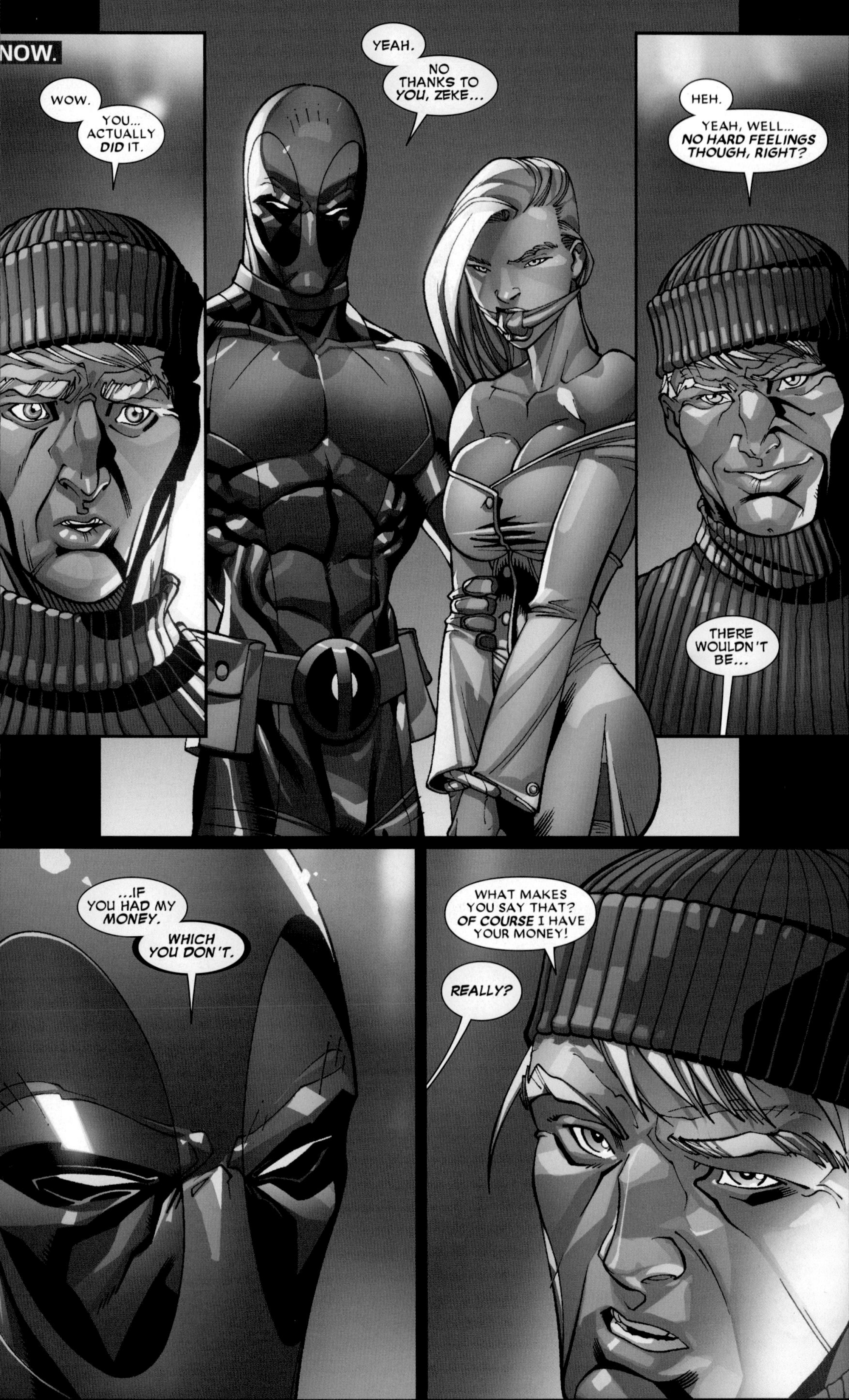
NOW.
WOW.
YOU... ACTUALLY DID IT.
YEAH.
NO THANKS TO YOU, ZEKE...
HEH.
YEAH, WELL... NO HARD FEELINGS THOUGH, RIGHT?
THERE WOULDN'T BE...
...IF YOU HAD MY MONEY.
WHICH YOU DON'T.
WHAT MAKES YOU SAY THAT? OF COURSE I HAVE YOUR MONEY!
REALLY?

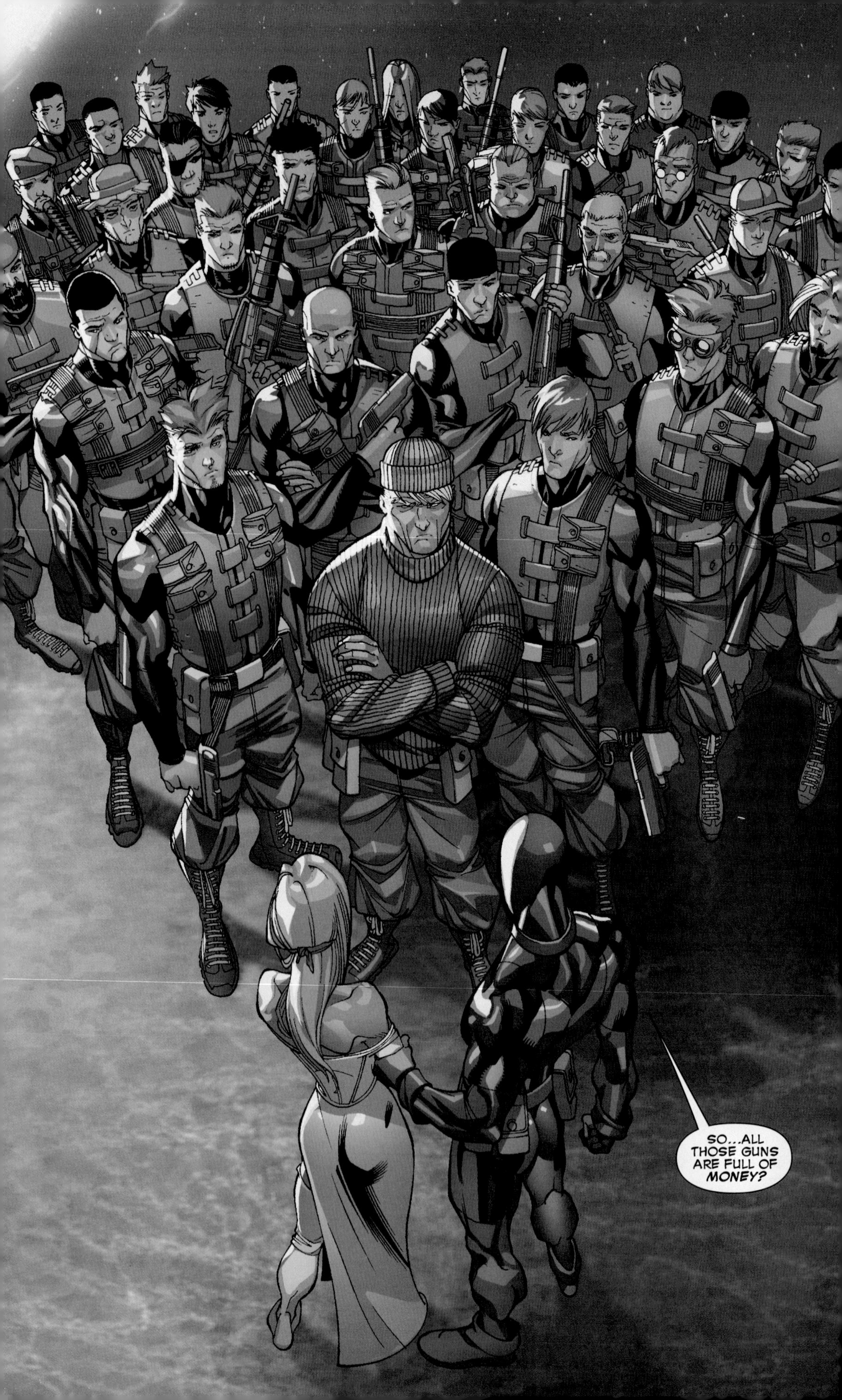
SO...ALL THOSE GUNS ARE FULL OF MONEY?

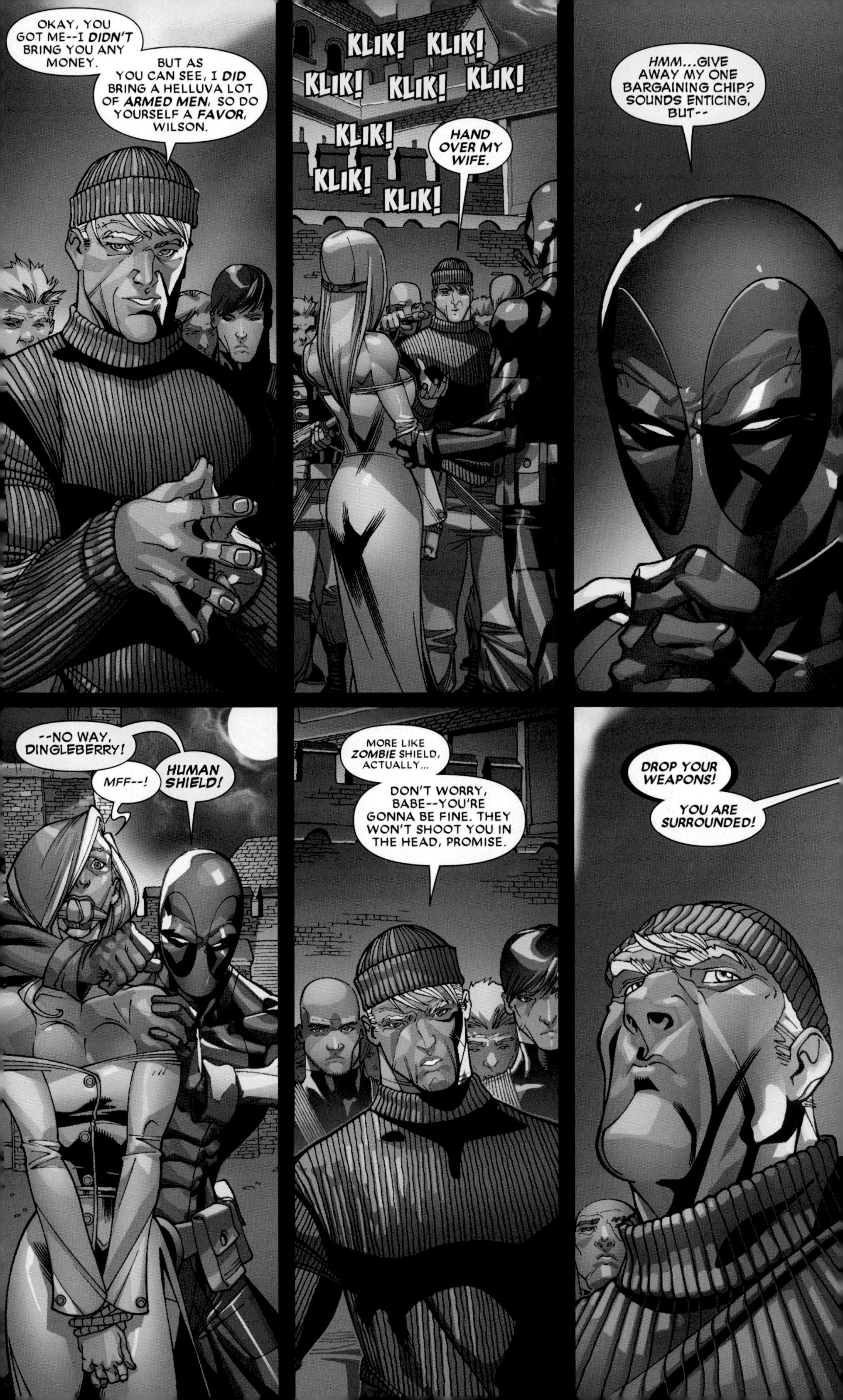
OKAY, YOU GOT ME--I DIDN'T BRING YOU ANY MONEY.
BUT AS YOU CAN SEE, I DID BRING A HELLUVA LOT OF ARMED MEN, SO DO YOURSELF A FAVOR, WILSON.
KLIK! KLIK! KLIK! KLIK! KLIK! KLIK! KLIK! KLIK!
HAND OVER MY WIFE.
HMM...GIVE AWAY MY ONE BARGAINING CHIP? SOUNDS ENTICING, BUT--
--NO WAY, DINGLEBERRY!
HUMAN SHIELD!
MFF--!
MORE LIKE ZOMBIE SHIELD, ACTUALLY...
DON'T WORRY, BABE--YOU'RE GONNA BE FINE. THEY WON'T SHOOT YOU IN THE HEAD, PROMISE.
DROP YOUR WEAPONS!
YOU ARE SURROUNDED!

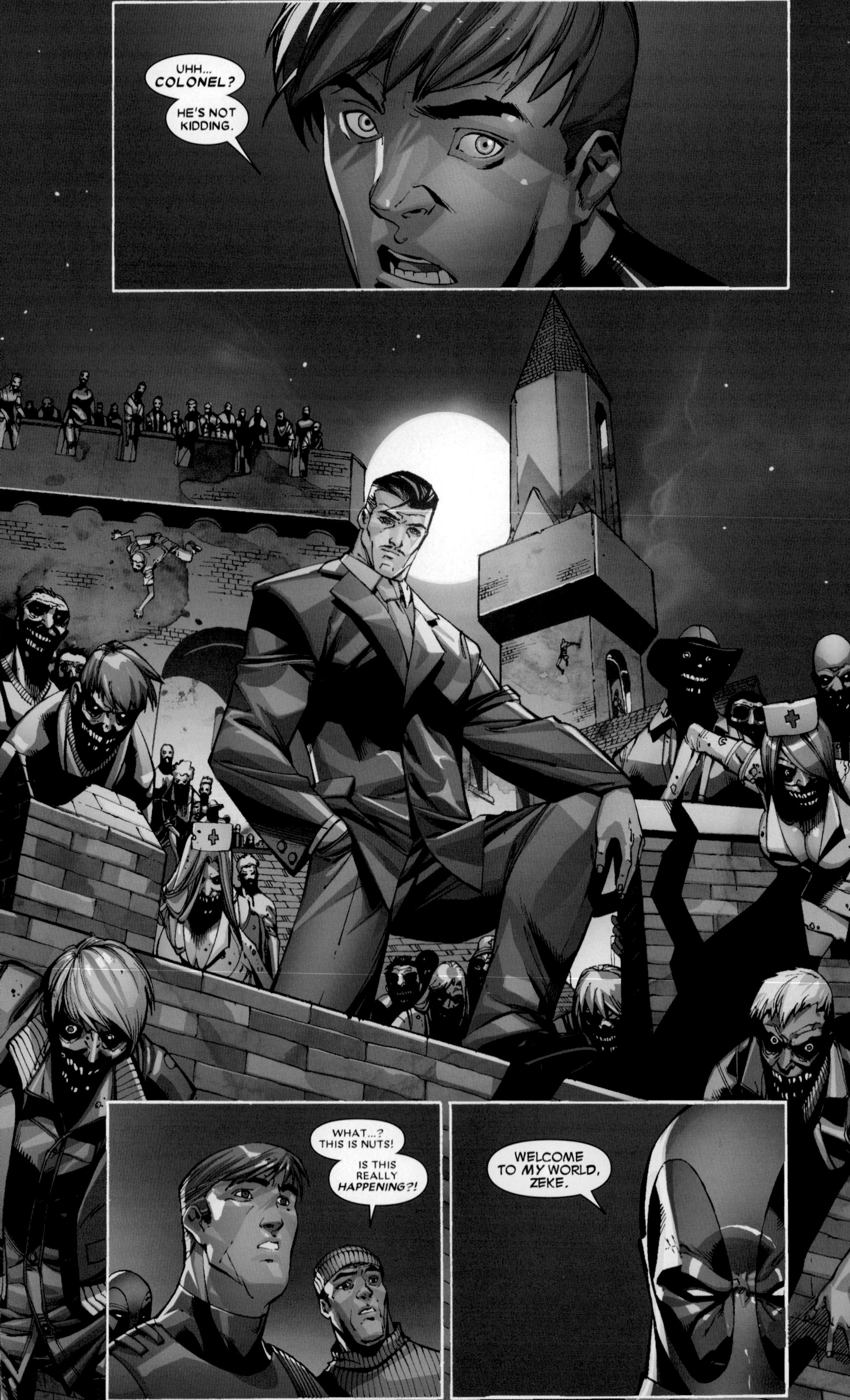
UHH... COLONEL?
HE'S NOT KIDDING.
WHAT...? THIS IS NUTS!
IS THIS REALLY HAPPENING?!
WELCOME TO MY WORLD, ZEKE.

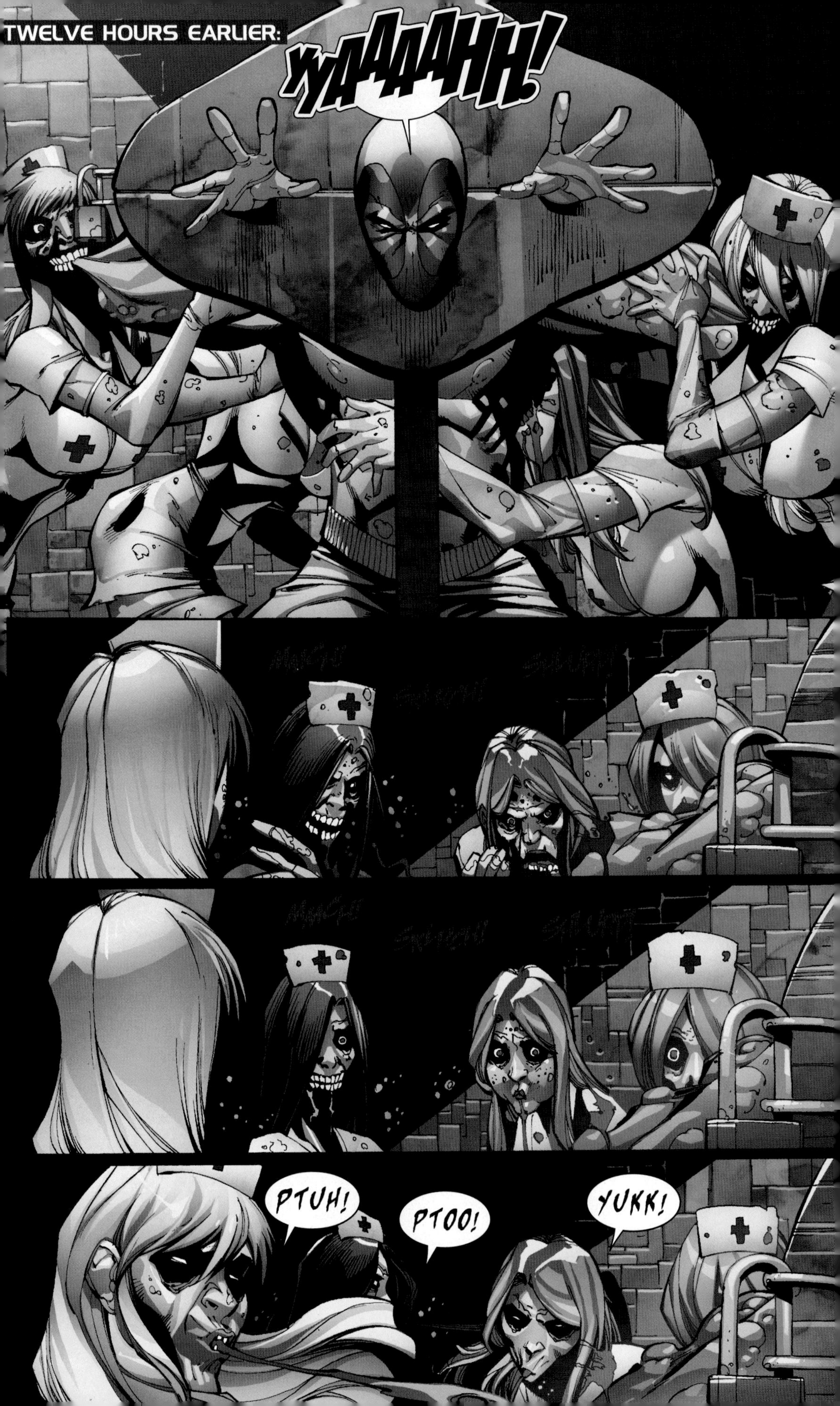
TWELVE HOURS EARLIER:
YYAAAAHH!
PTUH!
PTOO!
YUKK!

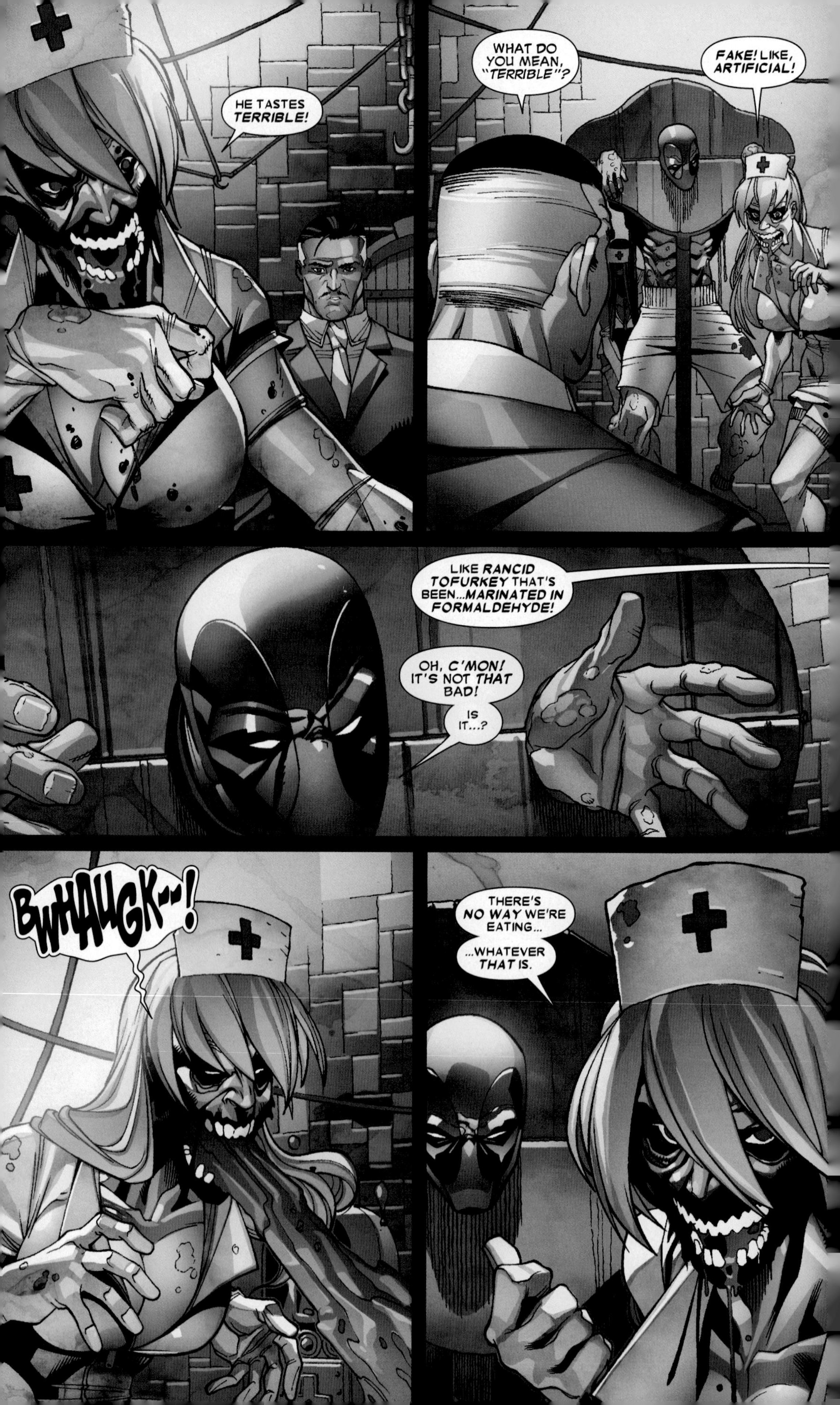
HE TASTES TERRIBLE!
WHAT DO YOU MEAN, "TERRIBLE"?
FAKE! LIKE, ARTIFICIAL!
LIKE RANCID TOFURKEY THAT'S BEEN...MARINATED IN FORMALDEHYDE!
OH, C'MON! IT'S NOT THAT BAD!
IS IT...?
BWHAUGK--!
THERE'S NO WAY WE'RE EATING...
...WHATEVER THAT IS.

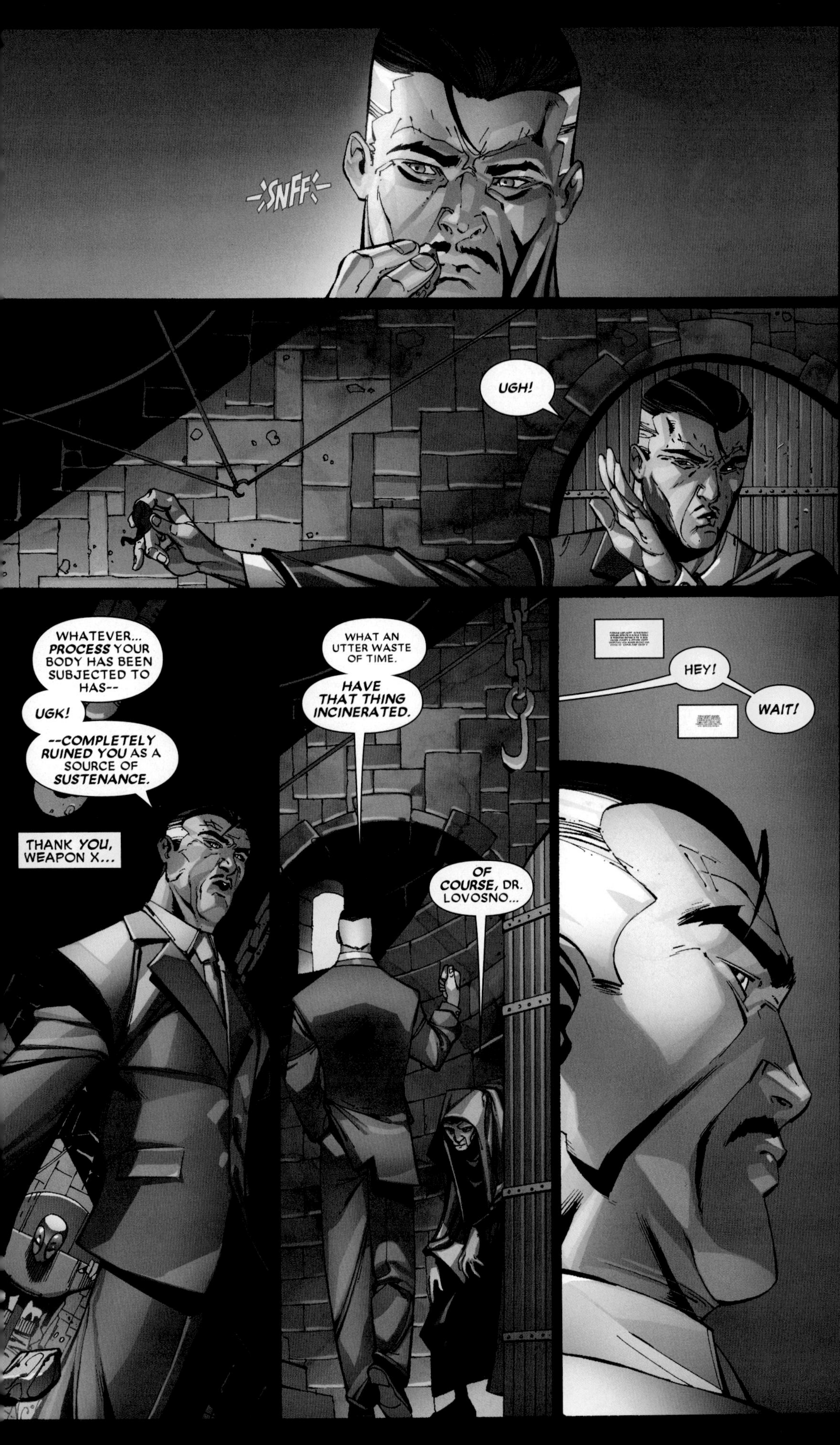
-SNFF-
UGH!
WHATEVER... PROCESS YOUR BODY HAS BEEN SUBJECTED TO HAS--
UGK!
--COMPLETELY RUINED YOU AS A SOURCE OF SUSTENANCE.
THANK YOU, WEAPON X...
WHAT AN UTTER WASTE OF TIME.
HAVE THAT THING INCINERATED.
OF COURSE, DR. LOVOSNO...
HEY!
WAIT!

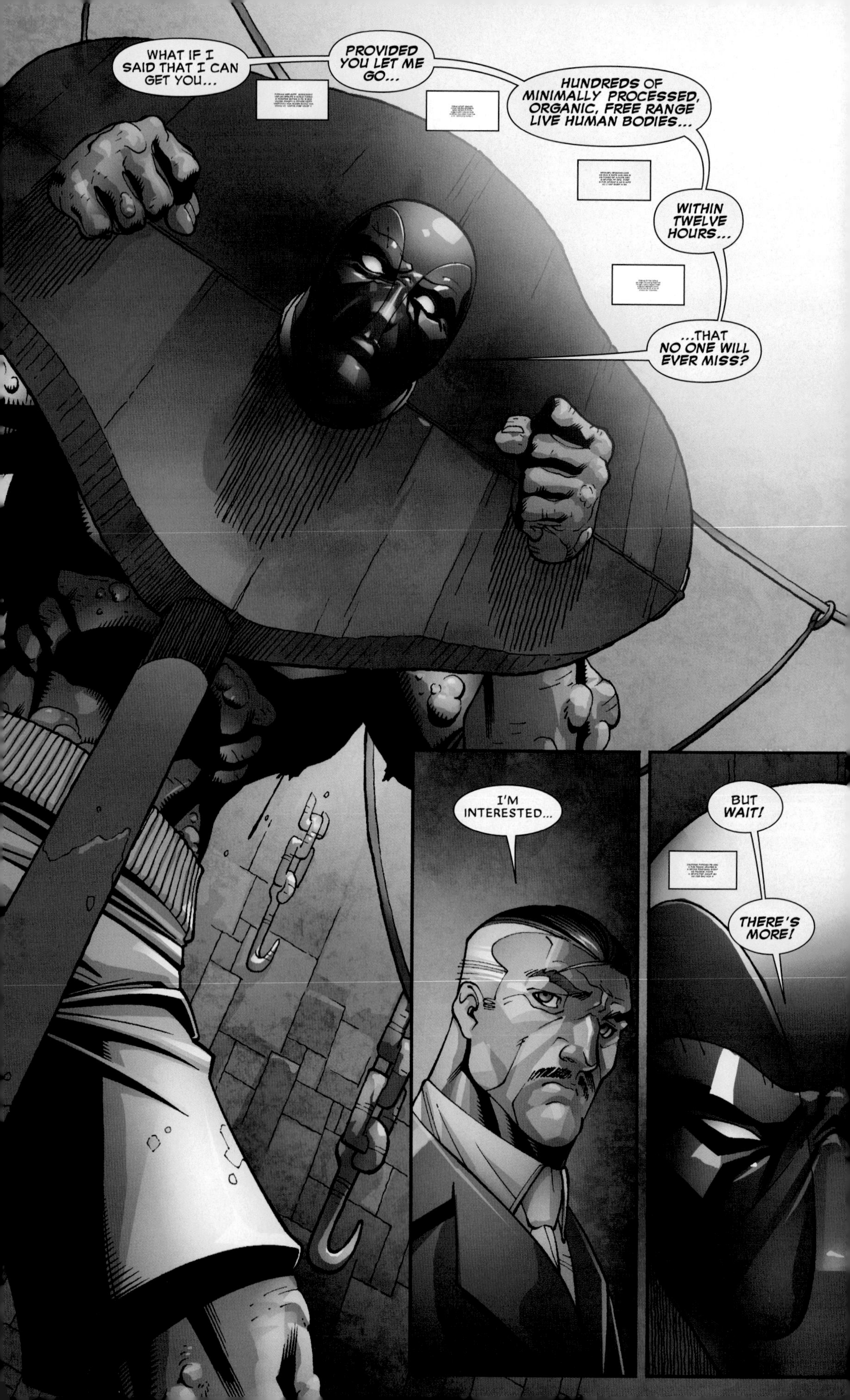
WHAT IF I SAID THAT I CAN GET YOU...
PROVIDED YOU LET ME GO...
HUNDREDS OF MINIMALLY PROCESSED, ORGANIC, FREE RANGE LIVE HUMAN BODIES...
WITHIN TWELVE HOURS...
...THAT NO ONE WILL EVER MISS?
I'M INTERESTED...
BUT WAIT!
THERE'S MORE!

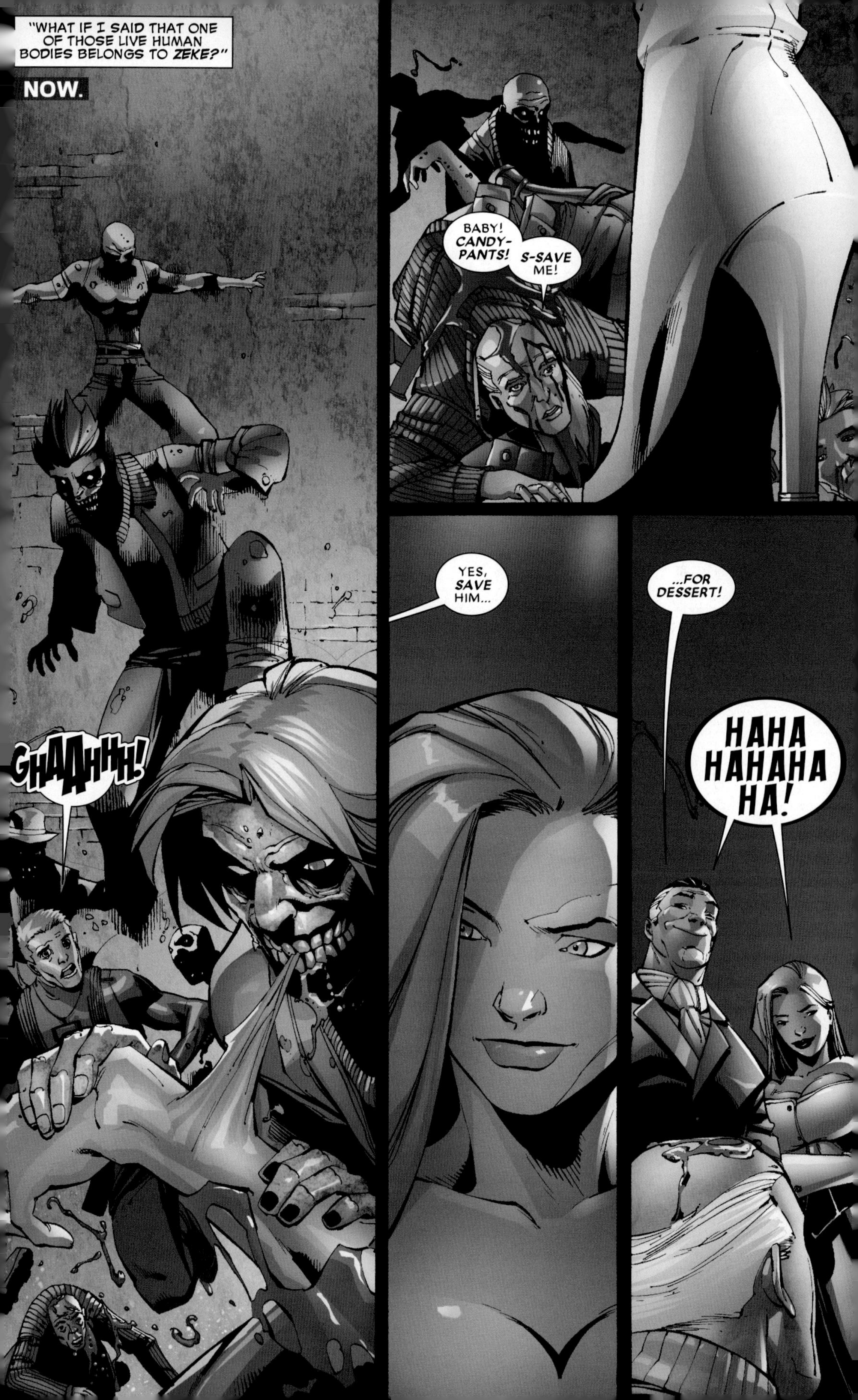
"WHAT IF I SAID THAT ONE OF THOSE LIVE HUMAN BODIES BELONGS TO *ZEKE?*"
NOW.
GHAAHHH!
BABY! CANDY-PANTS!
S-SAVE ME!
YES, *SAVE* HIM...
...FOR DESSERT!
HAHA HAHAHA HA!

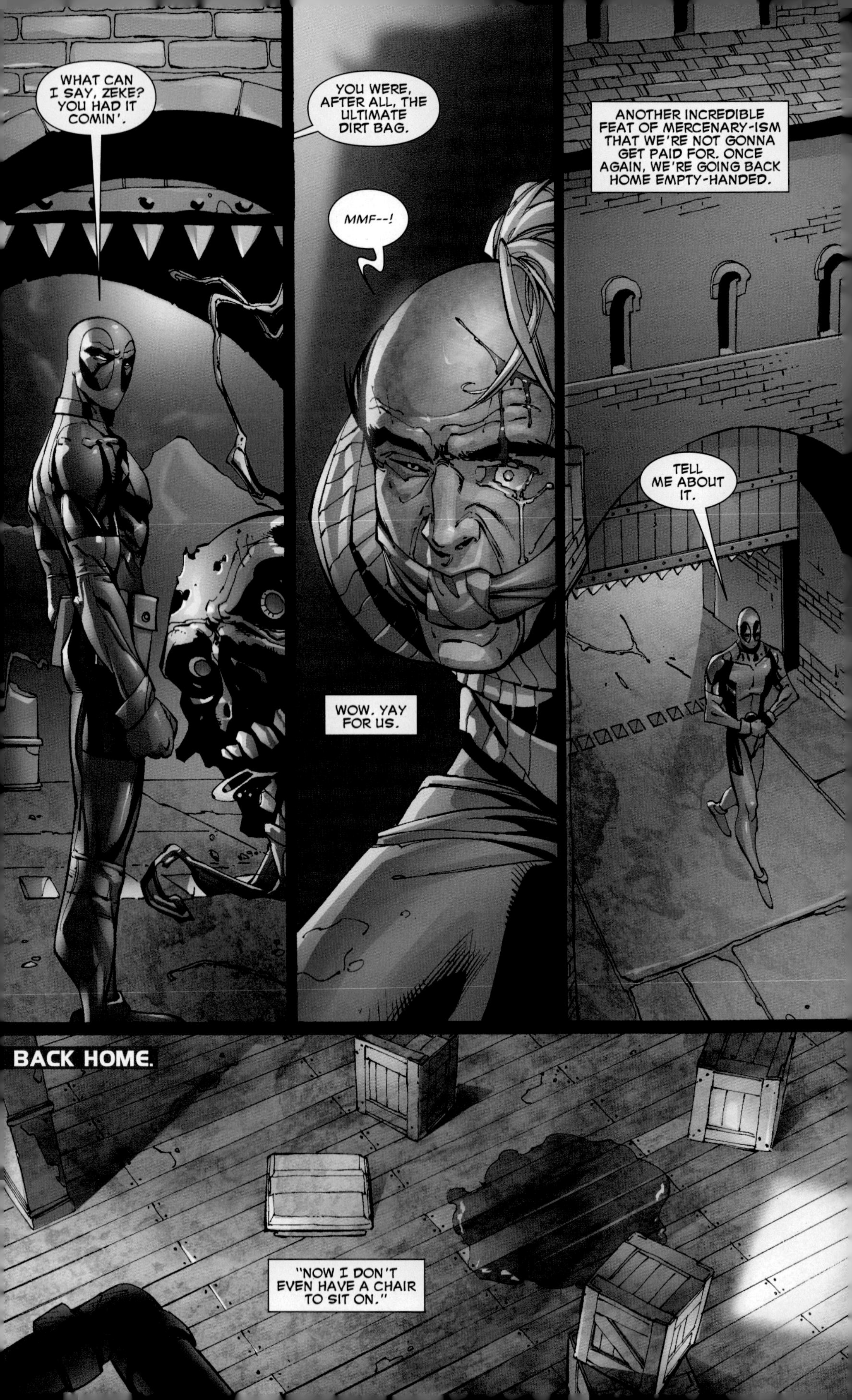
WHAT CAN I SAY, ZEKE? YOU HAD IT COMIN'.
YOU WERE, AFTER ALL, THE ULTIMATE DIRT BAG.
MMF--!
WOW. YAY FOR US.
ANOTHER INCREDIBLE FEAT OF MERCENARY-ISM THAT WE'RE NOT GONNA GET PAID FOR. ONCE AGAIN, WE'RE GOING BACK HOME EMPTY-HANDED.
TELL ME ABOUT IT.
BACK HOME.
"NOW I DON'T EVEN HAVE A CHAIR TO SIT ON."

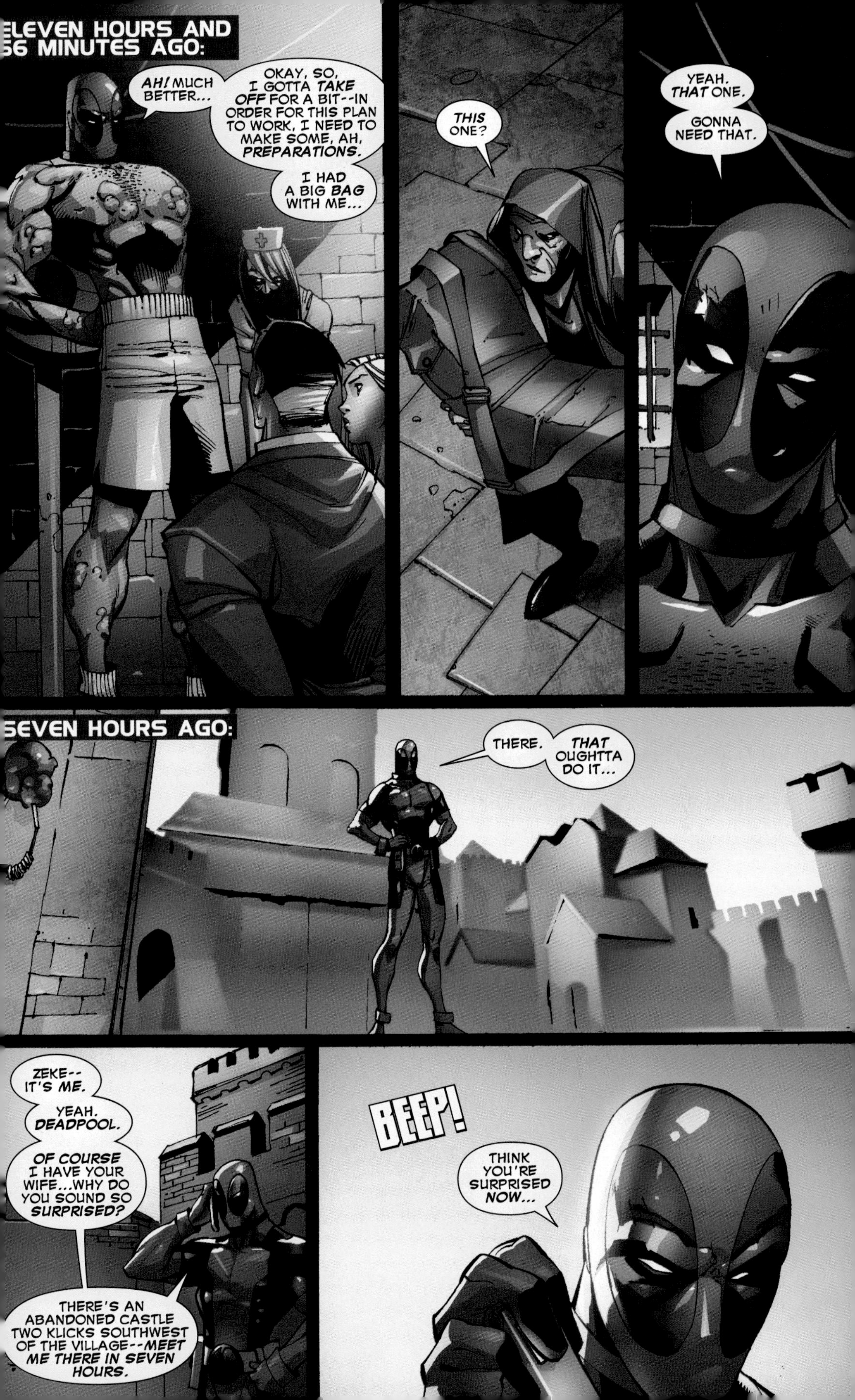
ELEVEN HOURS AND 56 MINUTES AGO:
AH! MUCH BETTER...
OKAY, SO, I GOTTA TAKE OFF FOR A BIT--IN ORDER FOR THIS PLAN TO WORK, I NEED TO MAKE SOME, AH, PREPARATIONS.
I HAD A BIG BAG WITH ME...
THIS ONE?
YEAH. THAT ONE.
GONNA NEED THAT.
SEVEN HOURS AGO:
THERE. THAT OUGHTTA DO IT...
ZEKE-- IT'S ME.
YEAH. DEADPOOL.
OF COURSE I HAVE YOUR WIFE...WHY DO YOU SOUND SO SURPRISED?
THERE'S AN ABANDONED CASTLE TWO KLICKS SOUTHWEST OF THE VILLAGE--MEET ME THERE IN SEVEN HOURS.
BEEP!
THINK YOU'RE SURPRISED NOW...

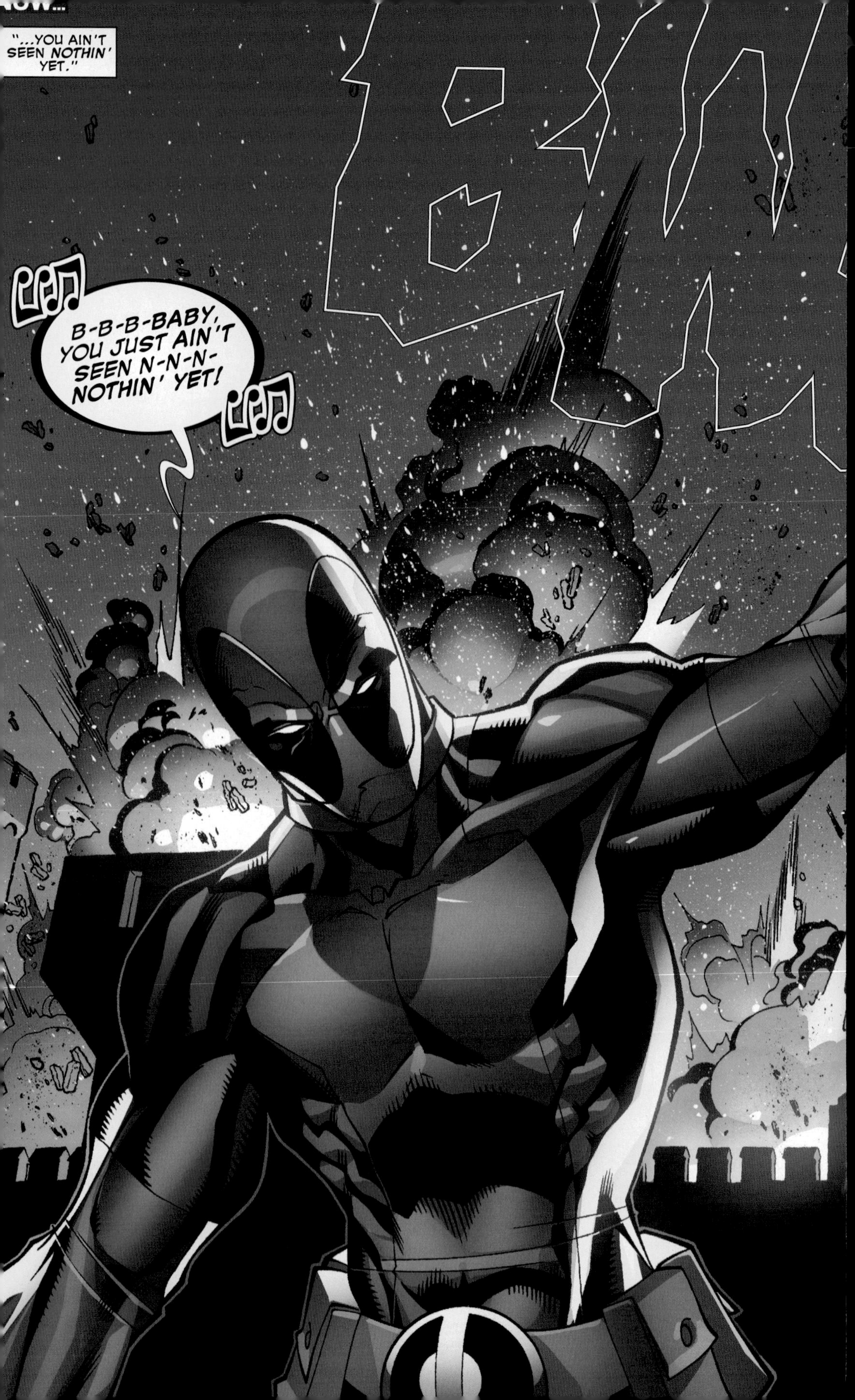
"...YOU AIN'T SEEN NOTHIN' YET."
B-B-B-BABY, YOU JUST AIN'T SEEN N-N-N-NOTHIN' YET!

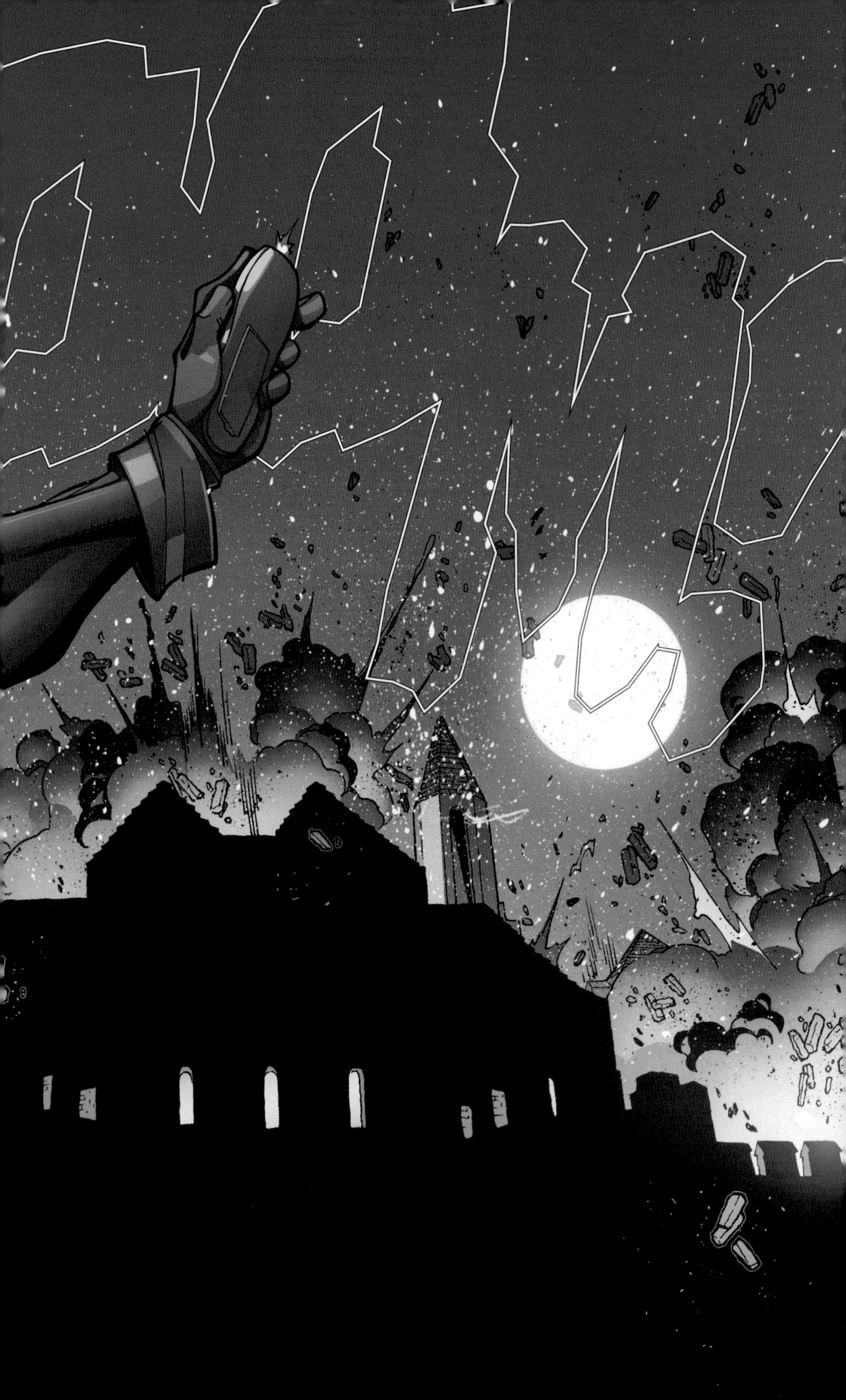

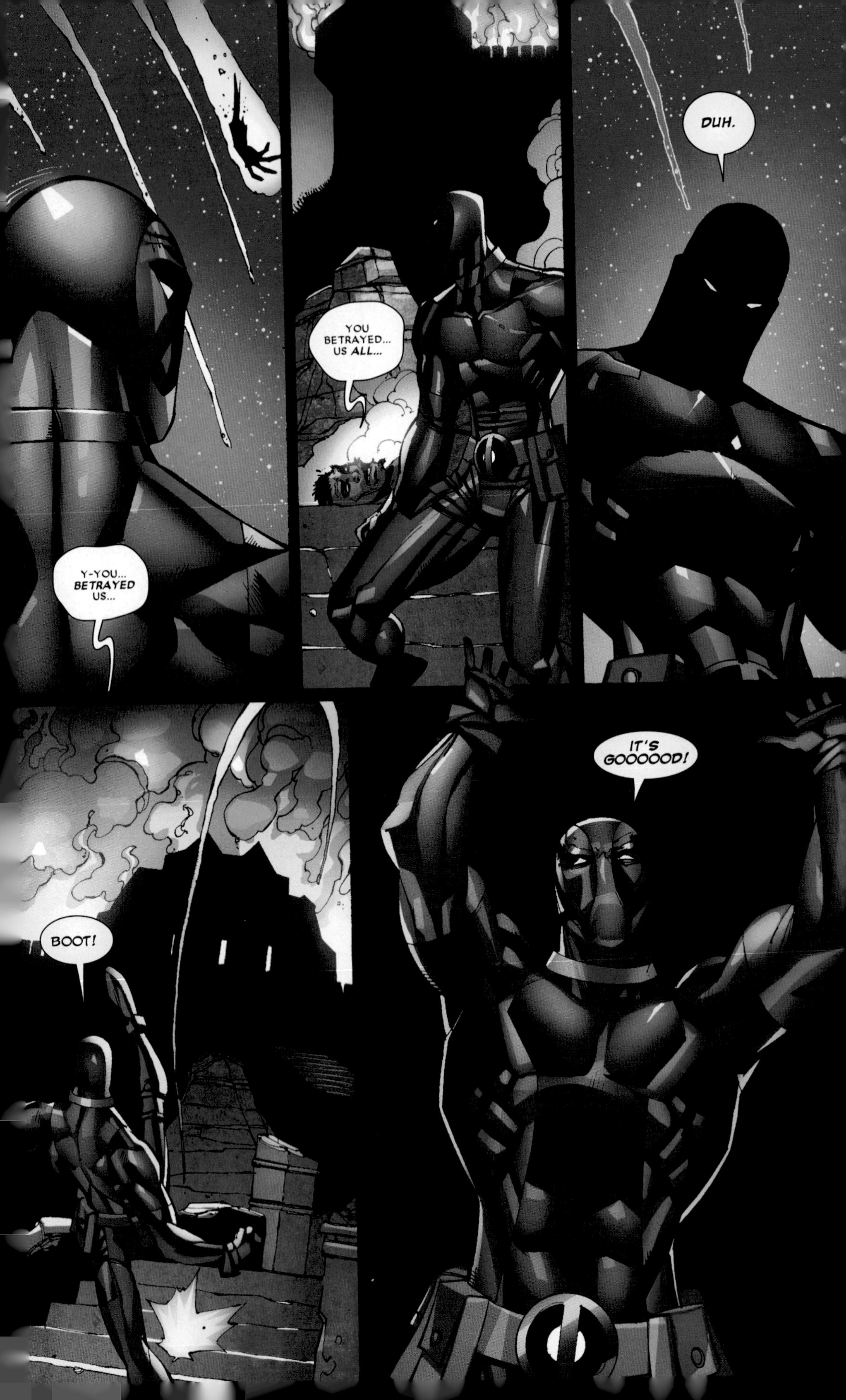

Y-YOU... BETRAYED US...
YOU BETRAYED... US ALL...
DUH.
BOOT!
IT'S GOOOOOD!

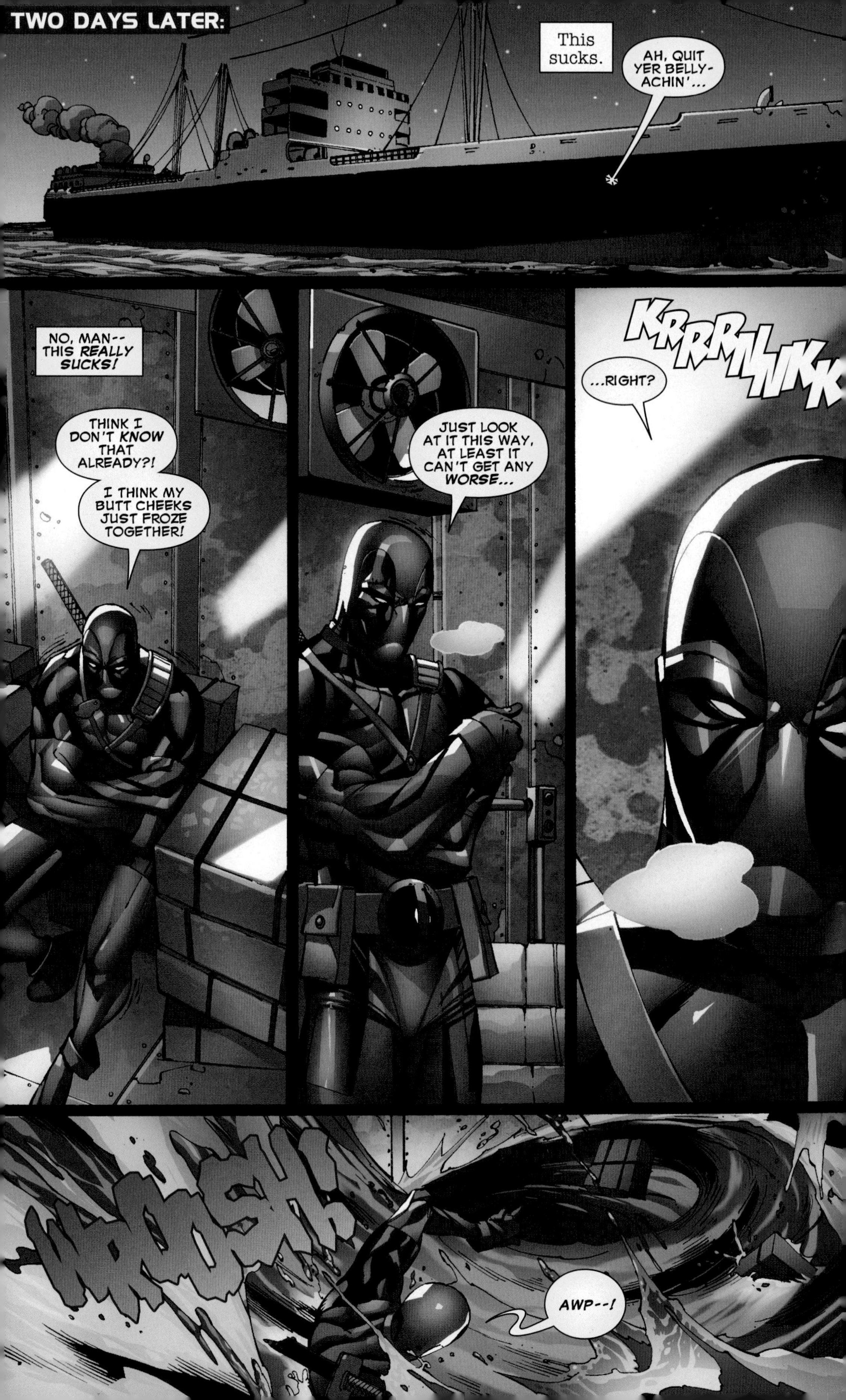
TWO DAYS LATER:
This sucks.
AH, QUIT YER BELLY-ACHIN'...
NO, MAN--THIS REALLY SUCKS!
THINK I DON'T KNOW THAT ALREADY?!
I THINK MY BUTT CHEEKS JUST FROZE TOGETHER!
JUST LOOK AT IT THIS WAY, AT LEAST IT CAN'T GET ANY WORSE...
KRRRNNKK
...RIGHT?
WHOOSH
AWP--!

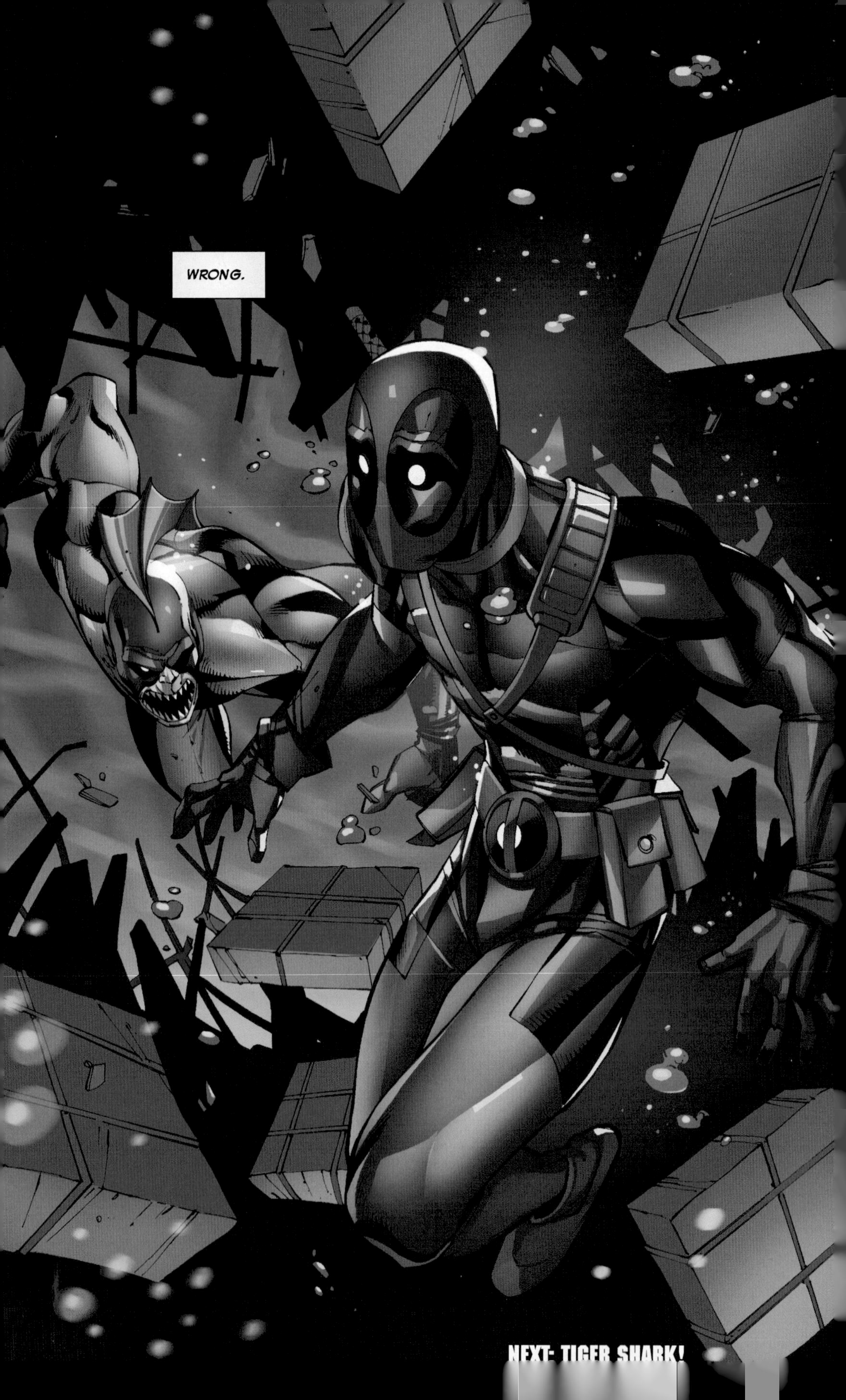
WRONG.
NEXT: TIGER SHARK!

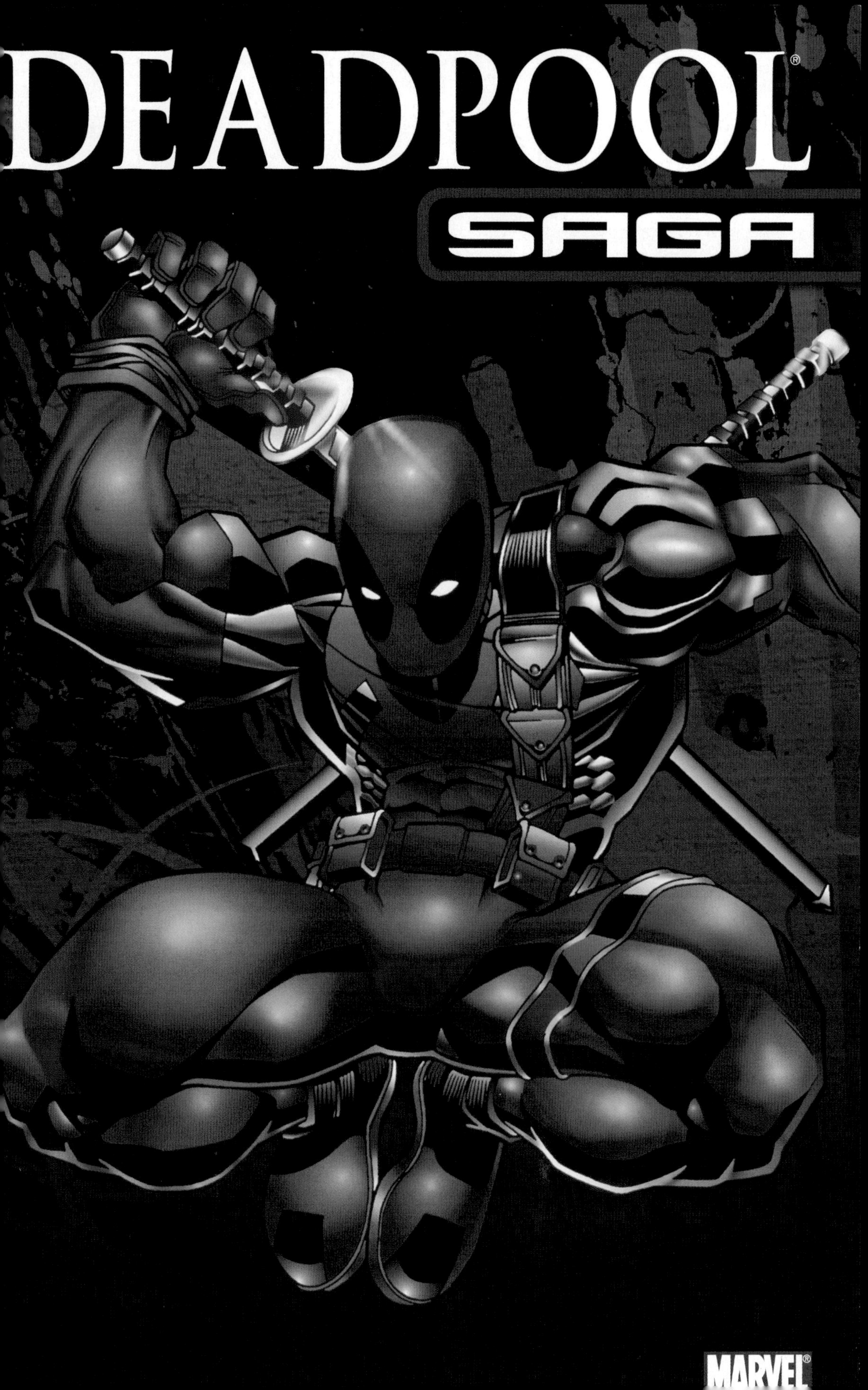
DEADPOOL®
SAGA
MARVEL®

Writer:
**RONALD BYRD**
Design:
**RODOLFO MURAGUCHI**
Assistant Editor:
**ALEX STARBUCK**
Editor:
**JEFF YOUNGQUIST**

Almost nothing is known for certain about the youth of the man called "Wade Wilson," not even if he was born with that name. He remembers a mother who died when he was five and a mother who beat him during his teen years, a father he hasn't seen since childhood and a father who was shot in a barroom altercation when his son was 17. Whatever his past, the youth who became Deadpool grew up to be a violent, conflicted man.

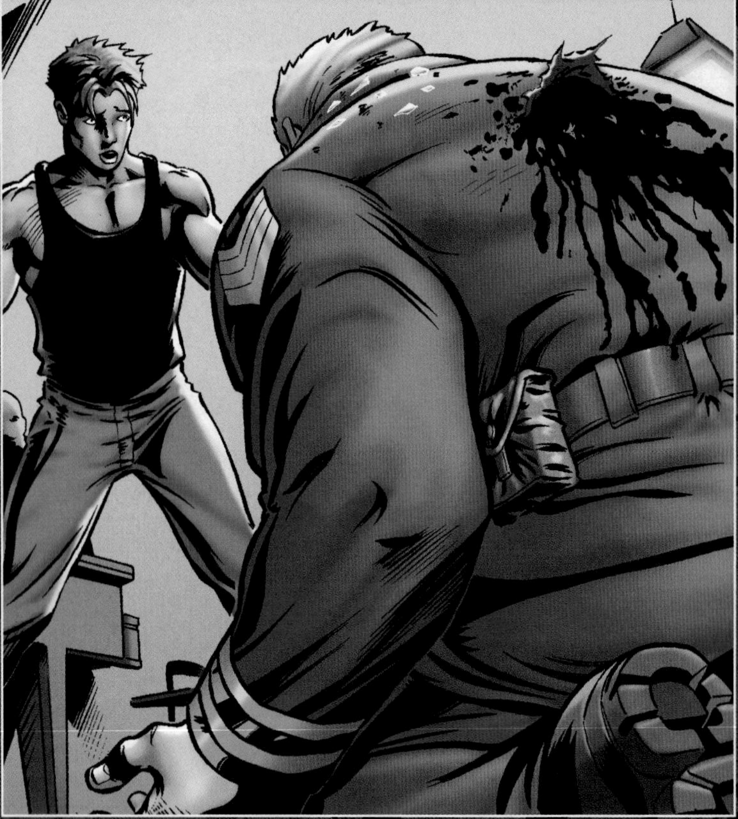

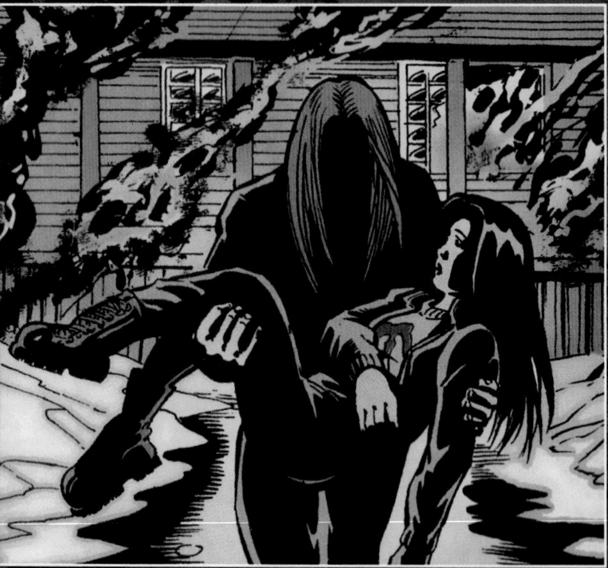

After serving in the military, that violent man became a teenage mercenary, taking assignments against those he felt warranted death. After failed assignments, he took new identities, and his true self, whoever that was, may have been lost in the process. A turning point came when, while on the run, he was nursed back to health by a husband and wife. Supposedly the husband's name was "Wade Wilson," and the mercenary craved that identity for himself. While trying to kill his benefactor, however, he inadvertently killed his wife Mercedes. Having broken his self-imposed rule against harming the innocent, the unhinged mercenary decided that **he** was Mercedes' husband, "Wade Wilson," and he mourned her before moving on.

Still a mercenary, Wilson traveled the world in the course of his assignments but never again abandoned the identity he believed was his. Eventually turning up in the USA, he fell in love with young Vanessa Carlysle, and although the couple lived their lives on the outskirts of society, they shared hopes for a better life. Unfortunately, Wilson contracted cancer, and he left Vanessa rather than force upon her what he perceived as the burden of a stricken man.

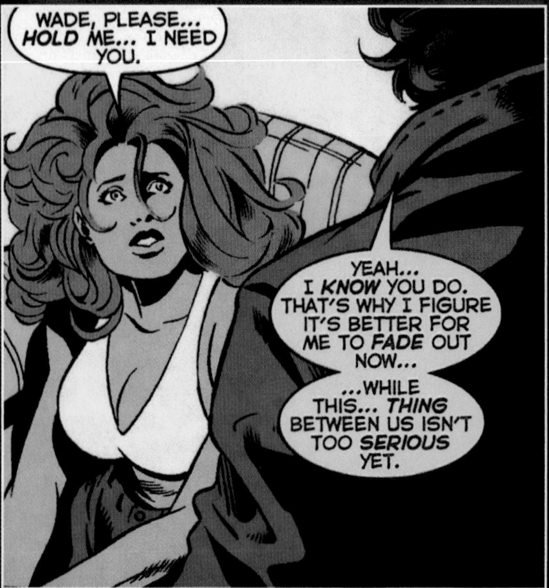
WADE, PLEASE... *HOLD ME*... I NEED YOU.
YEAH... I *KNOW* YOU DO. THAT'S WHY I FIGURE IT'S BETTER FOR ME TO *FADE* OUT NOW...
...WHILE THIS... *THING* BETWEEN US ISN'T TOO *SERIOUS* YET.

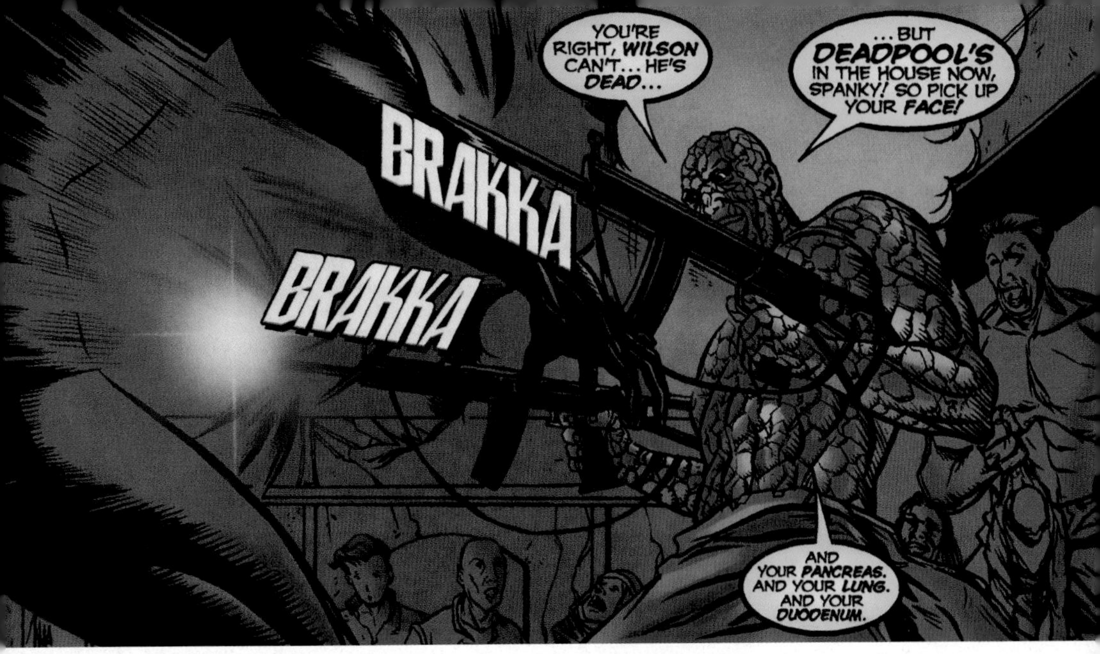
YOU'RE RIGHT, WILSON CAN'T... HE'S DEAD...
...BUT DEADPOOL'S IN THE HOUSE NOW, SPANKY! SO PICK UP YOUR FACE!
BRAKKA
BRAKKA
AND YOUR PANCREAS. AND YOUR LUNG. AND YOUR DUODENUM.

Wilson joined Canada's Department K and was mutated with a healing factor intended to cure his cancer. He worked with other operatives like Kane and Sluggo, but something went wrong. Whether due to a breakdown from his treatments or some other factor, Wilson apparently killed teammate Slayback. The government sent him to the Hospice for treatment, unaware of the sadistic experiments conducted by Dr. Emrys Killebrew. Killed for his rebellious streak, Wilson was revived by his healing factor, severely disfigured but no longer terminal. He tore the Hospice apart, freed his fellow test subjects, and proclaimed a new name for himself.

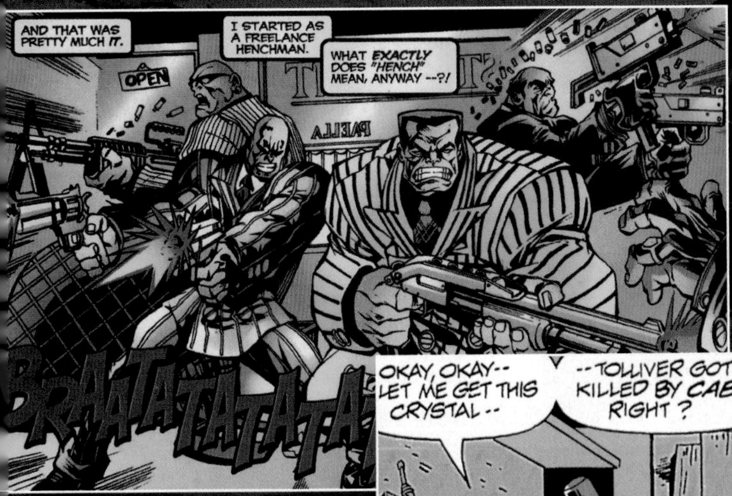
AND THAT WAS PRETTY MUCH IT.
I STARTED AS A FREELANCE HENCHMAN.
WHAT EXACTLY DOES "HENCH" MEAN, ANYWAY --?!
OPEN

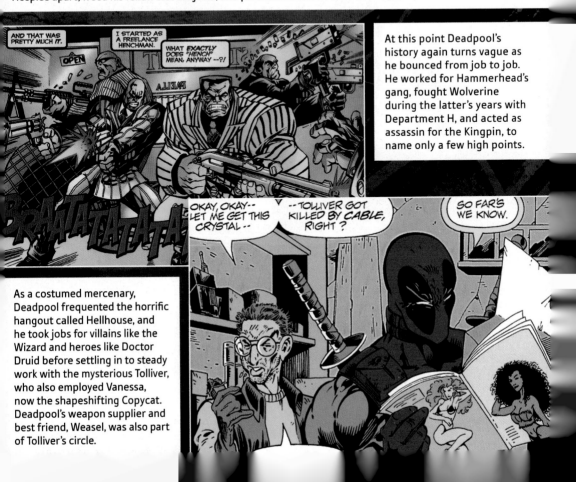

At this point Deadpool's history again turns vague as he bounced from job to job. He worked for Hammerhead's gang, fought Wolverine during the latter's years with Department H, and acted as assassin for the Kingpin, to name only a few high points.

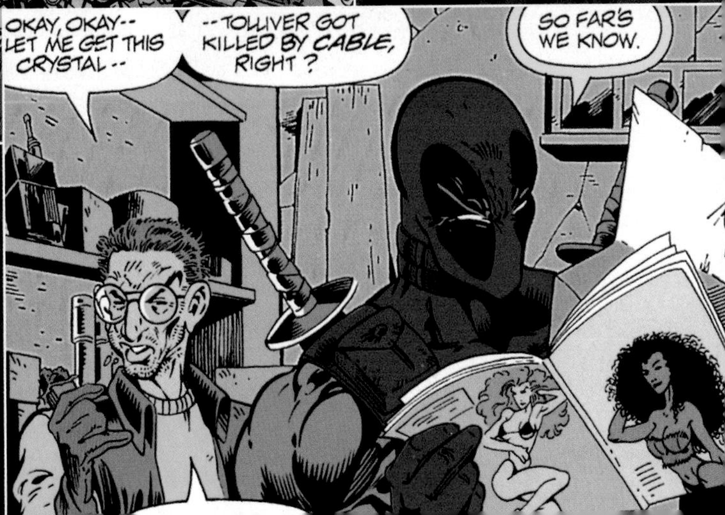
OKAY, OKAY-- LET ME GET THIS CRYSTAL--
--TOLLIVER GOT KILLED BY CABLE, RIGHT?
SO FAR'S WE KNOW.

As a costumed mercenary, Deadpool frequented the horrific hangout called Hellhouse, and he took jobs for villains like the Wizard and heroes like Doctor Druid before settling in to steady work with the mysterious Tolliver, who also employed Vanessa, now the shapeshifting Copycat. Deadpool's weapon supplier and best friend, Weasel, was also part of Tolliver's circle.

ntually Tolliver sent Deadpool :ill Cable, another super- vered mercenary and, retly, Tolliver's father. At time, Cable was acting as ntor to the New Mutants, so dpool burst into the Xavier titute, ready to rumble, but le defeated him and mailed back to Tolliver. Deadpool ıld little imagine how oortant Cable and his cohorts ıld become in his later life.

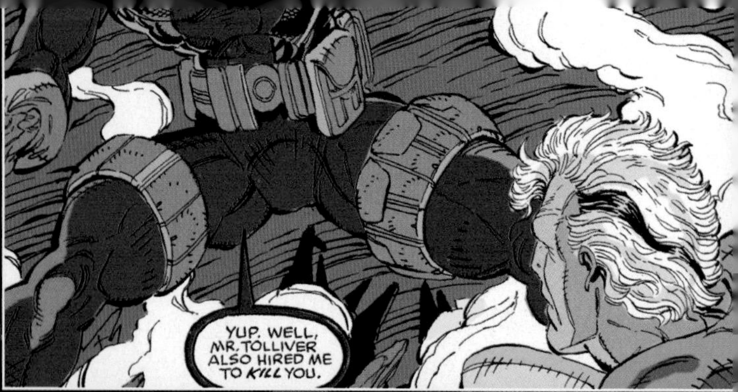
YUP. WELL, MR. TOLLIVER ALSO HIRED ME TO KILL YOU.

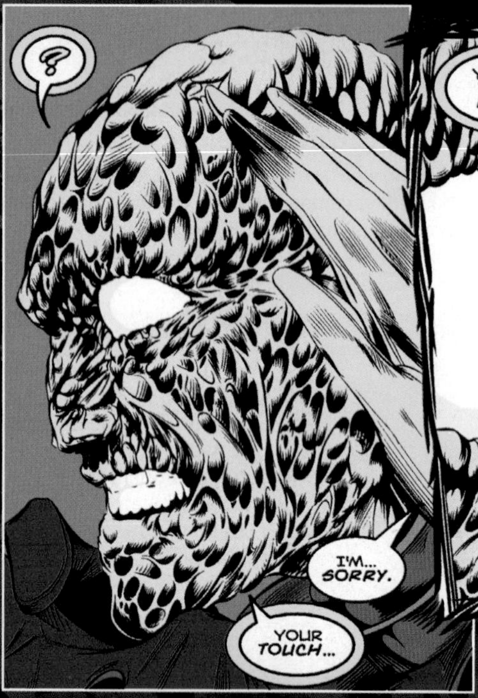
?
I'M... SORRY.
YOUR TOUCH...

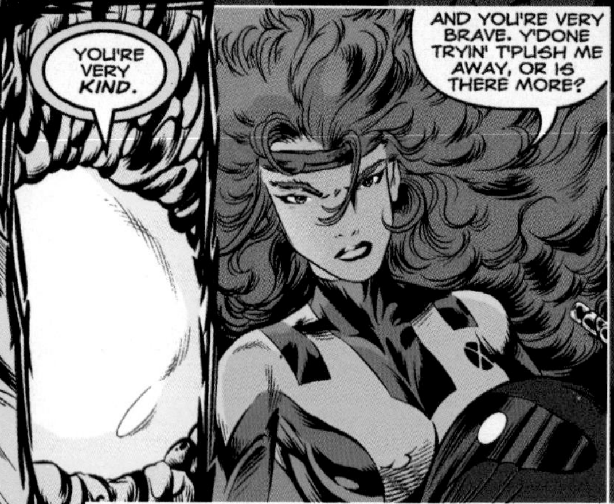
YOU'RE VERY KIND.
AND YOU'RE VERY BRAVE. Y'DONE TRYIN' T'PUSH ME AWAY, OR IS THERE MORE?

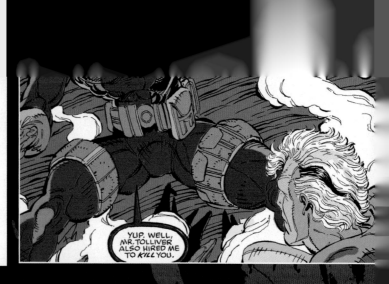

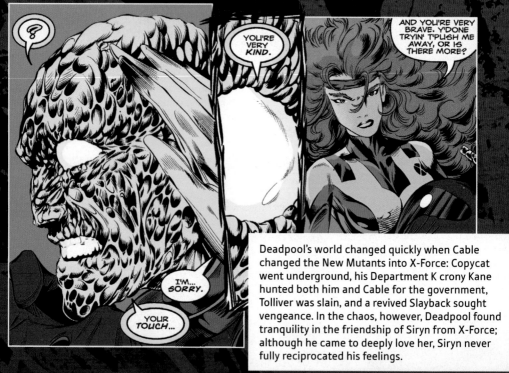

Deadpool's world changed quickly when Cable changed the New Mutants into X-Force: Copycat went underground, his Department K crony Kane hunted both him and Cable for the government, Tolliver was slain, and a revived Slayback sought vengeance. In the chaos, however, Deadpool found tranquility in the friendship of Siryn from X-Force; although he came to deeply love her, Siryn never fully reciprocated his feelings.

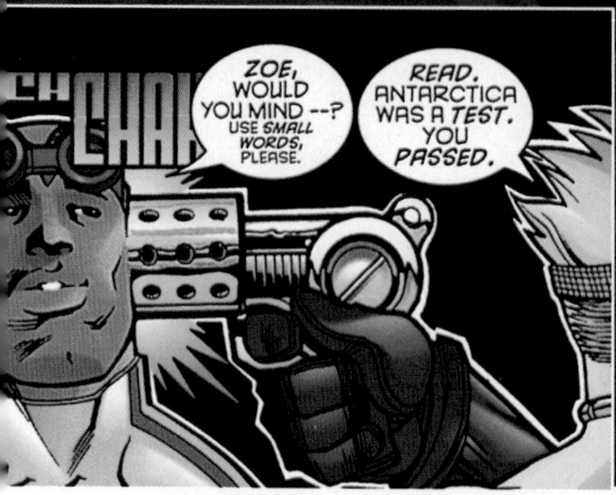
ZOE, WOULD YOU MIND --? USE SMALL WORDS, PLEASE.
READ. ANTARCTICA WAS A TEST. YOU PASSED.

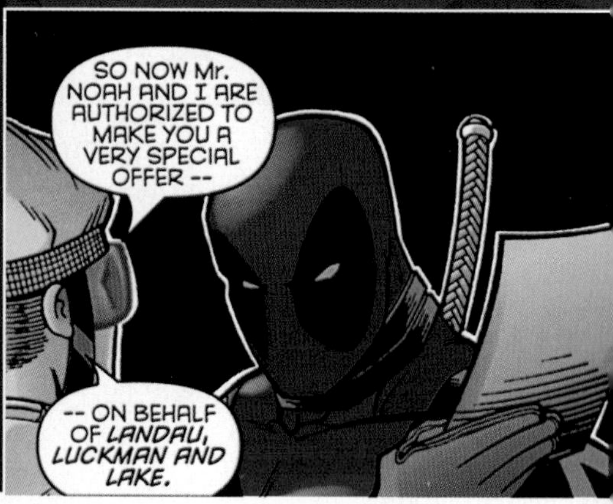
SO NOW Mr. NOAH AND I ARE AUTHORIZED TO MAKE YOU A VERY SPECIAL OFFER --
-- ON BEHALF OF LANDAU, LUCKMAN AND LAKE.

ıdpool's life settled back to normal, or as close to normal as he wanted it, but Zoe Culloden of the mystery ı Landau, Luckman, and Lake felt Deadpool was meant for more than mercenary misadventures. Zoe claimed eroic destiny awaited the dubious Deadpool, who was sure that, although he had worn many names, "hero" ıld never be one of them.

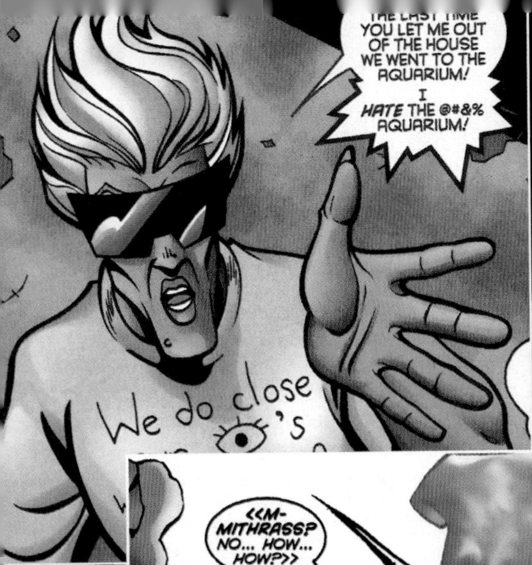
THE LAST TIME YOU LET ME OUT OF THE HOUSE WE WENT TO THE AQUARIUM!
I HATE THE @#&% AQUARIUM!

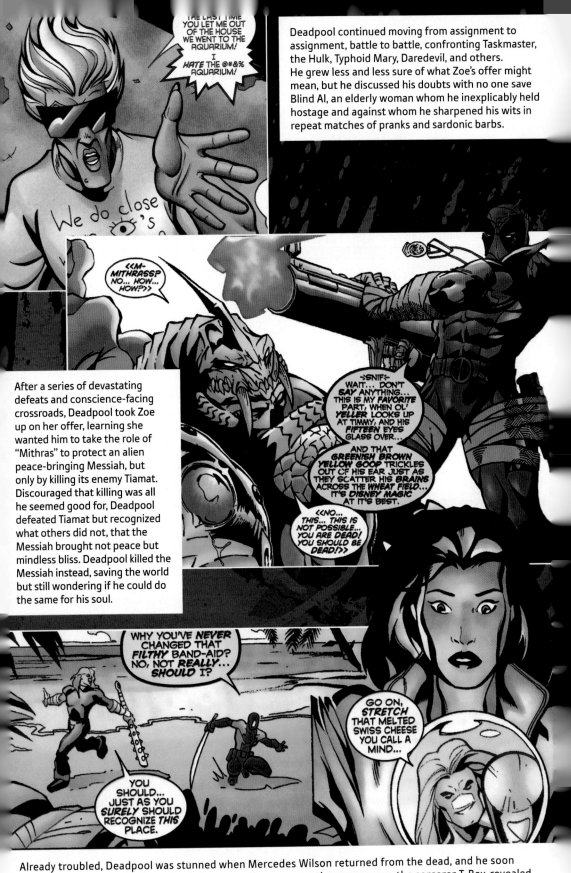

Deadpool continued moving from assignment to assignment, battle to battle, confronting Taskmaster, the Hulk, Typhoid Mary, Daredevil, and others. He grew less and less sure of what Zoe's offer might mean, but he discussed his doubts with no one save Blind Al, an elderly woman whom he inexplicably held hostage and against whom he sharpened his wits in repeat matches of pranks and sardonic barbs.

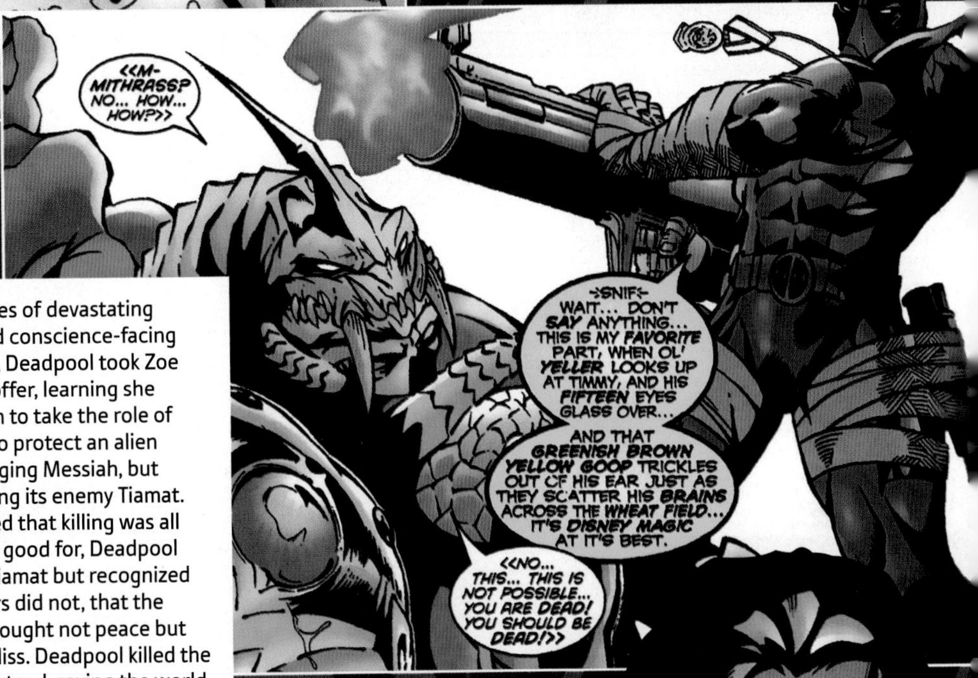
<<M-MITHRAS? NO... HOW... HOW?>>
-SNIF- WAIT... DON'T SAY ANYTHING... THIS IS MY FAVORITE PART, WHEN OL' YELLER LOOKS UP AT TIMMY, AND HIS FIFTEEN EYES GLASS OVER...
AND THAT GREENISH BROWN YELLOW GOOP TRICKLES OUT OF HIS EAR JUST AS THEY SCATTER HIS BRAINS ACROSS THE WHEAT FIELD... IT'S DISNEY MAGIC AT IT'S BEST.
<<NO... THIS... THIS IS NOT POSSIBLE... YOU ARE DEAD! YOU SHOULD BE DEAD!>>

After a series of devastating defeats and conscience-facing crossroads, Deadpool took Zoe up on her offer, learning she wanted him to take the role of "Mithras" to protect an alien peace-bringing Messiah, but only by killing its enemy Tiamat. Discouraged that killing was all he seemed good for, Deadpool defeated Tiamat but recognized what others did not, that the Messiah brought not peace but mindless bliss. Deadpool killed the Messiah instead, saving the world but still wondering if he could do the same for his soul.

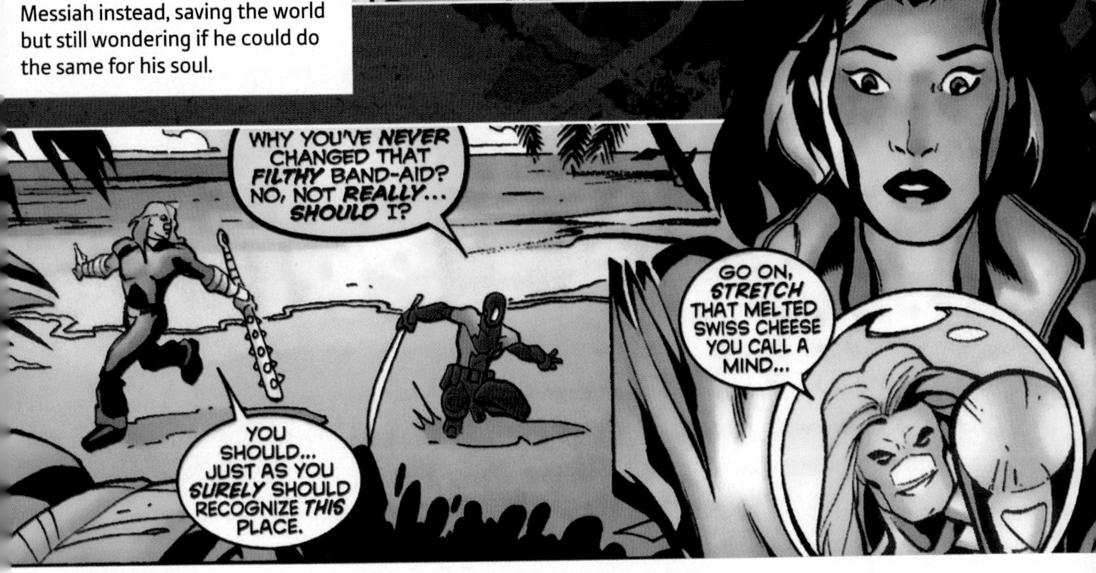
WHY YOU'VE NEVER CHANGED THAT FILTHY BAND-AID? NO, NOT REALLY... SHOULD I?
YOU SHOULD... JUST AS YOU SURELY SHOULD RECOGNIZE THIS PLACE.
GO ON, STRETCH THAT MELTED SWISS CHEESE YOU CALL A MIND...

Already troubled, Deadpool was stunned when Mercedes Wilson returned from the dead, and he soon felt sure he could find redemption in her arms. However, another mercenary, the sorcerer T-Ray, revealed that Deadpool could never find peace as Mercedes' husband...because **T-Ray** was her husband, the man Deadpool had left for dead long ago. Overwhelmed by the revelation, Deadpool nevertheless refused to break down in defeat the way T-Ray wanted.

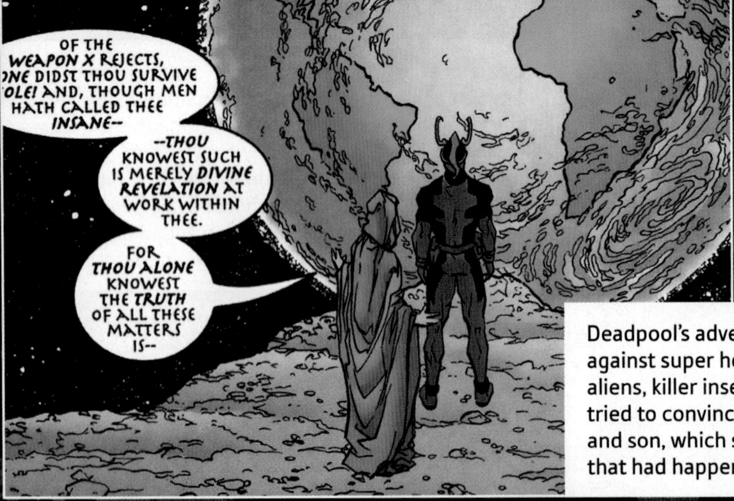
OF THE WEAPON X REJECTS, NE DIDST THOU SURVIVE OLE! AND, THOUGH MEN HATH CALLED THEE INSANE--
--THOU KNOWEST SUCH IS MERELY DIVINE REVELATION AT WORK WITHIN THEE.
FOR THOU ALONE KNOWEST THE TRUTH OF ALL THESE MATTERS IS--

Deadpool's adventures continued, setting him against super heroes, super-villains, werewolves, aliens, killer insects, and more. The god Loki even tried to convince Deadpool that they were father and son, which seemed as believable as anything else that had happened in Deadpool's life.

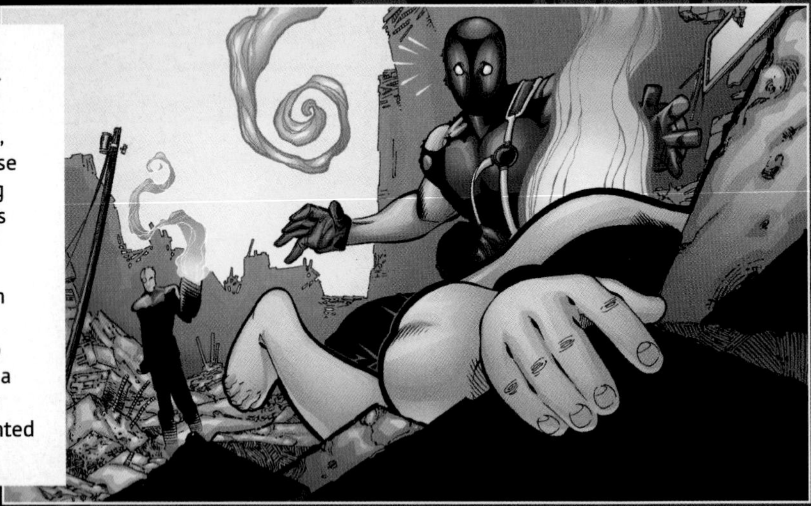

Deadpool then received an upgrade to his healing factor from Malcolm "Director" Colcord's Weapon X Program, which recruited him to oppose "the mutant menace." Joining Kane, who had turned callous while Deadpool had become more sympathetic to others, Deadpool was appalled when Kane murdered a mutant child. When Sabretooth, also in Weapon X, killed Copycat, a furious Deadpool was all but incinerated when he confronted her murderers.

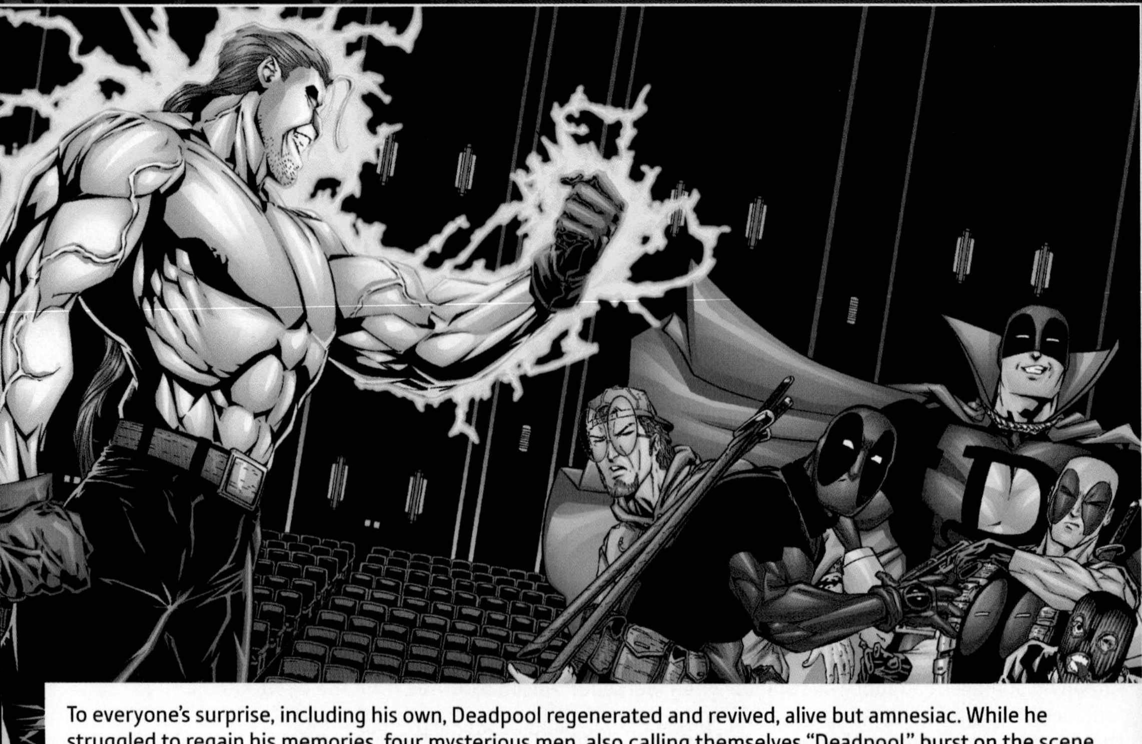

To everyone's surprise, including his own, Deadpool regenerated and revived, alive but amnesiac. While he struggled to regain his memories, four mysterious men, also calling themselves "Deadpool," burst on the scene in various venues. Deadpool learned they were aspects of his own personality, created by T-Ray in a scheme that ultimately failed.

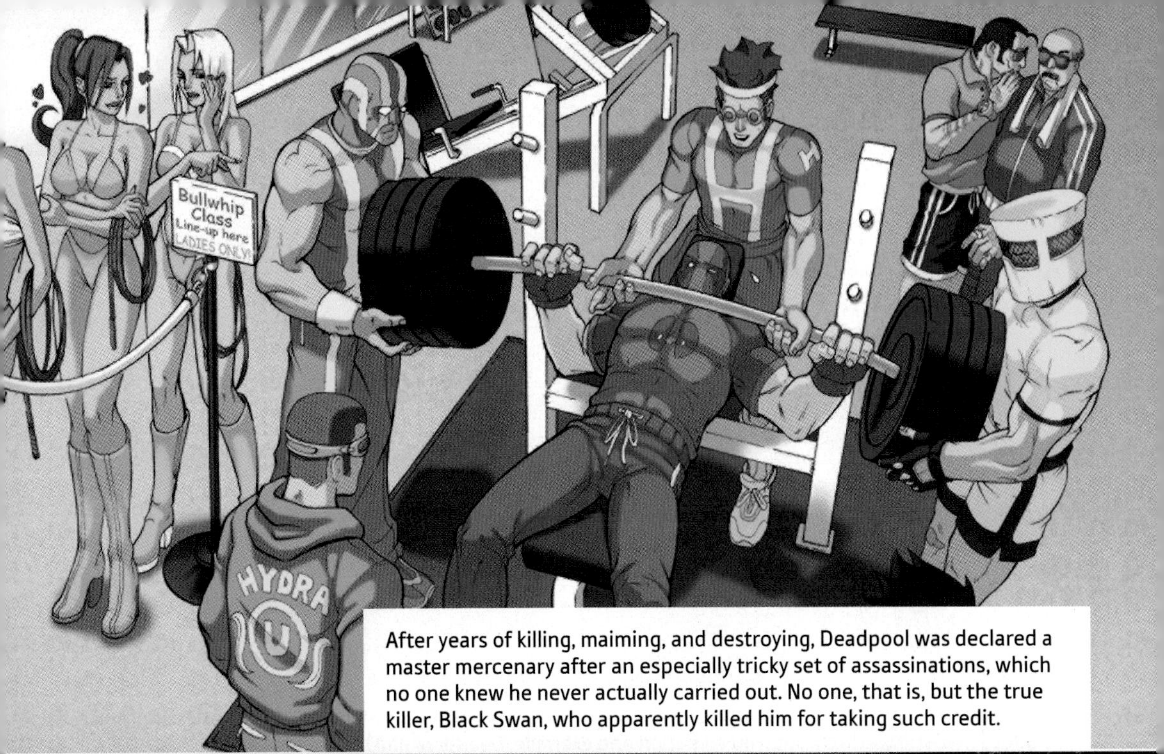
Bullwhip Class
Line-up here
LADIES ONLY!
HYDRA
After years of killing, maiming, and destroying, Deadpool was declared a master mercenary after an especially tricky set of assassinations, which no one knew he never actually carried out. No one, that is, but the true killer, Black Swan, who apparently killed him for taking such credit.

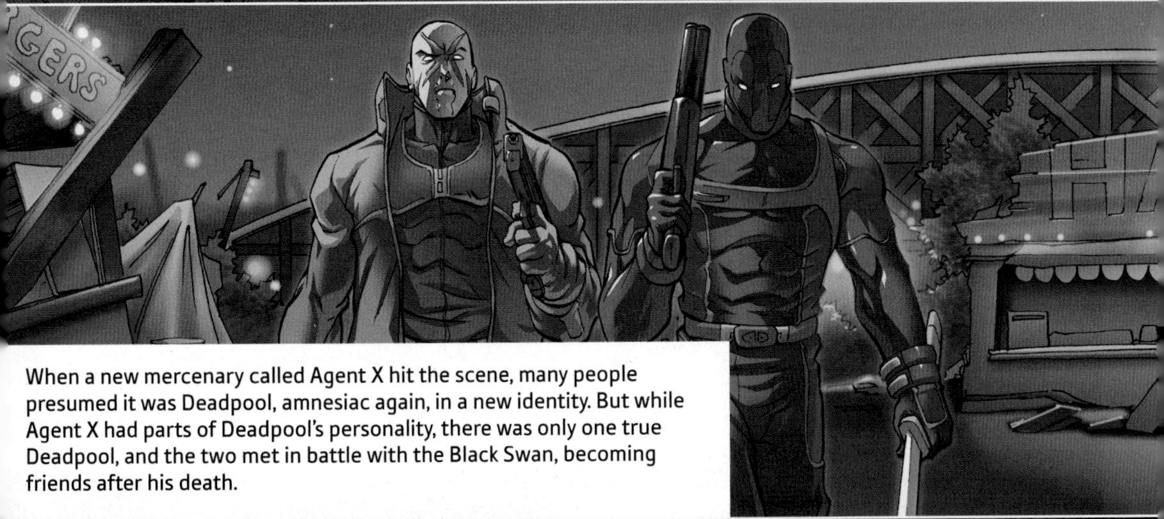
When a new mercenary called Agent X hit the scene, many people presumed it was Deadpool, amnesiac again, in a new identity. But while Agent X had parts of Deadpool's personality, there was only one true Deadpool, and the two met in battle with the Black Swan, becoming friends after his death.

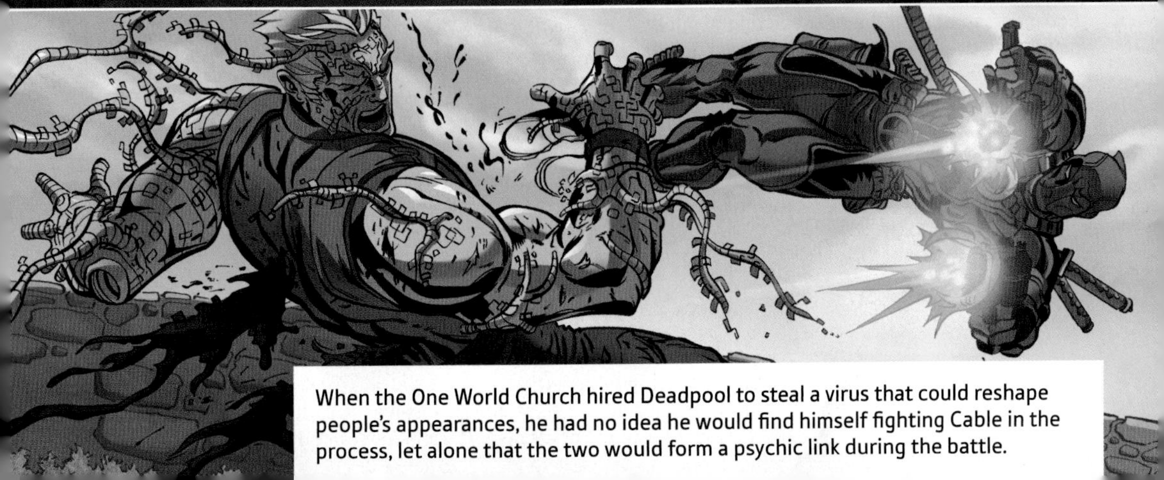
When the One World Church hired Deadpool to steal a virus that could reshape people's appearances, he had no idea he would find himself fighting Cable in the process, let alone that the two would form a psychic link during the battle.

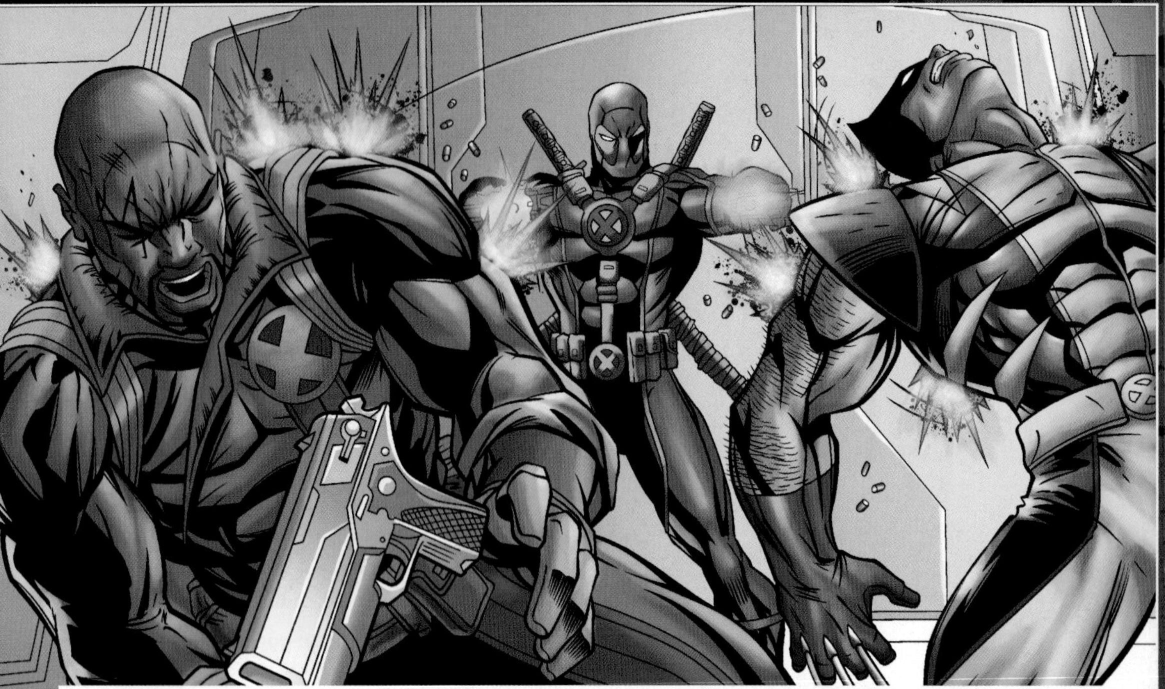

But a lot had changed since their battle at Xavier's school years before. His mercenary days far behind him, Cable was out to save the world through intervention and example. Deadpool had heard wild talk about saving the world before, but he became one of Cable's most ardent and unstable supporters, willing to fight friend or enemy on his behalf, and he became a frequent visitor to Cable's island paradise, Providence.

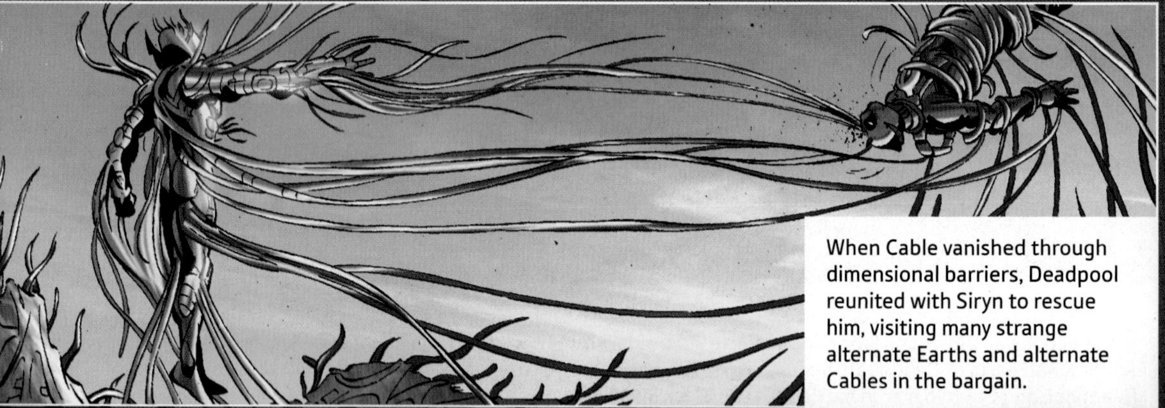

When Cable vanished through dimensional barriers, Deadpool reunited with Siryn to rescue him, visiting many strange alternate Earths and alternate Cables in the bargain.

During the "Civil War," Deadpool and Cable parted over differences regarding the Superhuman Registration Act and its effects on the future. Trying to put his newfound idealism behind him, Deadpool joined the government-sanctioned Six Pack to discredit him but inadvertently improved Cable's status in the eyes of the world.

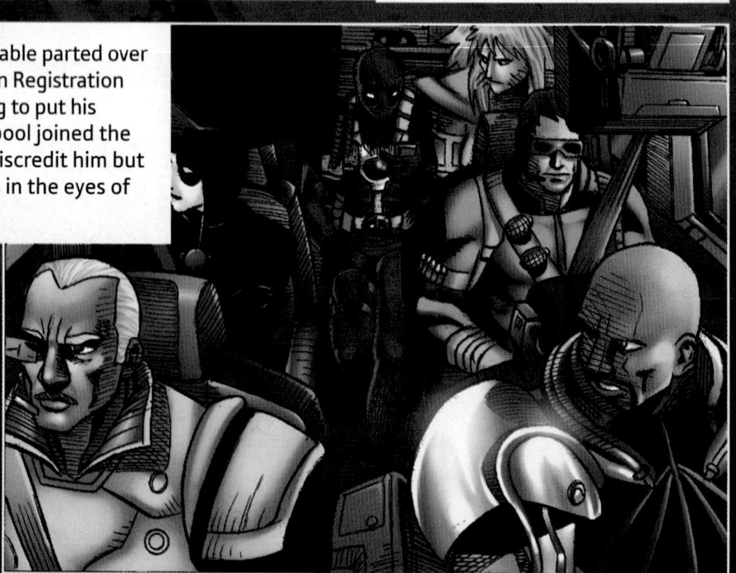

Unfortunately, Cable's dream reached an apparent end when Providence sank. Regardless of regrets over what might have been, Deadpool is now back in the mercenary game full-time, joining Weasel and other friends in Agency X. Cable may have disappeared into the future, but what future is waiting for Deadpool now?

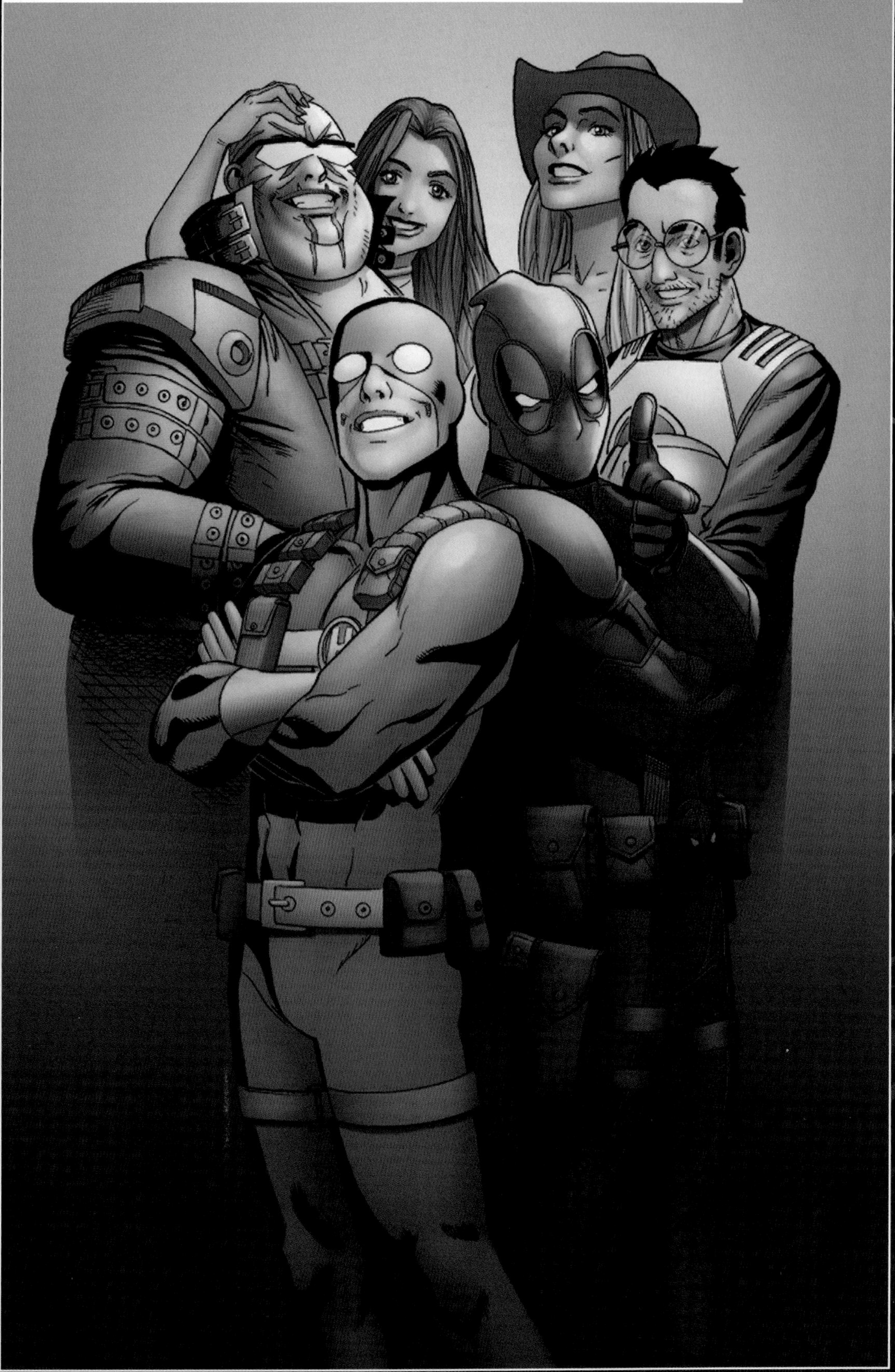

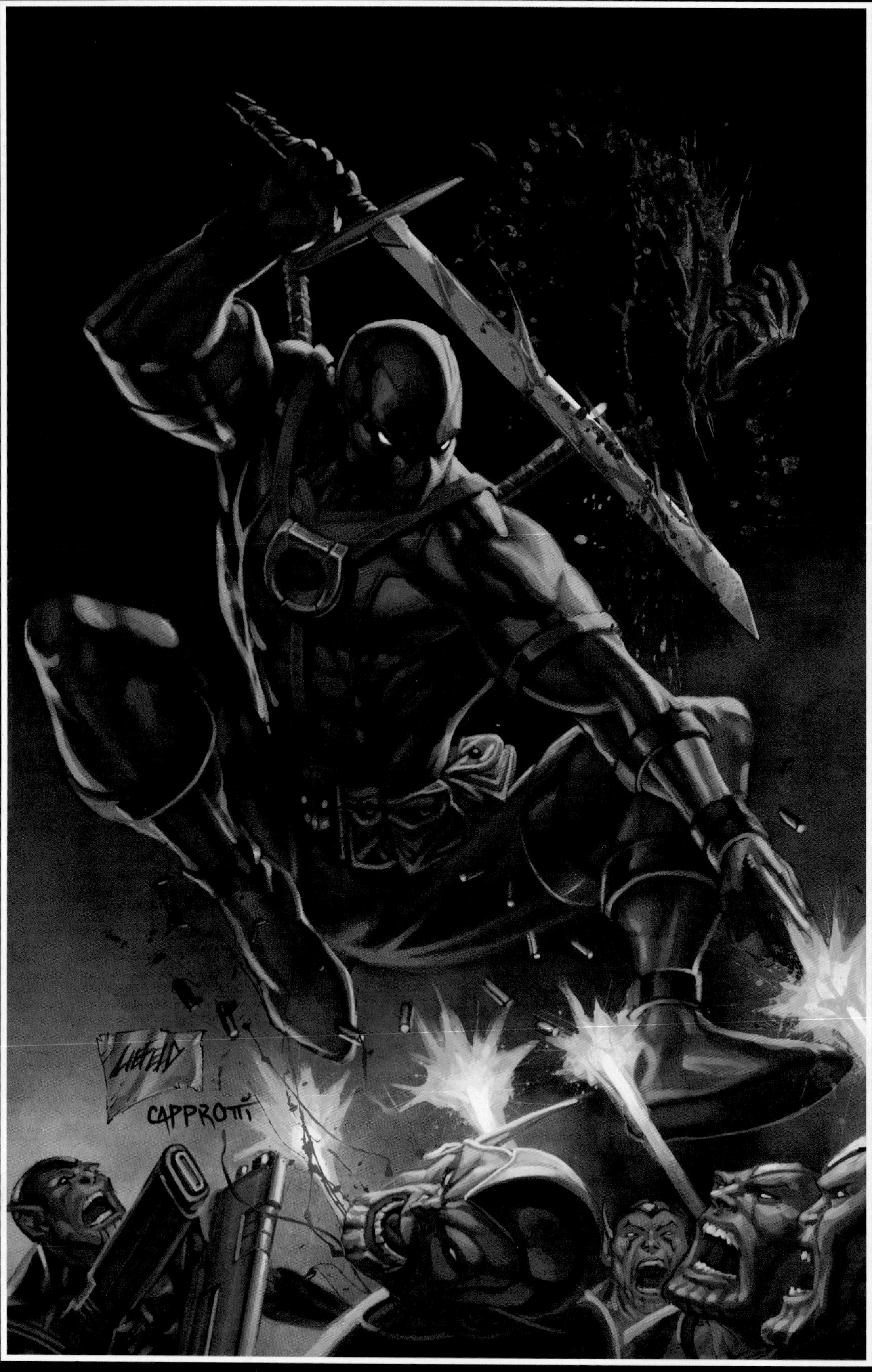
LIEFELD
CAPPROTTI

**DEADPOOL #1 VARIANT**
by Rob Liefeld

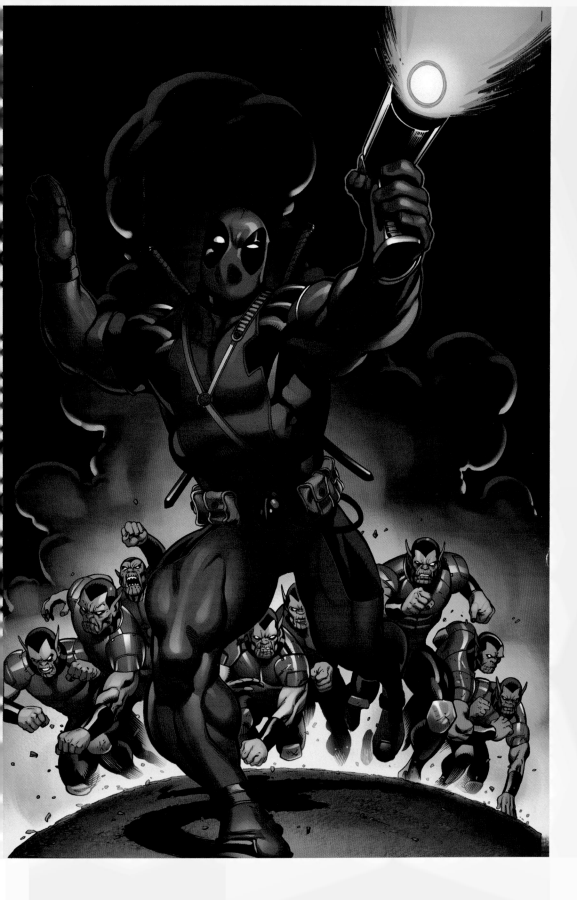

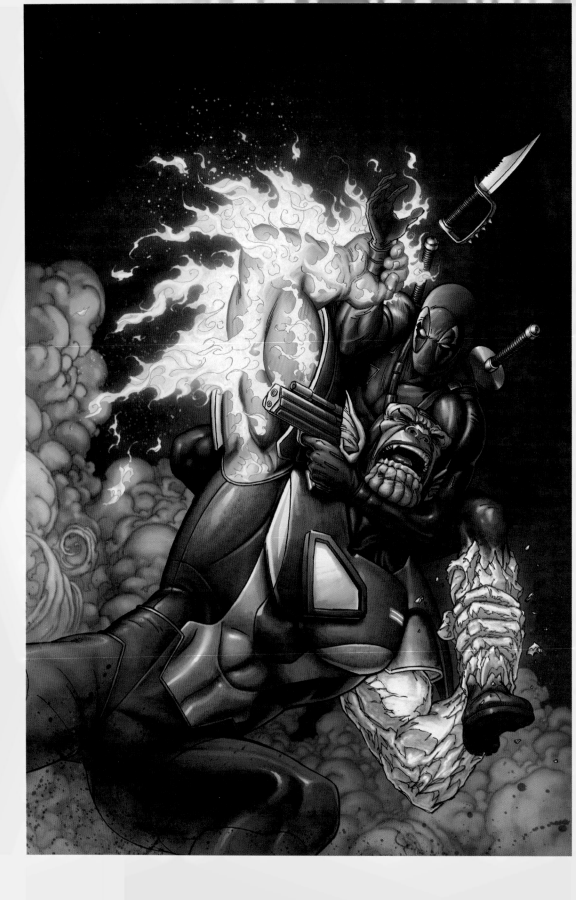

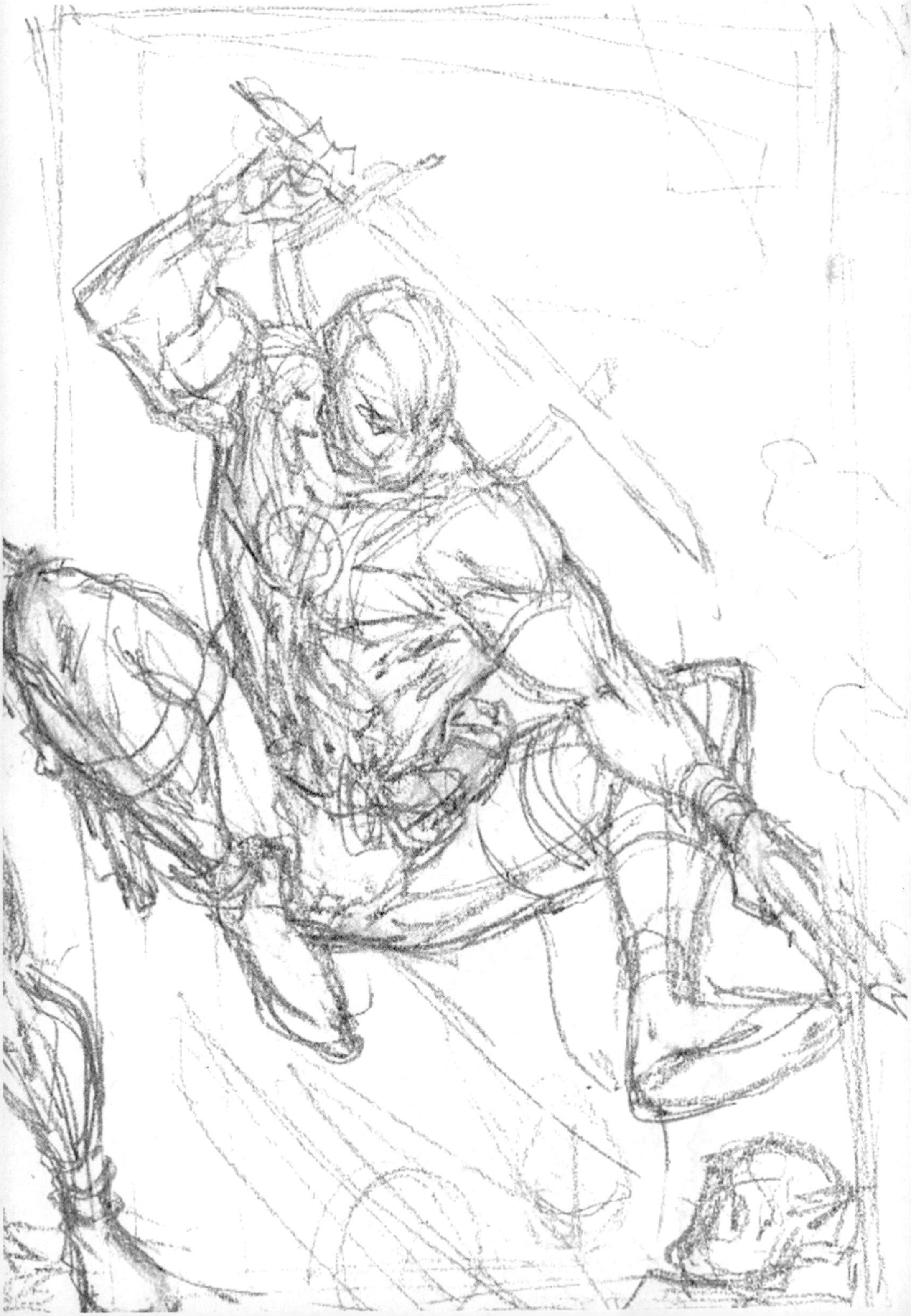

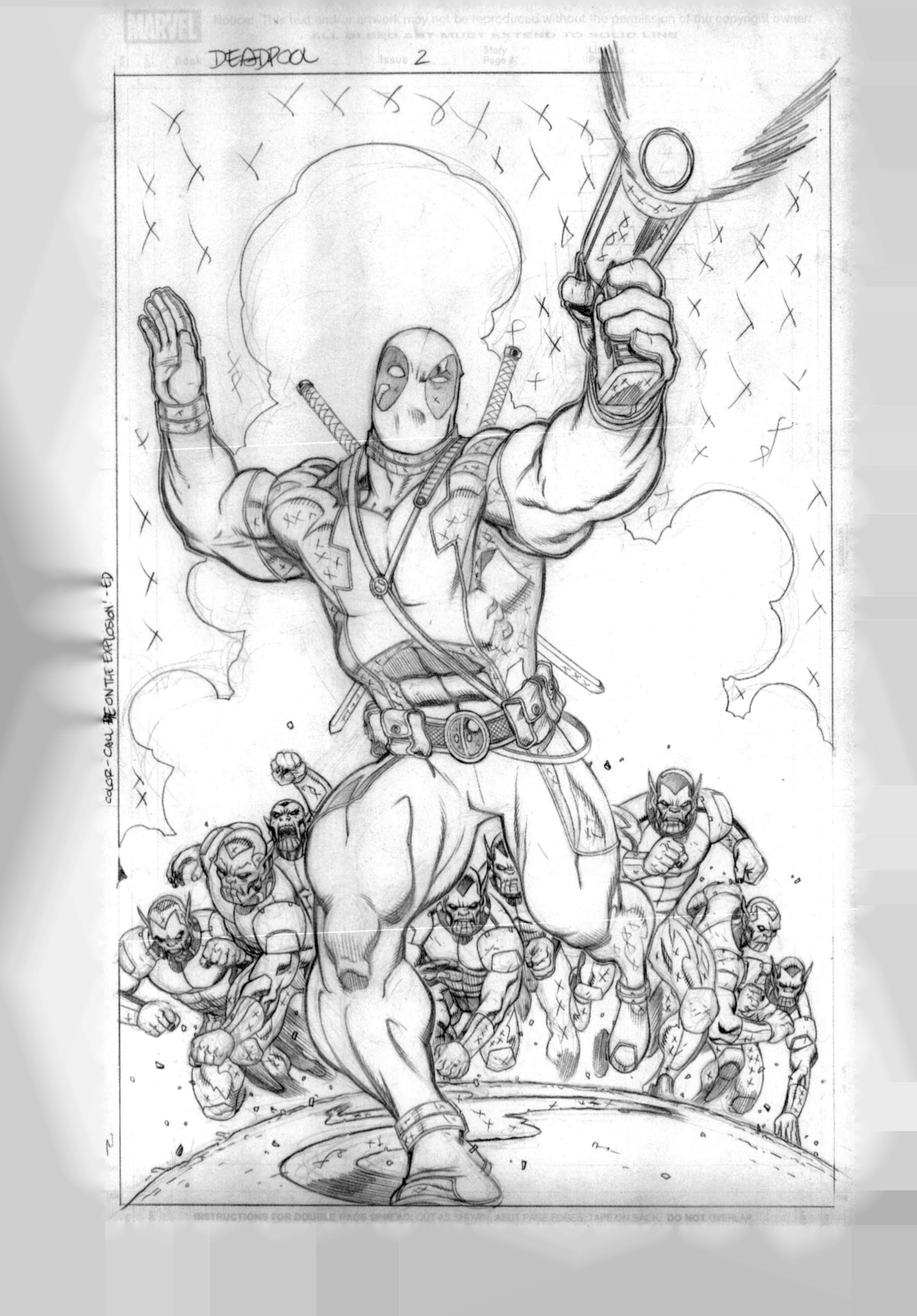
MARVEL
Notice: This text and/or artwork may not be reproduced without the permission of the copyright owner.
ALL BLEED ART MUST EXTEND TO SOLID LINE
Book DEADPOOL
Issue 2
Story Page #
COLOR - CALL ON THE EXPLOSION! - ED
INSTRUCTIONS FOR DOUBLE PAGE SPREAD: CUT AS SHOWN. ABUT PAGE EDGES. TAPE ON BACK. DO NOT OVERLAP.

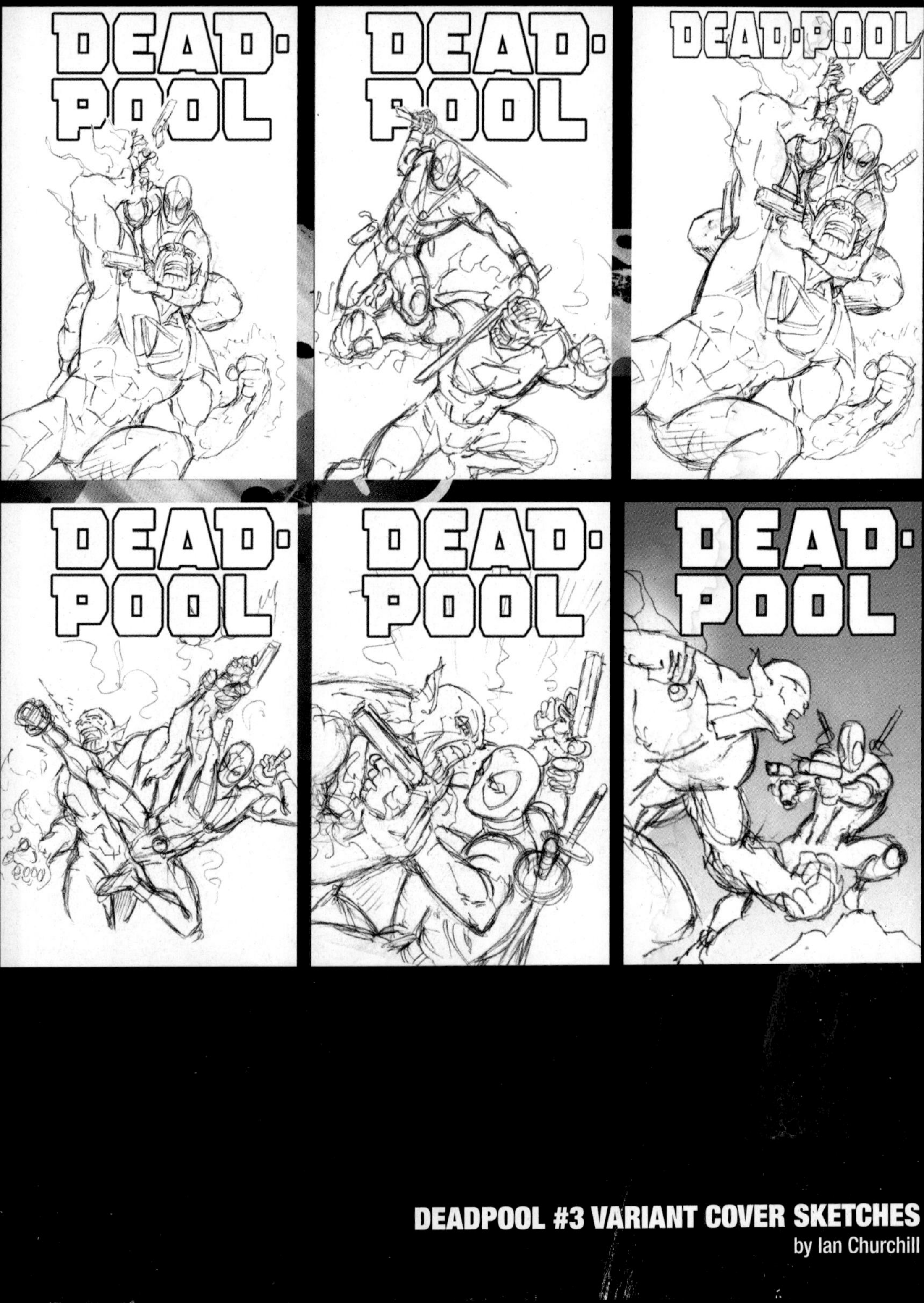
DEAD-
POOL
DEAD-
POOL
DEAD-POOL
DEAD-
POOL
DEAD-
POOL
DEAD-
POOL

**DEADPOOL #3 VARIANT COVER SKETCHES**
by Ian Churchill

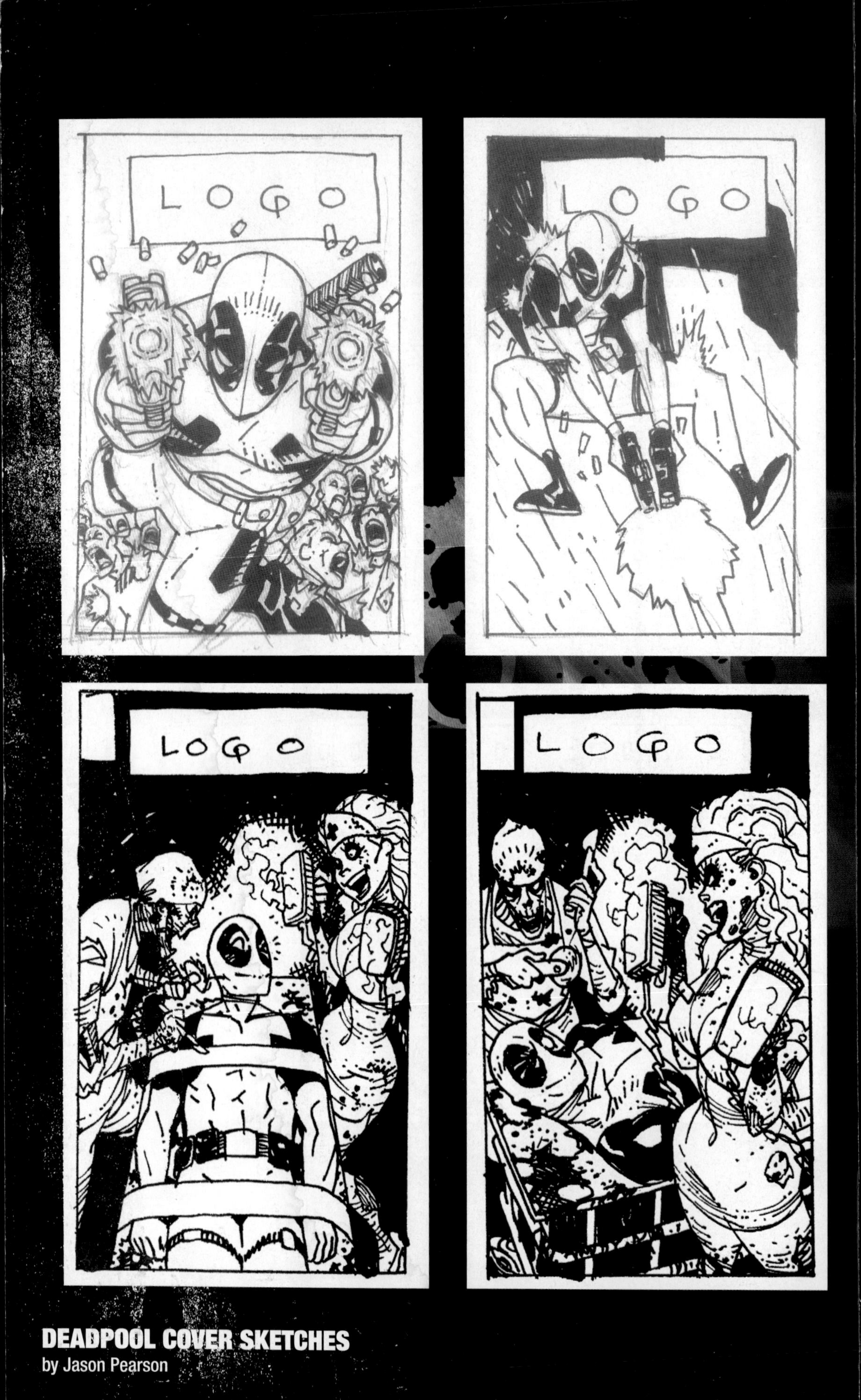
LOGO
LOGO
LOGO
LOGO

**DEADPOOL COVER SKETCHES**
by Jason Pearson